# THREE PLAYS by ARISTOPHANES

These three plays by the great comic playwright Aristophanes (c. 446–386 BCE), the well-known *Lysistrata* and the less familiar *Women at the Thesmophoria* and *Assemblywomen*, are the earliest surviving portrayals of contemporary women in the European literary tradition. These plays provide a unique glimpse of women not only in their familiar domestic roles but also in relation to household and city, religion and government, war and peace, theater and festival, and, of course, to men.

This freshly revised edition presents, for the first time in a single volume, all three plays in faithful modern translations that preserve intact Aristophanes' blunt and often obscene language, sparkling satire, political provocation, and beguiling fantasy. Alongside the translations are ample introductions and notes covering the politically engaged genre of Aristophanic comedy in general and issues of sex and gender in particular, fully updated since the first edition in light of recent scholarship. An appendix contains fragments of lost plays of Aristophanes that also featured women, and an up-to-date bibliography provides guidance for further exploration.

In addition to their timeless humor and biting satire, the plays are unique and invaluable documents in the history of Western sexuality and gender, and they offer strikingly prescient speculations about the social and political future of the female sex.

**Jeffrey Henderson** is the William Goodwin Aurelio Professor of Greek at Boston University and General Editor of the Loeb Classical Library. He is known for his pioneering work on Greek drama and for his editions and translations of the comic playwright Aristophanes.

# THE NEW CLASSICAL CANON

A Routledge book series edited by

David M. Halperin

# THREE PLAYS by ARISTOPHANES

## Staging Women

### Second Edition

Translated and Edited

by

Jeffrey Henderson

Routledge
Taylor & Francis Group

LONDON AND NEW YORK

First published in 1996
This second edition published in 2010
by Routledge
2 Park Square, Milton Park, Abingdon, Oxon OX14 4RN

Simultaneously published in the USA and Canada
by Routledge
711 Third Avenue, New York, NY 10017

Routledge is an imprint of the Taylor & Francis Group, an informa business

© 1996 Routledge, 2010 Jeffrey Henderson

Typeset in Joanna by RefineCatch Limited, Bungay,
Suffolk

British Library Cataloguing in Publication Data
A catalogue record for this book is available from the British Library

Library of Congress Cataloging in Publication Data
A catalog record for this book has been requested

ISBN10: 0-415-87132-8 (hbk)
ISBN10: 0-415-87131-X (pbk)
ISBN10: 0-203-86134-35 (ebk)

ISBN13: 978-0-415-87132-7 (hbk)
ISBN13: 978-0-415-87131-0 (pbk)
ISBN13: 978-0-203-86134-9 (ebk)

For William E. McCulloh

*caro magistro*

# Contents

# Preface to the Revised Edition

Since this volume was first published, scholarship on Aristophanes and Old Comedy has advanced on all fronts, not least as regards our three plays. I have accordingly revised the translations in light of the more recent critical editions of *Women at the Thesmophoria* by Austin and Olson (2004), of *Lysistrata* by Mastromarco (2006), of *Assemblywomen* by Sommerstein (1998), and of all the plays by Wilson (2007), as well as my own Loeb Classical Library edition of the plays and fragments (1998–2007); brought the introductions and notes current with recent scholarship; and updated the bibliography. I hope that in its freshened form this volume will continue to amuse, inform, and provoke its readers.

JJH
June 2009

# Preface to the First Edition

Aristophanes' comic plays *Lysistrata*, *Women at the Thesmophoria* (both from 411 BCE) and *Assemblywomen* (c. 392 BCE) contain the earliest positive portrayals of actual women (as distinct from the mythical or legendary figures of epic and tragedy, and the occasional prostitute or market woman of earlier comedy) in the European literary tradition, and they are the only such portrayals that survive complete from classical Athens. Thus they provide a unique glimpse into the lives and social roles of women in a culture that otherwise was elaborately silent about its women and permitted them no public voice. The focus of the plays is very broad, portraying contemporary women not only in their own various roles but also in relation to household and city, religion and government, war and peace, theater and festival, and, of course, men. And since these plays were written and performed by men for at least a notional audience of men as part of a civic festival, they also reveal much about male perceptions of women: women's role as "radical other" defining the civic space of men; women's roles in both domestic gender conflicts and public gender politics; and the figural, symbolic and ideological dimensions of femininity. In each play we find a fantastic but provocatively plausible inversion of the actual world, where women and men have exchanged their customary roles, in the process exposing and calling into question conventional gender boundaries. Aristophanes' comic gynecocracies put male fantasies of feminism (often intersecting with those of myth, tragic drama and Platonic idealism) into sharp and disturbing focus, using women and gender politics to stage a variety of personal, historical and cultural preoccupations in ways that only a comic poet was in a position to explore.

Yet in spite of their obvious value in the study of Athenian constructions of gender, there are few readily available translations of these plays and no collection of all three in a single volume. Furthermore, existing translations typically censor, translate around or otherwise misrepresent the texts, and they lack explanatory notes and informative introductions. One reason for this situation is a traditional squeamishness among classicists about those disruptive elements of Aristophanic comedy that threaten to complicate, if not undermine, the construction and maintenance of an idealized Glory of Greece: blunt and often obscene sexual language and action, forceful social criticism and political protest, rough satire and outrageous fantasy. Classicists have long thought that these elements are incompatible with the universalizing and humanistic reading deemed appropriate to the Greek classics. For this reading, epic and tragedy are the favored poetic genres. Neglect of Aristophanes' three "women's plays" in particular stems from the traditional emphasis on the masculine "high" culture of competition, warfare and statecraft that has been so central to the idealized picture of classical Greece. Even the female characters of epic and tragedy suit this emphasis better than those in comedy: the former were part and parcel of the heroic, masculine culture of a bygone mythical era, while the latter represented ordinary Athenian women who were highly critical of male hegemony. And so Aristophanes' plays have tended to be marginalized within the professional canon and largely hidden from nonspecialists.

But in recent decades, advances in the fields of cultural and comparative studies, social history, women's studies and critical theory have prompted new questions about the social realities and symbolic mentality of Greek culture and have begun to reveal an Athens that is at once more problematic than its idealized versions and more interesting to modern students of culture. Since many of these advances have taken place outside the discipline of classical studies, nonspecialist researchers often lack access to texts of great relevance to their studies because adequate translations and explanatory materials are unavailable. For this reason students of women and gender in classical Athens have for the most part used tragedies but not comedies as their central texts. But it is surely significant that tragedy and comedy were staged together at the same festivals: Athenian drama as an institution embraced both comic and tragic views of the world, and Athenians defined themselves in terms of the mundane as well as the heroic. And so there is no good reason why those who ponder, say, the Theban Antigone's Bronze Age heroics should not also make room in their studies for Aristophanes' heroines, who after all were supposed to represent actual Athenian women hurling their complaints at actual Athenian men.

And so I offer this annotated translation in order to make these three plays available to general readers and useful to all students of Greek literature and culture, within and outside the field of classical studies. For each play I supply an introduction and explanatory notes, and the collection as a whole has general introductory essays about Aristophanes, the comic theater and women in Aristophanic comedy. In the introductions and notes I have not tried to develop particular interpretations of the plays but rather to supply the basic information and bibliography that readers will need to interpret the plays for themselves. I have also included, in an Appendix, translations of fragments from Aristophanes' lost comedies that bear on his portrayal of women. Since the volume is geared particularly to readers interested in gender studies and in women's history, the introductions and notes concentrate especially on those areas.

I wish to thank my readers and editors for their encouragement, advice and expertise, and to express my special gratitude to David M. Halperin, who first suggested this project and along the way gave it the great benefit of his learning, critical acumen and sensitivity to the complexities of cultural self-expression.

# INTRODUCTION

# I. ARISTOPHANES

Aristophanes was judged in antiquity to be the foremost poet of the "old" Attic (or Athenian) comedy, of which he was one of the last practitioners and of which his eleven surviving plays are our only complete examples. Aside from his theatrical career little is known about his life. He was born c. 447/46, the son of one Philippos of the urban deme[1] Kydathenaion, and died probably between 386 and 380. By his twenties his hair had thinned or receded enough that he could be called bald. He seems to have had landholdings on, or some other connection with, the island of Aigina. He was twice prosecuted by the popular leader Kleon for the political impropriety of two of his plays, but he was never convicted (see II, below). Early in the fourth century he served as one of his deme's representatives on the Council of 500, a representative body that steered and supervised the agenda for the sovereign assembly. He had two sons, Araros and Philippos, both of whom had careers as comic poets in the mid-fourth century. In his dialogue *Symposium* Plato portrays Aristophanes as being at home among the social and intellectual elite of Athens. Although the historical veracity of Plato's portrayal is uncertain, Aristophanes' plays generally do champion the social and political views of contemporary upper-class, landowning conservatives, insofar as these could be portrayed as serving the interests of the citizen populace at large.

Aristophanes' first comedy was produced in Athens in 427 and his last in 386 or soon thereafter. At least once he produced a comedy in the deme-theater of Eleusis. Forty-four comedies ascribed to Aristophanes were known to the Alexandrian scholars of the third and second centuries BCE who first collected and edited his plays; four of these they thought spurious. From these Alexandrian editions eleven complete comedies and some 1000 brief fragments of the lost comedies survive. In competition Aristophanes was very successful, winning at least six first prizes and four second prizes, with only two last-place

3

finishes attested. After his victory with *Frogs* in 405, the people voted him an honorific crown of sacred olive for the advice he had given in that play and decreed that it should have the unique honor of being performed a second time.

Here is a list of Aristophanes' eleven extant plays, with their dates and (where known) the festivals at which they were performed (see II, below): *Acharnians* (Lenaia 425), *Knights* (Lenaia 424), *Clouds* (Dionysia 423; the surviving version is an incomplete and never-staged revision dating from 419–17), *Wasps* (Lenaia 422), *Peace* (Dionysia 421), *Birds* (Dionysia 414), *Lysistrata* (Lenaia 411), *Women at the Thesmophoria* (Dionysia 411), *Frogs* (Lenaia 405), *Assemblywomen* (392 or 391), and *Wealth* (388).

## II. OLD COMEDY: PRODUCTION AND COMPETITION

### *The Dramatic Festivals*

The period of organized Old Comedy at Athens began in 486 BCE, when comedy first became part of the festival of the Greater Dionysia; by convention it ended in 388 BCE, when Aristophanes produced his last extant play. During this period some 650 comedies were produced. We know the names of some fifty comic poets and the titles of some 300 plays. We have eleven complete plays by Aristophanes, the first one dating from 425, and several thousand fragments of other plays by Aristophanes and other poets, most of them only a line or so long, and very few from plays written before 440.

The principal occasions for the production of comedies were the Greater Dionysia, held in March or April and lasting six days, and (from 440) the Lenaia, held in January or February and lasting four days.[2] These were national festivals that were at once civic and religious—a dual identity that must be kept in mind, for it is of vital importance in understanding the meaning of the dramas and their functions in the polis, especially as regards their portrayal of gender. Because of their antiquity and Panhellenic roots, the dramatic festivals in many respects elided, and could even challenge, the distinctions between men and women, and their notional spaces within the Athenian democratic polis, that were on other occasions strictly maintained, and this peculiar freedom allowed the dramatic poets to explore social and ideological tensions that would otherwise be unexplorable in a communal setting.

The dramatic festivals honored the wine and fertility god Dionysos, whose cult from very early times had included mimetic features, but they were officially sponsored, hosted and regulated by the executive *demos* ("sovereign people") of Athens and were a showcase for the culture and ideology of its democracy. The theatrical productions themselves were civic competitions in

which poets, dancers, actors, producers and musicians—all of them male—
competed for prizes that were awarded at the close of the festival by judges
representing the people. The Greater Dionysia was held in the Theater of
Dionysos on the south slope of the Akropolis, which in Aristophanes' time, at
least, accommodated as many as 10,000 spectators, including both Athenians
and foreigners. While the performances were created, organized and performed only by men, the festival itself welcomed everyone as spectators: at the
Greater Dionysia more of the Attic populace was gathered as an audience in
one place at the same time than at any other event, and participation was
uniquely inclusive. Unlike such purely civic events as meetings of the assembly
(accommodating up to 6000) or the lawcourts (some 600), which only adult
male citizens could attend, the Dionysia was open to anyone who could get a
seat: citizens, slaves, foreigners, children and even women (see III, below). The
Lenaia, which only Athenians attended, was held elsewhere in the city (we do
not know where) probably until 440, when it too was given an official dramatic
contest and moved to the Theater of Dionysos.

### The Dramatic Genres

At these festivals comedy shared the theater with tragedy and satyr-drama,
which had been produced at the Greater Dionysia since the sixth century. The
first contest in tragedy is dated to 534 (the poet Thespis was victorious), but it
is not certain that this contest was held as part of the Greater Dionysia, which
in any case seems to have experienced major changes after the overthrow of
the Peisistratid tyranny and the establishment of democracy in 508. Tragedy
dramatized stories from heroic myth, emphasizing dire personal and social
events that had befallen hero(in)es and their families in the distant past and
mostly in places other than Athens. By convention, the poetry and music of
tragedy were highly stylized and archaic. Satyr-drama, which was composed by
the same poets who wrote tragedy, had the same features, except that the
heroic stories were treated in a burlesque fashion and the chorus was composed of satyrs—mischievous followers of Dionysos who were part human and
part animal.

All three dramatic genres were written in verse (iambic trimeter for dialogue,
lyric forms for choral song and dance), but comedy differed from the other two
in many of its performance-conventions (see III, below) and was less restricted
in its choice of linguistic and musical registers and of subjects. That is probably
why the composers and performers of tragedy and satyr-drama were never the
same ones who composed and performed comedy. The language of comedy
was basically urbane and colloquial, though it often parodied the conventions

of other (particularly tragic) poetry, and was free to include indecent, even obscene language and action, especially a sort of stylized "nudity" that regularly included the large artificial phallos worn by male characters and chorus-members (see further III, below).³ The music and dancing, too, tended to reflect popular styles.

The favorite subjects of comedy were free-form mythological burlesque; domestic situations featuring everyday character types; and (apparently beginning in the 450s) political satire portraying people and events of current interest in the public life of the Athenians. Our eleven surviving comedies all fall into this last category. Mythological and domestic comedy continued to flourish after the Old Comic period, but political comedy largely vanished: a casualty of social and political changes following the Athenians' loss of the Peloponnesian War, and with it their empire, in 404. Given Old Comedy's obvious synchronicity and topical engagement with fifth-century Athenian culture, its significance must be sought primarily in the context of the political and ideological system of which it was an organic feature: the phase of radical democracy inaugurated by the reforms of Ephialtes in 462/61 and lasting until the end of the century.⁴

### Drama and Democracy

Democracy means "rule by the demos" (sovereign people). In fifth-century Athens democracy was radical in that the sovereignty of the demos was more absolute than in any other society before or since. The Athenian democracy was, however, much less representative than modern democracies, since the sovereign demos consisted solely of citizen males at least eighteen years of age; women, slaves and noncitizen males were excluded from membership in the demos and therefore from any participation in government (see further IV, below). All decisions affecting the governance and welfare of the state were made by the direct and unappealable vote of the demos meeting either together in the assembly or separately as juries in a lawcourt. The polis was managed by members of the demos in good standing and at least thirty years of age, who (in addition to being able to vote in assembly and as members of a jury in legal cases) were chosen by lot from a list of eligible citizens and who held office in periods ranging from one day to one year. The only exceptions to the lottery system were military commanders, who were elected to one-year terms, and holders of certain ancient priesthoods, who inherited their positions.⁵ The demos determined by vote whether or not anyone holding any public position was qualified to do the job, and after completion of his term, whether he had done it satisfactorily.

By custom, though not by legal statute, all military commanders and most assembly speakers and holders of powerful allotted offices came from the wealthy classes, but their success depended on the good will of the demos as a whole, which always had the final vote. By thus empowering all citizens individually to participate in managing the state and collectively to decide between proposals and arguments made to them by ambitious, elite individuals, the democracy tried to balance egalitarianism and elitism. All members of the demos, whatever their individual differences in wealth and power, were politically and ideologically equals at the civic level, so that all could pride themselves on belonging to an exclusive and all-sovereign corporation.

Important for understanding drama's portrayal of women is the degree to which the development of this sort of exclusive and gender-marked civic culture encouraged the ideological marginalization and political subordination of private households and the women who managed them. In the pre-democratic period the polis had been run by noble families, and there was no strict dichotomy between polis and household: women could play important social and symbolic roles as mothers, wives or daughters eligible for dynastic marriages. Under the democracy, by contrast, "civic" (male/executive spheres) and "private" (female/family spheres) tended to be sharply distinguished, so that women were increasingly removed both physically and notionally from those civic spaces that were defined as male. Drama, however, which could appeal to polis norms and ideals older than democracy and which remained institutionally positioned both within and outside the civic spheres of the demos, took advantage of its position to explore tension-points within the developing democratic dichotomies of civic and domestic, public and private, polis and household, internal and external, and thus provides our most detailed view of the gender oppositions that lay at their center.

### The Dramatic Competition

One of the most important allotted offices was that of *choregos* (sponsor of a dramatic chorus).[6] Choregoi were allotted from a list of men wealthy enough to hold this office, for they had to recruit and pay for the training, costuming and room and board of the chorus that would perform at one of the festivals. In the case of a comic chorus this involved twenty-four dancers and the musicians who would accompany them. Good dancers could be compelled by a choregos to join his chorus and were excused from military service in order to do so. Being a choregos gave a man an opportunity to display his wealth and refinement for the benefit of the demos as a whole and to win a prize that would confer prestige on himself and his dancers. Some wealthy men therefore volunteered to be choregoi instead of waiting for their names to be drawn. Conversely, a man who put on a cheap or otherwise unsatisfactory chorus could expect to suffer a significant loss of public prestige. Worse, a choregos, like any other officeholder, could be prosecuted for failing to discharge his duties to the satisfaction of the demos.

All other expenses, including stipends for the poet and his actors and for prizes, were undertaken by vote of the demos and paid for from public funds. A poet got a place in the festival by submitting a draft some six months in advance to the relevant archon (the office-holder in charge of the festival). Ancient sources say that at least the choral parts of the proposed play had to be submitted. How much more was submitted we do not know. But revision up to the day of the performance was certainly possible, since many allusions in comedy refer to events occurring very shortly before the festival, most notably the death of the tragic poet Sophokles shortly before the performance of *Frogs* in 405.

If a poet got on the program, he would be given his stipend and assigned his actors. He and the choregos would then set about getting the performance ready for the big day, the poet acting as music master, choreographer and director, the choregos rounding up, and paying the expenses of, the best dancers he could find. While tragic poets produced three tragedies and a satyr drama, comic poets produced only one comedy.

### Formative Traditions

In these ways comedy, as a theatrical spectacle, was an official and organic feature of Athenian democracy. But its poetic, musical and mimetic traditions were much older, deriving from ancient forms of popular, rustic carnival that were fashioned into increasingly sophisticated entertainments by cultivated members of the aristocratic families that had governed Attika in proto-democratic fashion before the democracy. One such form was the *komos* (band of revellers), which gave comedy its name (*komoidia*: "song of the komos"). A komos was made up of some solidary group (a military, religious or family group, for example), often in disguise, which entertained onlookers on many kinds of festive and religious occasions, particularly those honoring Dionysos. The Greater or City Dionysia was developed in the course of the sixth century by the "tyrant" Peisistratos as part of his program to unify the cultural life of Attika across class lines. The Greater Dionysia was the crucible in which carnival, komos and mimetic drama coalesced to produce the theatrical genre of Old Comedy.

From time immemorial carnival had been a period of ritual license, when society's normal rules and hierarchies were suspended or inverted so that ordinary people got a chance to vent, in festive enactments, those frustrations and hostilities that would have been difficult or impossible to express at any other time: the oppressiveness of laws and rules, the unfairness of social hierarchies, the unworthiness or misbehavior of powerful individuals, disruptive but unactionable gossip, the shortcomings of citizens in groups or as a whole. In this capacity carnival served as a social safety valve, allowing a relatively harmless airing of tensions before they could become dangerous, and also as a means of social communication and social control, upholding generally held norms and calling attention to derelictions. But in addition to its critical and rebellious aspects, carnival (like all festive activities) had an idealistic side, its very inversions helping people to envision the community as it would be if everyone agreed on the norms and lived up to them. Carnival also had a utopian side, imagining how wonderful life would be if reality were as human beings would like it to be and if there were no need for rules and social distinctions. In this capacity carnival provided a welcome relief from the cares, burdens and frustrations of everyday life.[7]

Among Old Comedy's carnivalesque legacies are its hero(in)es, who typically represent marginal or powerless groups; its utopian inversions of the status quo; and its criticism of the system and its official enforcers. The theatrical festivals themselves also preserved the carnival's spirit of popular freedom, solidarity and rebellion. Since the Dionysia was the only public assembly that everyone could attend—women, children, slaves and foreigners as well as members of the demos—it became the venue of choice for civic representations of all kinds, including the announcement of public honors.[8] But while the prominent and powerful were being recognized, popular control was reasserted in the ritual of the *phallephoria*, a procession in which costumed men brought huge phalloi (models of the erect penis and testicles) into the theater and directed ridicule and abuse at the honorands. In this way Dionysiac ritual prefigured the content of the dramas to follow: tragedy's portrayal of the disasters that afflict the great, and comedy's exposure of the unworthiness of the powerful.[9]

Readers of Old Comedy have always been especially impressed, even appalled, by its earthy and obscene language and by its open display of sexual and other animal functions—features absent from all other genres of classical Greek literature save the archaic *iambos* (see below).[10] In part, these features are an inheritance from rural fertility cults, especially those celebrating Dionysos and Demeter: the phallos, carried in procession and also worn by celebrants, was the primary emblem of fertility, ritually empowered both to encourage human and animal reproduction and to frighten away baleful spirits that might impede it. Ritual obscenity, too, was thought to possess these powers. Then too, there was the sheer fun of enjoying a release from the inhibitions and taboos that ordinarily surrounded sexual life: the use of obscenity is the primary linguistic method, and nudity (actual or symbolic) the primary visual method, of "revealing" what is normally hidden.[11] Communal "defiance" of the normal rules allowed a relatively harmless release of tensions and facilitated the social levelling that the cult of Dionysos especially promoted. As noted above, mockery of the powerful by the humble was an important dimension of the phallic procession and its associated ritual abuse.

But it was the artistic side of these cults—dancing, masking, cross-dressing, role inversion, song and poetry—that elaborated their central themes of sexuality and fertility in more formal ways; comedy and iambos were the genres that preserved and refined the use of obscenity and transgressive sexuality for their own purposes. Unlike other poetic genres, which dealt with heroic mythology and the world of gods and nobles, comedy and iambos looked at the contemporary world through the eyes of ordinary people, and so developed personal, colloquial and popular styles in which obscenity and sexuality were very much at home, and which preserved an important dimension of Dionysiac worship.

The festive komos, from which comedy got its name, was the chief transitional form linking carnival and Old Comedy, and was the vehicle by which the free-form criticism of carnival—popular criticism of authority as such—acquired political focus, since it featured abuse and criticism of individuals or groups standing outside the solidarity of a particular komos. The victims might be among the onlookers or they might be members of a rival komos. The komos sang and danced as a group, and its leader (who was no doubt also the poet) could speak by himself to his komos, to the onlookers or to a rival komos-leader. No doubt at a very early stage komos was a competitive entertainment by which a given group could, in artistic ways, make those claims and criticisms against rival groups which at other times they might make in more overtly political ways.

Old Comedies were theatrical versions of komos: the band of dancers with their leader was now a comic chorus involved in a story enacted by actors on a stage. The chorus still resembled a komos in two ways. As performers, it competed against rival choruses, and in its dramatic identity it represented a distinct group or groups. The comic chorus differs from a komos in that at a certain point in the play it drops its dramatic identity and thereafter represents the celebrating community as a whole. At this point, its leader steps forward in a speech (called the parabasis and often made on behalf of the poet himself) to advise and admonish the spectators, and his chorus might sing abusive songs about particular individuals in the audience.

The actors who performed in the stage-area were a secondary ingredient of Old Comedy, having been amalgamated with the chorus during the sixth century but playing no prominent role until the fifth. Their characteristic costumes (III, below) and antics were depicted in vase-paintings of that earlier period in many parts of Greece, suggesting a much older tradition of comic mimesis. As early as the Homeric period (eighth and seventh centuries) we find mythological burlesque and such proto-comedy as the Thersites-episode in the second book of the *Iliad*. In this period, too, the iambic poets flourished. Named for the characteristic rhythm of their verses, which also became the characteristic dialogue rhythm of actors in Athenian drama, the iambic poets specialized in self-revelation, popular storytelling, earthy gossip and personal enmities, often creating fictitious first-person identities and perhaps also using masks and disguise. They were credited with pioneering poetic styles of invective, obscenity and colloquialism. Comedy is the only other poetic genre to use this sort of language in the classical period, and in this respect is a direct literary descendant of the iambic poets.

The characters on the Old Comic stage preserved many of these traditions, but like the chorus they were an adaptation to the democratic system, most clearly in political comedy. In Aristophanes' plays, the world depicted by the plot and the characters on stage was the world of the spectators in their civic and social roles: as heads or members of families, as participants in governing the state or running its households. We see representations of the demos in its various capacities; of the competitors for public influence; of the men who hold or seek office; of social, intellectual and artistic celebrities. We are also taken, as in tragedy, into the private world of women, children and slaves—a world conventionally invisible in purely civic arenas (IV, below). We hear everything from formal debate on current political issues, complete with its characteristic invective, to conversations in household, marketplace, symposion or brothel. We get a decision, complete with winners and losers, and we see the outcome. This satirical depiction of democratic life—in both its political and social aspects—was designed both to arouse laughter and to encourage reflection about people and events, and the system itself, in ways not possible in other public contexts. Thus comedy was at once a distorted and an accurate depiction of life. Like a modern topical cartoon, an Athenian comedy humorously distorted reality in order to draw attention to perceptible gaps between truth and lies, ideals and realities.

## Comic Politics

Aristophanic comedies typically depict Athens in the grip of a terrible and intractable problem (e.g. misconceived warfare, bad political leaders, an unjust jury system, dangerous artistic or intellectual trends) which is solved in a fantastic but essentially plausible way, often by a comic hero(ine). The characters of these heroic plays fall into two basic categories, sympathetic and unsympathetic. The sympathetic characters—the hero(ine) and his/her supporters—are always fictitious creations embodying ideal civic types or representing idealized versions of ordinary, marginal or powerless Athenians. The unsympathetic characters embody disapproved civic behavior (political, social, artistic, religious or intellectual) and usually represent specific leaders or categories of leaders. The sympathetic characters advocate positions allegedly held by political or social minorities (e.g. women) or by ordinary, disempowered citizens (e.g. small farmers). But these are shown winning out against the unsympathetic characters, who represent the current social or political hegemony. Characters or chorus-members representing the demos as a whole are portrayed as initially sceptical or hostile to the sympathetic character(s), but in the end they are persuaded. As for those who are responsible for the problem, they are exposed, then disgraced or expelled, and Athens is recalled to a sense of her true (traditional) ideals and is thus renewed.

In the (essentially democratic) comic view, the people are never at fault for their problems: they have been deceived by bad leaders or entranced by unworthy celebrities. By such portrayals the comic poets often tried to persuade the actual demos, sitting among the other spectators, to rethink or even change its mind about the way it was running the polis or about issues that had been decided but might be changed, to discard dangerous novelties, and to be more critical of its leaders. Aristophanes at least once succeeded: after the performance of *Frogs* in 405, he was awarded a crown by the city for the advice given by the chorus-leader in that play and subsequently adopted by the demos.

The use of satire and partisan criticism within a plot addressing itself to important issues of national scope was thus a democratic adaptation of such predemocratic traditions as carnival, komos and iambic poetry. That the comic festivals were state-run and not privately organized is striking evidence of the openness and self-confidence of a full democracy: the demos was completely in charge, so it did not fear attacks on its celebrities or resent admonition by the poets. On the contrary, the institution of Old Comedy performed functions essential to any democracy: public airing of minority views; promotion of the concept of society as inclusive and suprapolitical; and criticism of those holding power. In this function, the Old Comic festivals were organized protest. But like tragedy, comedy also articulated and explored civic ideals: through their comic fantasies and inversion of the norms, the poets identified the shortcomings of the status quo by holding it up against a vision of things as they ought to (or used to) be. This vision is normally crystallized by viewing the status quo through the eyes of ordinary people or people ordinarily excluded from public power, like women, and before an inclusive audience.

Still, many modern scholars (in contrast to their ancient counterparts) are often astonished by the extent of comic outspokenness on political issues and the degree of vilification in comic attacks on individuals, and often imagine that such criticisms could not have been intended, much less taken, at all seriously: if comedy was not merely an innocuous festive activity detached from the real world, then there must have been some special exemption, legal or cultural, for comic outspokenness. Neither alternative is satisfactory: certainly the comic festival was not a political meeting, but neither was it a purely festive "time out of time": it was rather a special opportunity for the whole polis to look at itself in a critical way, with serious matters often on the agenda. Moderns, in whose world art, religion, humor and politics are largely separate activities, find it hard to grasp the different situation of fifth-century Athens, where such dichotomies did not exist. There, festival and state were inseparable and included one another; the Athenians expected their poets to be "teachers" on all matters affecting life and society; and as a rule they were much less inclined than we are to treat their political leaders with fear and deference. Since the Athenian people were themselves the government, they tended to see their elite leaders more as advisers and competitors for public status than as august representatives of "the state."[12] Even the gods come in for their share of jesting. Indeed, the "right of every citizen to speak freely" (*parrhesia*) was a proud hallmark of the Athenian democracy, and the comic poets exemplified the reality of this right.

There was, however, an important difference between Athenian *parrhesia* and American freedom of speech that is relevant to comic speech: the Athenians did not recognize what we know as "protected speech" or "intellectual freedom," nor did their slander laws seek to protect the individual from harm. In Athens, any sort of speech could be (and often was) punished if (and only if) it could be construed as threatening the democratic polis or unfairly compromising the ability of any member of the demos to participate in democratic governance; otherwise it was not punished.[13] Failure to appreciate this peculiarity of Athenian *parrhesia* has led some to think that comic outspokenness (particularly as regards the abuse of individuals) went beyond what would have been permitted in strictly political discourse and so must have been somehow exempt from the rules. But the comic poets in fact articulate themselves comfortably within the prevailing norms of *parrhesia*: their "improper" language aside, all the modes of comic caricature, criticism, mockery and abuse are found also in contemporary political and forensic oratory; and conversely, whatever strictly political speakers avoid the comic poets also avoid, which would not be the case if they enjoyed a special license to say whatever they wanted without fear of being taken seriously. That comic advice could be taken seriously, at least on occasion, is demonstrated most prominently by the case of *Frogs* (above) and by the case of the philosopher Sokrates: the Athenians seem to have taken to heart the criticisms Aristophanes made in *Clouds* of 423, however exaggerated they may have been. As Plato reported in his *Apology*, Aristophanes' portrait of Sokrates may have been "nonsensical" but nevertheless was a significant factor in the people's decision to condemn him to death in 399.

That comic criticisms were trenchant rather than innocuous is also suggested by their tendentiousness. It is not true, as some claim, that comic poets launched their satirical attacks against all prominent people and all popular policies indiscriminately. Aristophanes in fact shows strong and consistent biases against the left—radical populists (e.g. Kleon), innovators artistic (e.g. Euripides) and intellectual (e.g. Sokrates), unfair manipulators of democratic freedoms (e.g. professional litigators)—while entirely sparing from criticism, and championing the ideology of, conservative landowners. In addition, comic poets, like any other public voices, tried to avoid actionable slander (statements that might affect the political standing of a member of the demos) and did not criticize either the democratic constitution or the inherent rightness of the demos' rule. Nor did they speak ill of the (honorable) dead, compromise the integrity of the state religion, or violate sensitive social protocols by (for example) compromising the integrity of respectable women or girls (IV, below). Following each festival there was an assembly in which anyone who had a legal complaint could come forward.

The comic poets thus seem to follow the operative rules for public voices: to avoid annoying (1) the demos or (2) anyone who might persuade the demos that he had been attacked in a manner threatening to democratic ideals or processes. In other words, all public advice, criticism and abuse had to be expressed in terms of the rules governing *parrhesia*, which safeguarded the discourses proper to the hegemonic ideology of the democracy.[14] If the criticism and abuse we find in Old Comedy and in Athenian oratory often seems outrageous by our standards, it is because we differ from fifth-century Athenians in our definition of outrageous, not because orators and comic poets were held to no standards.

Aristophanes, for example, was twice prosecuted by the politician Kleon, once for slandering the demos and its officers in front of visiting foreigners (in

*Babylonians* of 426) and once for slandering Kleon himself (in *Knights* of 424). In the first instance the demos decided not to hear the case. In the second the poet and the politician settled out of court. (Aristophanes subsequently boasted that he had not abided by the agreement.) The demos could also punish comic poets by authorizing smaller stipends or by enacting laws restricting comic freedoms. One of these was enacted in 440, when Perikles led Athens to war against her own ally Samos, and another in 415, in the aftermath of the scandal involving parody of the Eleusinian Mysteries of Demeter. It is perhaps relevant that three of the men condemned in this affair seem to have been comic poets. At the same time, restrictive actions against comedy seem to have been sporadic and short-lived, and suits against comic poets rare: clearly the genre had broad support and its transgressive elements enjoyed a wider latitude than would be allowed in other venues.

## III. PERFORMANCE

### *Theater and Audience*

The theater of Dionysos on the south slope of the Akropolis of Athens was a large amphitheater that, in Aristophanes' time at least, could accommodate as many as 10,000 spectators. The two annual theatrical festivals (II, above), which were national holidays, opened with religious and civic ceremonies, patriotic displays and tribal competitions in dithyramb (each of the ten tribes entered a chorus of fifty older men and a chorus of fifty boys). On the following days came the dramas: three tragic tetralogies (but only two at the Lenaia) and five comedies.[15] Spectators would typically arrive at the theater early each morning and spend the whole day in attendance. Uniquely in the festive calendar of the Athenians, there was a fee for admission. The price of a seat seems never to have exceeded two obols, roughly equivalent to the cost of attending a major concert today and thus not an impossible expense for people of at least moderate means who were strongly motivated to attend. At some point a "theoric" (spectator) fund, administered through the local demes, was created to subsidize the attendance of citizens who could not afford a seat. This fund is not mentioned in any of our sources until 343 BCE, but a few later sources trace it back to the fifth century. The creation of the theoric fund implies the previous nonattendance of the poorer class of citizens. If the fund was created only after the time of Aristophanes, it could be that the conservative and upper-class biases of fifth-century political comedy (II, above) were designed to play to an audience that did not include a significant number of lower-class citizens. On the other hand, contemporary public oratory, whose audiences did contain lower-class citizens, shows essentially similar biases, and the "new comedy" that flourished after the establishment of the theoric fund, and when theaters were larger and more numerous, still largely depicts the life, and reflects the attitudes, of the middle or upper classes.

The composition of the theatrical audience was in other respects as exceptional as its size. Unlike all purely civic congregations, which were open only to adult male citizens in good standing, and unlike most other public congregations, like religious and sporting festivals, where certain classes of residents were typically excluded or unwelcome, the dramas were open to everyone: not only to women and children but also to slaves and (especially at the Dionysia) foreigners. Front-row seating was reserved for important civic, military and religious figures (including priestesses in charge of major cults) and for visiting dignitaries; there were also special sections for the 500 Councillors, newly commissioned male citizens and war orphans. Presumably the rest of the good seats were occupied by other male citizens and any male guests they might bring along. Women, small children and slaves probably sat in a separate area behind the men.

The presence of women in the theater has been a controversial issue since the turn of the nineteenth century, though not before then: no classical source states or even implies that women could not or did not attend; Plato several times explicitly says that women formed part of the traditional audience for drama; the later anecdotal tradition about the classical theater assumes women's presence; and there are several apparent (though arguably ambiguous) allusions to female spectators in fifth-century comedy.[16] Even if we put this testimonial material aside, it is difficult to imagine a plausible reason why women would have been subject to what amounts to a unique exclusion, especially in the context of a festival for Dionysos, whose cults (like the dramas themselves) were always deeply involved with women, households and issues of gender and, where they were exclusive, typically excluded not women but men.

It used to be thought that women must at least have been excluded from the comic performances because of their "indecency," but that is anachronistic: there is no sort of indecency in comedy that was not also abundantly on offer in the cults and indeed in the everyday life of what was still largely an agricultural society, and women's participation in these (especially the highly sexualized and transgressive cults of Demeter and Dionysos) is solidly documented. A more recent argument for women's exclusion claims that the dramatic festivals belonged exclusively to the "civic space" of the democracy and therefore automatically excluded such nonenfranchised residents as women. But this explanation will not do either, since it fails to explain the well-documented presence of children, foreigners, slaves and resident aliens (who could even perform at the Lenaia), which already demonstrates the suprapolitical character of the festivals. In this connection it must be borne in mind (1) that the "civic space" of the democracy was not a monolithically demarcated zone but a complex of notional spaces whose identity shifted according to the occasion; (2) that the rigid separation of civic and noncivic spaces that we find articulated in Athenian law and "official" ideology often masks their more complementary and interpenetrable character in everyday life; and (3) that the Athenian democracy was not merely a political system and a set of institutions for enfranchised males but a way of life, and an ideology, for everyone—and nowhere was that more true than in its festive activities. One of the important functions of drama was its ability to address an inclusive audience on the meaning of this way of life, so that to exclude only women from participation would be most paradoxical, and something we would surely have heard about.

The idea that Athenian dramas were written exclusively for male audiences seems even more paradoxical in view of the prominence of women in them and their frequent focus on gender conflicts. Only one extant tragedy (Sophokles' *Philoktetes*) lacks female characters altogether, and more than half of the tragedies known to have been produced in the fifth century have as their title either a woman's name or the designation of a woman's chorus. As for comedy, the three plays in this volume concentrate primarily on women and their world and attribute to their female characters complaints and advice that ring true to life; the plot of one of them, *Women at the Thesmophoria*, actually revolves around the reaction of Athenian women to their portrayal in Euripides' plays. In these circumstances, nonattendance by women requires us to assume that the female characters created, and the gender conflicts addressed, by Athenian dramatists were directed at men only, and that Athenian women (unlike many modern women) would have found nothing of interest in them. Arguments to this effect have nevertheless been formulated, and will be dealt with in section IV, below; but meanwhile they gain no support from the particulars of the performances themselves.

That all female characters, even the "naked women" of comedy, were played by men does not mean that Athenian drama was a drag show or tell against the possibility that these portrayals of women were intended to be believable. After all, Shakespeare's women were also played by men (before audiences that included women), but no one finds them especially untrue to life: like the female characters of Athenian drama, they are now played by female actors without any need of adjustment. If male portrayal of females was not simply an Athenian theatrical convention but a drag show for men, we would expect to find the dramatists (especially the comic poets) calling attention to its artificiality. But there are no examples of this: male and female characters are at all times understood to be, respectively, men and women, and every character's gender was always obvious at least from the mask: pale for women, dark for men.[17] Finally, the convention by which men played women's roles was less a strain on the imagination in the theater of Dionysos than it would be in today's theatrical media: the wearing of masks, together with the huge amphitheater setting, put a premium on the actor's voice and on broad, stylized gestures.[18]

Nevertheless, despite the frequent appearance of believable slave, foreign and female characters in the plays and the presence of their counterparts in the audience, it remains true that the dramatic poets seem to address their plays to the male citizens, only rarely and obliquely acknowledging the presence of others. Thus the notional audience of drama (the executive male demos) differed by convention from the actual audience (the demos plus its wards and guests), so that the spectacle was at once civic/political (exclusive) and festive (inclusive). This convention is not hard to understand in view of Athenian norms both social and institutional.

That the female spectators of drama were conventionally invisible follows the general pattern of Athenian public etiquette: a citizen did not publicly name or explicitly allude to any living, respectable woman not holding a public office (such as a priesthood).[19] There was also an ideological component to female invisibility: in its attempt to control all public and potentially political aspects of women's behavior, the democracy tended to sequester them wherever practicable and officially to ignore them otherwise; on their part, women were not to take political advantage of such public events as funerals but to be publicly silent.[20] For these reasons direct appeals or references to female spectators would have been both offensive to everyone's sense of propriety and threatening to the men of the polis in their capacity as official representatives and hosts. In addition, the dramas were a male competition, and in any competitive male context, input from or appeal to women would have been resented as demeaning.[21] In the particular case of comedy, whose topical criticisms and advice sought to have an impact, even if unofficial, on the governance of the polis, the poets were primarily interested in reaching the citizen males. Finally, Athens was essentially patriarchal, so the fact that its official dramas were essentially male-oriented is neither surprising nor incompatible with the assumption that the women in the audience will have internalized many of the same values; women in patriarchal societies must in the end be consumers of male culture. Like the lawcourts, then, which women could attend but not address, the theater was an assembly sponsored by and representing the official community, so that in its civic aspect it was an assembly where women and their world could be portrayed, but only by men for a notional audience of men.

### *Actors and Chorus*

The stage-area was a slightly raised platform behind the large *orchestra* ("dancing area"), which was originally (and in Aristophanes' time) rectangular but circular in later times. Behind it was a wooden two-story building called the *skene* ("tent," from which our word "scene"). It had two or three doors at stage level, windows at the second story, and a roof on which actors could appear. On the roof was a crane called the *mechane* ("machine"), on which actors could fly above the stage (as gods, for example, whence the Latin expression *deus ex machina*, "god from the machine"). Another piece of permanent equipment was a wheeled platform called the *ekkyklema* ("device for rolling out"), on which actors and scenery could be wheeled onstage from the skene to reveal "interior" action. A painted or otherwise decorated plywood facade could be attached to the skene if a play (or scene) required it, and movable props and other scenery were used as needed. Since plays were performed in daylight in a large outdoor amphitheater, all entrances and exits of performers and objects took place in full view of the spectators. All in all, more demand was made on the spectators' imagination than in modern illusionistic theater, so that performers must often tell the spectators what they are supposed to see.

The actors wore masks that covered the entire head. These were generic (young man, old woman, etc.) but in comedy might occasionally be special, like a portrait-mask of a prominent citizen (Sokrates may well have been so caricatured in *Clouds*, for example). The costumes of tragic actors were grand, as befitted personages from heroic myth; comic costumes[22] were contemporary and generically suited to the characters except that, wherever possible, they accommodated the traditional features of padded stomach and rump and (for men) the phallos, made of leather, either dangling or erect as appropriate, and circumcised in the case of outlandish barbarians.[23] As noted above, all dramatic roles were played by men; the "naked" women who often appear were men wearing body stockings to which false breasts and genitalia were attached. The city supplied an equal number of actors to each competing poet, probably three, and these actors played all the speaking roles. In *Birds*, for example, there are twenty-two speaking roles, but the text's entrances and exits are so arranged that three actors can play them all. Some plays (like *Lysistrata*) do, however, require a fourth actor in small roles. It could be that in given years the allotment changed, or novices were periodically allowed to take small parts, or poets or producers could add extra actors at their own expense.

In the comic orchestra was a chorus of twenty-four men who sang and danced to the accompaniment of an *aulos*, a wind instrument that had two recorder-like pipes played simultaneously by a specially costumed player; and there could be other instruments as well. Like actors, members of the chorus wore masks and costumes appropriate to their dramatic identity. There could be dialogue between the chorus-leader and the actors onstage, but the chorus as a whole only sings and dances.[24] The choral songs of comedy were in music and language usually in a popular style, though serious styles were often parodied, and the dancing was expressive, adding a visual dimension to the words and music.

### The Formal Structures of Comedy

Old Comedy in Aristophanes' day had a number of conventional features of form and structure. Typically we find: a scene in which the initial situation is revealed to the spectators (Prologue); the song of the chorus as it enters the orchestra (Parodos); a dispute leading to a formally structured debate (Agon); the self-revelation of the chorus, usually containing a speech to the spectators delivered by the chorus-leader on behalf of the poet (Parabasis); a series of scenes (Episodes) illustrating the results of the comic scheme and articulated by choral songs more or less detached from the plot (often mocking individuals in the audience); and finally an exit-song by the chorus (Exodos). In some plays, like *Clouds*, there can be a second Parabasis and/or a second Agon. Not all of these structural components are found, or found in the order given above, in each of Aristophanes' plays: during his career he creatively manipulated them for his own purposes, and as time went by, those components designed for plays featuring a prominently involved chorus (Parodos, Agon and Parabasis) tended to shrink or disappear, so that in his late play *Assemblywomen* we already see the beginnings of the comic form that was to become standard for centuries to come: Prologue followed by Episodes (later, acts) articulated by detached, and often optional, choral songs.

A fifth-century comedy was played through without intermission, the performance probably lasting about two hours.

## IV. WOMEN IN ARISTOPHANIC COMEDY

### The State of the Evidence

Real-life Athenian women are all but invisible. They cannot speak directly to us, for although a woman's service in a public cult might be recorded, or she might leave an epitaph,[25] women were otherwise debarred from all media of public expression and so were largely unable to document their own existence.[26]

Athenian men, for reasons of social protocol connected with the new demo-cratic laws and ideology (II, above), took great pains to conceal the women of their households from public view and even from being publicly mentioned by name: although women had personal names (often feminine versions of male names), these were for "internal" family use only; respectable women could be publicly referred to (when a reference was unavoidable) only as X's wife or X's daughter.[27] In the public sphere women and their lives could be portrayed only by the men themselves, so that virtually all we know about Athenian women must be derived from male sources: art, literature, laws, courtroom cases, social regulations—all were masculine creations; in drama, "women" were male performers enacting female roles written by male poets (III, above). And such portrayals were almost always generic rather than personal—characters from heroic myth or fictional types—since any portrayal that might be con-strued as alluding to living Athenian women could be thought questionable, if not outrageous.[28] Exceptions were made only for women holding a public (i.e. priestly) position in her own right, and for the wife or mother (but never the unmarried daughter) of an enemy.

In these conditions it is very difficult to recover the sort of details about women's lives that they themselves might have considered important, and quite impossible to know how women viewed themselves and their world. Theirs is at best an objective and not a subjective record. Nevertheless, our sources, male-derived though they are, still tell us a great deal about women: if it is not the whole picture, it is at least half the picture. And even by itself the male view is interesting: it enables us to study the rules and roles that men created for women and to glimpse the desires and fears that prompted their enforcement, and thus we can form some appreciation of the gender dynamics of a cultural system that, after all, long served as an important role model for Western culture as a whole. Old Comedy is an especially valuable source, being uniquely free to create topical portrayals even of citizen women, including what purport to be their complaints against Athenian men and the male-dominated system of democratic Athens.[29]

The following overview, necessarily brief, will consider first the social and legal outlines of the normative gender system that the men created and operated, as a background against which to assess at least the typological verisimilitude of the women portrayed in comedy;[30] more detailed information is given in the introductions and notes to the plays in this volume. Then we will try to ascertain whether and to what degree the comic portrayals are about women at all, or merely a sort of artifice by which men communicated with one another about essentially male concerns.

## The Normative System

As outlined in II, above, the culture of democratic Athens distinguished sharply between the public and the private spheres of life, and this distinction was gender-oriented. In terms of persons and places the private sphere embraced the individual household or *oikos*, a complex entity managed by the citizen wife of its citizen head (the husband and father), governed by family relations, and aligned with other households by ties such as kinship, marriage, friendship, or participation in common cults. This private sphere was the proper domain of women, children and slaves. The oikos was represented and safeguarded by its male head in the public sphere of the official polis, which was the exclusive domain of citizen males, consisting of those areas of life where, in competition with other men, he sought reputation and honor: in law, politics, business, warfare and various prestige-contests. While citizen males had authority in both spheres, citizen women (ideally at least) could operate only in the private sphere and had no autonomous authority in either. Noncitizens of either sex— resident aliens and slaves—had no civic rights or authority: slaves were completely subject to their owners and masters, and aliens were at liberty only at the sufferance of the polis.

The executive Athenian polis was thus a legal, political and military entity comprised of and regulated by the individual citizen-male heads of households, and among its chief goals was to insure the integrity and continuity of each household. To this end, inheritance was strictly regulated: a household passed from its head male either to his legitimate sons (his children by a wife who was also a citizen) or, in the absence of sons, to his nearest male relative. A woman had no official claim to a household: she belonged to household and polis only by virtue of being the daughter, wife or mother of a citizen male, or the ward of the citizen male who was otherwise entitled to her. Marriages were arranged by fathers with an eye to establishing suitable alliances with other households. In marriage the husband's job was to safeguard the integrity and the property of his household, and the wife's job was to manage her husband's household and to produce its male heirs. Athenian law for the most part watched over the public sphere: apart from its interest in the proper maintenance and transmission of a household's property, the law did not normally regulate the private sphere, where families were left to their own devices and the "unwritten laws" of social and religious custom. In this respect, women and children were outside the law, and in having no absolute autonomy or acknowledged subjectivity their status resembled that of slaves.

Though not answerable to polis law, however, an ill-behaved woman could be socially sanctioned: divorced by her husband, shunned by her community or debarred from religious life, where as celebrants, officials or priestesses women had their only opportunity to achieve a degree of independence, even prominence, in their own right.[31] Conversely, private scandal could result in a man being debarred from participation in the public sphere, which amounted to social emasculation, since he was now relegated to the sphere of women and slaves. Busybodies were a notorious feature of democratic life in Athens, encouraged as they were by the legal provision for voluntary prosecution of anyone whose speech or behavior could be portrayed to a jury as being harmful to the democracy. A man's household was always a great potential liability.

In these circumstances the chastity of one's daughter and wife were of crucial importance: female derelictions could impair a daughter's marriage-ability, a son's eligibility to inherit, and a household's fiscal and social stability. This sort of trouble in a man's private sphere could compromise his public standing, with potentially disastrous consequences. Needless to say, chastity and sexual fidelity were concepts that applied only to citizen women: although marital love was the norm and ideal of sexual happiness (as *Lysistrata* takes as a given), men who could afford the price were free to enjoy mistresses and prostitutes—these were always either noncitizens or slaves—since any off-spring with them would be illegitimate and so could not affect a man's property or inheritance. But men who seduced another man's wife (calling into question the legitimacy of his children) or daughter (ruining her chances of a good marriage) were considered to have violated the integrity of that man's oikos and so were subject to severe penalties, including death.

Managerial competence was also an important responsibility of a house-hold's women. Running a household in ancient Athens was a far more complex and labor-intensive job than it is in today's industrialized world: it included provisioning and bookkeeping, clothes-making, food preparation, cleaning and maintenance, supervision of slaves, often running an oikos based agricultural or manufacturing business, and keeping track of the household's extended familial, social and religious ties with other households: weddings, funerals, celebrations, assistance at births, participation in cults. The less well a man's womenfolk discharged these duties, the less fully was he able to participate in public activities and the less well could he maintain his civic standing. In this area, too, he was in some sense at the mercy of his wife.

Men therefore took elaborate measures to avoid any public exposure of their private worlds, principally by discouraging public exposure of the women of their households. A woman seen too often away from her house might be considered neglectful of her duties, and one conversing at any time with strange males would expose herself to suspicion of infidelity. And so the private sphere was considered officially separate, hidden by protocols of public invisibility and silence. Ideally, the women of a man's household would, as the orator Lysias somewhat defensively put it, "live so respectably that they are shamed at being seen even by members of the family" (3.6) and, in the words of Perikles, would be "least talked about by men either for praise or for blame" (Thucydides 2.46). The boundaries between public and private were fluid but could always be established by the movements of each gender: wherever men were, respectable women were not, and vice versa. Part of a woman's own home became part of the public sphere, and off-limits to her, whenever men unrelated to the family came to visit. Typically this would be for a *symposion*, a party where men drank and talked, often in the company of mistresses or prostitutes. Conversely, normally public spaces became off-limits to men whenever women occupied them, as for the festival of Thesmophoria, when for three days the matrons occupied the Pnyx Hill, the site of the civic assembly. At public events attended by men and women together, such as state funerals and festivals, unrelated men and women would avoid each other's company.[32]

The ideal separateness of public and private engendered a normative definition of gender-roles that was mutually exclusive and absolutely complementary: men, and the skills and virtues that defined manhood, were what women, and the skills and virtues that defined womanhood, were not, and vice versa. Since women did not do the same things a man did, they could not reap the rewards that men aspired to, and men consequently thought that women lacked the necessary virtues; indeed, anything a woman could also achieve would not be of value to a man. Women were credited with virtues, and these were highly esteemed: the august goddesses Athena, Demeter and Aphrodite embodied most of them. But women's virtues were different from men's, and men considered them lower-order virtues by comparison with their own. And since men were vulnerable on their household side, they kept a close watch on the women, and consequently came to believe that the women needed watching; women were therefore thought naturally to lack self-control and loyalty. At the same time, Athenian men expressed great esteem for women and the vital roles they played in their own spheres, and if asked why they kept women under wraps would reply that the women deserved no less than the most vigilant protection and respect.

In this gender-system, there was no overlap, no space or sphere of action that was common to men and women, so that the two genders tended to define one another. A man whose behavior seemed womanish or slavish (e.g. who shaved or had a sparse beard, who masturbated, who was timid in battle or in a competition, who was emotional, deceptive, easily tempted, bossed by his wife[33]) could suffer considerable social degradation; worse, he could be debarred from public life if he had ever allowed himself to be sexually penetrated. Just so, a woman who was unchaste (sexually autonomous and therefore unwomanly) could be shunned, or lose her marital position, in the private sphere.

This ideal system of strict seclusion and sexual segregation of women had great normative force but in reality only the most affluent households could afford to put it entirely into practice. Most households had few slaves to take care of errands and outdoor chores, and though slave and alien women typically worked the "outside" jobs that required them to be in public spaces, the women of the poorest citizen classes might have to work alongside them.[34] For most households, then, decorum was less a matter of living up to the ideal than of managing appearances: a woman had to make sure her public conduct would always seem legitimate enough in the eyes of a watchful community as to offer no opportunity for malicious gossip, and in no event could she seem to be challenging the ideal. She would not be seen too often in public spaces and never alone, and she would avoid conversation with any unrelated males.

Otherwise, a woman was free to associate with companions of her own sex: neighbors for the most part, but a much wider circle if she had family in other demes or could secure a role in one or more of the many cults that were managed by women at the local and national level.[35] The most prominent national priesthoods might even gain a woman a certain public competence and legitimate public visibility.[36] As for men, whatever their behavior in their own homes might be, their public behavior must always appear to be fully manly, that is, both manly and not womanly in any way.

### Comic Portrayals

Drama and oratory were the principal "literature" of the Athenian polis. Oratory, being confined to the public worlds of assembly and lawcourts, had little to say about women and their world except where these might impinge on a man's political or legal standing in the polis, and in such cases the viewpoint was strictly male and ideal. Drama, by contrast, was performed for an inclusive audience on occasions that were at once civic and festive (III, above), and it portrayed not only public life but also, and primarily, family life. And so it is natural that drama would portray women as well as men. But it is curious that although respectable women characters had long been featured in tragedy, it was only in 411 that we find them (in Lysistrata and Women at the Thesmophoria) as prominent characters in comedy.[37]

The likeliest explanation is that tragic women, who were drawn exclusively from the repertory of heroic myth, were not traditionally regarded as a threat to the propriety of Athenian women, whereas any portrayal of respectable women in the topical genre of comedy would have been disturbing. The appearance of more lifelike women in Euripides' plays seems to have strained this generic protocol: by 411 he had acquired a reputation for misogyny and (according to the women in Aristophanes' plays of that year) for embarrassing respectable Athenian women. And so it would seem that a degree of verisimilitude was a significant factor in the portrayal of women in drama, and that more lifelike portrayals were an innovation of the progressive drama first of Euripides and then of Aristophanes.[38] Since such portrayals seem to have appeared first during the long Peloponnesian War (431–404), they may well reflect a relaxation of the normal proprieties, and actual female discontent, in a time of extraordinary pressures: the movement of the rural population into the city, the continuous absence of men on campaigns, the disruption of domestic routines, economic pressure on households, the unprecedented casualties among men who were, or would have been, husbands and fathers—all these are actually mentioned by Aristophanes as factors motivating the actions and protests of his female characters, and they cannot have been entirely the product of his own imagination.

Aristophanes and Euripides were in fact the dramatists most acutely aware of the ambivalence, contradictions and tensions inherent in the Athenian social and political system, and they constantly explored them as a key element of that radical and often satirical critique of ideological stances that was central, and unique, to their genres.[39] To this critique each playwright, in response to the upheavals occasioned by the war, contributed memorable female characters and unique formulations of gender-conflict. Aristophanes' criticism of Euripides' daring portrayals (particularly in *Acharnians*, *Women at the Thesmophoria* and *Frogs*) is to a degree disingenuous, for he is usually "guilty" of the same charges himself, often to the point of creative borrowing from Euripides; certainly he was inspired by Euripides' portrayals. But in his own pungently satirical genre Aristophanes was free to go much farther than a tragic poet, even Euripides, could go. Aristophanes based his female characters (as he does his males) on their real-life counterparts for verisimilitude, but he also exploited prevailing stereotypes in order to create ideological complexity, with attention constantly being drawn to the gaps and misfits between actual and ideal behavior on both sides of the gender divide. Thus "Aristophanes' dramas are not an unthinking product of male ideologies, but rather a conscious manipulation and satire of them."[40] Aristophanes' basic strategy is to create women who would simultaneously stress their own importance to the polis and challenge its male-authored status quo.

Comedy, like tragedy, portrays women not as a monolithic category but according to typical criteria of age, class and social context. Only citizen women appear as speaking characters, and they belong to the respectable, even the upper-class strata of Athenian society; Lysistrata appears to be recalling the most prominent and high-born woman of her day, the priestess of Athena Polias, Lysimache. Like composers for all other public media,

Aristophanes and his characters adhere to the protocol by which a free man does not refer by name to a living respectable woman not holding a public (i.e. priestly) office,[41] though women whom a comic poet considered disreputable—the wife or mother (but not maiden daughter) of a political enemy, for example—could be insulted by name, and even portrayed onstage.

Comedy, like tragedy, portrays women and their world always in an oppositional relation to men and the masculine world; there were plays that treated only men's concerns, but no plays that treated only women's. Mythical tragedy had little problem arranging a common ground for meetings between men and women: its heroic scenarios allowed both public and private issues to be confronted from within a royal household. But Aristophanes' comedies, being topical and political, respect his culture's strict separation of public and private. To take his women out of the household in a plausible way Aristophanes associates them with the cults of goddesses: in real life these provided the only avenue by which citizen women could achieve public visibility and some measure of autonomy in their own right, and so they provided Aristophanes with a realistic venue from which his women could publicly confront men.

Though maidens frequently appear in tragedy, they appear only rarely and circumspectly in fifth-century comedy; the horny citizen girl in *Assemblywomen* is a striking anomaly in all of extant comedy. Older women, being past the age of childbearing and therefore posing no sexual threat to their households, in real life enjoyed greater freedoms, responsibilities and respect than young wives; in both tragedy and comedy they are portrayed as forthright (sometimes excessively so), responsible and sage, so that when men are to be confronted or admonished it is older women, not young wives, who do the job.[42]

As in tragedy, where marriage is a strife-ridden and dangerous institution for both husbands and wives,[43] the young wives in comedy receive almost all of the negative traits associated with women as a gender: they are typically frivolous, spendthrift, naive, ignorant of realities outside the household, devious, impulsive and sex-obsessed. They talk of stealing food and wine from the household stores,[44] lying to their husbands about where they have been when they go out, purchasing male slave-babies to supply their husbands with an heir, using dildoes, and dreaming of lovers, sometimes expressing resentment at competition from pretty slave-girls. But even here Aristophanes preserves the minimal decorum: though we hear a lot about wives' misbehavior, and in some respects (particularly their bold sexuality) they are compared to courtesans, we never actually see them misbehaving,[45] and they are never shown alone in the company of any men other than their husbands. And the marital relationships portrayed in comedy are for the most part benign: wily wife, obtuse husband. The terms of Aristophanes' satire of husbands and wives is not monolithic but depends very much on a play's particular theme: in *Lysistrata* (where war is shown disrupting wholesome normality) the marital bond is held up as the ideal of sexual happiness, while in *Assemblywomen* (where marriage and the household are declared failed institutions) the women strive to free themselves from it. But by comparison with the femmes fatales of tragedy and with his own savage caricature and abuse of male characters, Aristophanes' portrayal of wives is decidedly gallant.

Although conflict between husbands and wives was a staple in both tragedy and comedy, both genres were careful to give their wives believable and often sympathetic complaints about the institution of marriage and about women's position in the polis: resentment about restricted courtship, arranged marriage and the sexual double standard; annoyance at the restrictions imposed by male suspicions and at the deceit and manipulation of appearances that were so often the necessary response; frustration about women's inability to participate in or directly influence decisions in the public sphere that had a direct impact on their lives, especially decisions about warfare, which cost them fathers, husbands and sons; and a feeling that their own contributions to family and society were not sufficiently acknowledged, public honor belonging almost exclusively to the male sphere. No doubt wives in real life (especially wives with handsome dowries and powerful relatives) made similar complaints; even under the strictest patriarchies resourceful women can wield considerable power within their own families and exert influence on their husbands even on public matters, and women socially or ritually active seem to have had considerable authority in their local communities. But as long as such influence remained in the private sphere it was ignorable and deniable in the public sphere if the men so chose.[46] Here drama played an important role in bringing women's concerns and complaints out of the shadows: in dramatizing the female point of view, the dramatic poets provided a vicarious public voice for the one class of citizens otherwise debarred from public expression, thus (in good Dionysiac fashion) exposing the artificiality of, and in effect inverting, the public and "official" pattern of authority.

The contrast between the male and female worlds was also dramatized at the ideological level. In tragedy, as in myth generally, the female world is typically portrayed as a threat to the men's: women are essentially wild (the Amazons are paradigmatic) and must be tamed in the interests of civilization (defined as male); and the claims of the household, important though they may be, must be subordinated to the larger justice of the (male-ordered) polis (as Aischylos' *Oresteia* memorably argues). Aristophanes, by contrast, typically portrays the household and its female managers as superior to the polis and its male managers in terms of solidarity, prudence and good sense, competence, adherence to tried-and-true traditions, loyalty to the highest civic ideals, reverence for life, and devotion to the gods. And by contrast with tragedy, where gender strife usually ends in disaster for both genders, comic gender-wars result in the restoration of harmony (*Lysistrata* and *Women at the Thesmophoria*) or the establishment of a social utopia (*Assemblywomen*) that even the men accept (the sympathetically characterized ones, at least). In comedy, when men are bested by women, it turns out to be for their own good.

In part, Aristophanes intends this ideological comparison to shame the men in the audience into accepting his political advice and criticisms—it is noteworthy that he attributes to his heroines many of the same ideas that he or one of his heroes argues in other plays—but since we find the same comparison in such serious authors as Plato, we should not automatically assume it to be merely paradoxical or a humorous inversion. After all, the preeminent symbol of Athens was Athena, whose Akropolis cult was the ideal household writ large.[47]

### Gender-specific Characteristics of Comedy

As an institution drama was a male enterprise: written and performed by men before a notional audience of men (see III, above) for prizes that were awarded by judges representing the male spectators and that conferred esteem in the public world of men. Female characters are plentiful, and their world is frequently explored, but always in relation to men and the male world, which the women always challenge and threaten to disrupt. Consequently, it has been argued that, despite the prominence of women in Attic drama, these plays were never really about women at all, but about men.[48] According to this model, women were not represented in Attic drama for their own sake, but instead were complex modes of male self-representation. The female mask could license male speech that would otherwise be improper (because too emotional, for example, or too politically sensitive),[49] or enable men conveniently to speak about women by speaking for them.[50] Moreover, women and their hidden world served as "the radical other," an area of absolute difference by which the poets could problematize and challenge the boundaries, behavior and values of the male gender and its civilization, and so provoke their (re)definition, (re)construction and (re)affirmation. By showing male characters confronting female characters, the dramatists invite the male audience to confront both their own constructions of the female and their own anxieties about the justice of the civic and family worlds over which they had claimed exclusive control. In this way, the dramatists were fulfilling their traditional role as educators of the male citizens in charge of the democracy.

This model is certainly valid in some respects but is probably too narrowly drawn. The dramatists' portrayal of women as "radically other" would have been neither possible nor plausible if Athenian men were not generally anxious about women and their problematic relationships to household and polis, and if women did not express their own anxieties as well. If the role of heroines in drama is always to challenge, and never uncritically to support, the male status quo, the same after all can be said of heroes. Clearly, life as lived by women was a subject for drama too. Comedy in particular seems to include verisimilitude in its satirical agenda; gives women complaints and suggestions that ring true to life; imitates their characteristic patterns of speech;[51] and takes for granted that a substantial number of Athenians of both sexes understood at least Euripides' plays about women not primarily as challenges to male constructs of identity but (also) as plays about women. And for what it is worth, modern audiences generally accept the female characters of Attic drama as believable women. Whether the women in the audience really reacted in their own way to their dramatic representation, as Aristophanes says they did, we are no longer in a position to verify; but none of the information we do possess rules this out. That dramatists writing for the largest and most inclusive audience of Athenians that assembled during the year would focus so prominently on women and yet ignore their reality seems inherently improbable. If drama was an education for Athenians, it was an education for all Athenians, not only the men.

## V. NOTES ON THE TRANSLATION

Like all classical playwrights Aristophanes wrote his plays in verse: for spoken dialogue he used a standard iambic trimeter line roughly similar to English "blank verse"; for speeches and formal debates he used a longer line in iambic, trochaic or anapestic rhythm, probably accompanied by the pipe (*aulos*); and for songs accompanied by music (songs for the chorus and arias or duets for the actors) he used various lyric rhythms, typically those reflecting popular styles except when he was parodying the more elaborate styles of tragedy or archaic lyric. Choral singing was strophic, meaning that the songs were normally written in pairs of matching stanzas called "strophe" and "antistrophe"; I have indicated strophic pairs in the translation. In the interest of clarity and accuracy, however, I have not attempted a verse translation, which restricts a translator's options, but have instead rendered the Greek in straightforward, idiomatic prose.

Aristophanes' basic linguistic register was urbane, colloquial Attic, but the conventions of his genre allowed, and evidently encouraged, a strong admixture of other registers both higher (e.g. parody of tragedy and other serious poetry) and lower (e.g. imitation of vulgar speech) than the colloquial norm. In the latter category we find in Attic Old Comedy quite a lot of rough and abusive language, including outright obscenity, that will strike some readers—at least those from urban middle-class America and Europe—as being shockingly crude, sexist, homophobic, xenophobic or otherwise dis- criminatory. But we should bear in mind (1) that Aristophanes was writing not for us but for contemporaries living in a society at once very sophisticated and very different from our own, and (2) that outrageousness was a traditional ingredient of Old Comedy and one fully in keeping with comedy's tendency to expose, deflate and provoke. Thus nothing that we hear or see in an Aristoph- anic comedy can automatically be assumed to reflect the norms and behavior of the average, or indeed any, Athenian. In my translation I have therefore made no attempt to spare the modern reader by censoring or translating around potentially disturbing material; instead I have tried to render each of Aristophanes' linguistic registers by using the nearest English equivalent.

The earliest texts of Aristophanes' plays, since they were made not for readers but for those who would perform them at a single festival, included only the words of the scripts; there were no notes, stage directions or even assignments of lines to speakers. In tragedy, whose plots follow traditional myths and feature relatively few characters, actions and props, it is usually possible to assign speakers and stage directions confidently. In comedy, by contrast, plots and characters are original and not always consistent, the action more complex and less predictable, and props much more numerous, so that it is sometimes hard to infer what was happening on stage and who speaks a given line. Among the four speakers in the prologue of *Lysistrata*, for example, Lampito's Spartan accent tells us when she is speaking, as (for the most part) does Lysistrata's role as ringleader, but the assignment of lines to Kalonike and Myrrhine for the most part depends on our sense of their roles: in the first edition I assigned the role of Lysistrata's principal sidekick in this part of the play to Kalonike, but in this revision I follow the most recent editors in assign- ing it to Myrrhine, since she (and not Kalonike) is to reappear later in the play as the representative Athenian wife.

We have no authorial texts of Greek literature: in Aristophanes' case, our earliest texts were written c. 950 CE and derive from lost intermediate copies of a scholarly edition made over a century after his death. Until the first printed editions (nine of the eleven extant plays, including *Assemblywomen*, in the Aldine edition of 1498; then *Lysistrata* and *Women at the Thesmophoria* in the Juntine edition of 1516), the plays were transmitted through handwritten copies, each copy differing to some degree from every other copy, so that every editor or translator must choose from the available texts (manuscript or printed) the readings, and when no transmitted readings are satisfactory, the editorial emendations that (s)he thinks most likely reproduce Aristophanes' own lost text. In making these translations I have based myself eclectically on the complete editions of the Greek text by Henderson 1998–2007 and Wilson 2007, and of the editions of Henderson 1987, Sommerstein 1990 and Mastromarco 2006 of *Lysistrata*; Sommerstein 1994 and Austin/Olson 2004 of *Women at the Thesmophoria*; and Ussher 1973 and Sommerstein 1998 of *Assemblywomen*, except where I translate what I consider to be a preferable reading or attribution of speaker. I supply stage directions as best I can infer them from the texts.

# LYSISTRATA

# INTRODUCTION

## 1. *The Historical Context*

*Lysistrata* was produced in 411 (almost certainly at the Lenaia), twenty years into the Peloponnesian War, a panhellenic struggle pitting Athens and her island empire against Sparta and her allies.[1] Athens and Sparta had emerged from the Persian invasions (490–478) as the two superpowers of Greece. Athens, relying on her navy, had turned a defensive alliance against Persia into a tribute-paying empire composed mainly of small subject states with democratic governments controlled by the Athenian demos. Sparta, the chief city of the Peloponnese (the lower half of mainland Greece) and the greatest land power in Greece, feared the growing power of Athens and disapproved of its imperialism and its democratic government. Although Perikles, the major proponent of the war, had initially predicted a quick victory, the war lasted for twenty-seven years, ending in 404 with Athens' loss of her navy, her empire and even (for a time) her democracy.

At the start, many Athenians questioned Perikles' war plan. First, it granted the Spartans supremacy on land and allowed them to invade the Attic countryside, so that farmers and landowners had to abandon the countryside to the invaders and move into the city, where they spent the first six years of the war as virtual refugees. Second, it proved too passive for a quick victory, so that by 428 the Athenians had run through their financial reserves and were forced to raise new funds. The burden fell mainly on the wealthy, especially the landed aristocracy, on the farmers and on the subject allies, while the benefits went mainly to those who could profit financially or politically in wartime conditions: military provisioners, ambitious commanders, popular leaders. In his early plays Aristophanes championed the former group and denounced the latter. After ten years of indecisive warfare and internal division at Athens, the Peace of Nikias was arranged in 421. But some fundamental issues were not addressed and not all the major combatants signed on, so that the Peace proved to be merely a time-out, lasting only until 418, when Athens accused Sparta of violating its terms and embarked on aggressive new campaigns.

The war began to go decisively against the Athenians in 413, when their great armada, launched in 415 in hopes of conquering Sicily, was wiped out at Syracuse, with crippling losses of men, material and wealth. Important territory fell out of Athenian control; several major allies quickly defected from the empire and others threatened to follow suit; the Persians were negotiating with Sparta; and many believed that Athens would soon be helpless. By the end of 412, however, the Athenians had somehow managed to stave off defeat by winning back some strategic territory and rebuilding an effective navy. The political and fiscal discipline required to do this was facilitated by the agreement of the Assembly to accept the imposition of restraints on its own autonomy, in particular by appointing an extraordinary board of ten elderly statesmen (including the tragic poet Sophokles) called Probouloi ("executive councillors"), who could expedite the war effort by bypassing the Assembly. An unnamed member of this board is the heroine's antagonist in *Lysistrata*.

But in spite of their political housecleaning and their renewed hope of achieving an honorable peace, the Athenians at the time of *Lysistrata* (winter of 411) were still in a bad way, once again surrounded by a Spartan army of occupation, unsure of their remaining allies, financially straitened and politically volatile. And the audience that watched *Lysistrata* did not yet know the worst: that officers of the main Athenian naval base at Samos had entered into talks with the exiled Athenian aristocrat, Alkibiades, who promised to bring Persia into alliance with Athens if the Athenians would arrange his recall and agree to "a more moderate constitution with a rather smaller number eligible to hold office."[2] The general Peisandros—the only politician singled out by name for abuse in the play—had recently returned from Samos to engineer the acceptance of Alkibiades' demands but had not yet put them before the people in Assembly. The months following the performance would see the formation of an antidemocratic conspiracy complete with a campaign of propaganda, intimidation, and assassination. Although Alkibiades was ultimately unable to deliver Persian support for Athens, the conspirators moved ahead with their plans anyway, and by the summer they had succeeded in installing (temporarily) an oligarchic government.

## 2. The Play

Although *Lysistrata* has a heroine, portrays a battle of the sexes and has much to say about men and women, sex and gender, its main theme is peace—both political peace at home and an end to the great war between Greeks—and its characterizations are constructed to develop that theme.

An Athenian woman named Lysistrata organizes and successfully prosecutes a Panhellenic conspiracy of wives that forces the men of Athens and Sparta to negotiate a peaceful settlement of the war and promise never to fight one another again. Since her conspiracy requires reconciliation at home (in both senses) and abroad, it consists of two separate initiatives. One is a conjugal strike, whose divine supporter is Aphrodite, goddess of sexual enjoyment: the young wives from all the warring states will refuse to perform their domestic (especially sexual) duties until their warrior husbands lay down their arms and come home to stay. The other initiative is the occupation of the Akropolis, the sacred citadel and treasury of Athens, and its divine supporter is Athena, goddess of domestic arts and protector of the polis: by denying access to the state treasuries, which were kept on the Akropolis under Athena's aegis, the politicians will no longer be able to fund the war effort. The occupation is carried out by those women of Athens who are too old to participate in the conjugal strike; when they have secured the Akropolis the young wives join them there. The strike plot, described in the prologue and illustrated later in the play by Kinesias and Myrrhine, succeeds virtually unopposed: after only six days the young warriors are sexually desperate enough to agree to whatever terms Lysistrata demands. The occupation plot contains the agonistic component of the play: strife between semi-choruses of old men who storm the Akropolis and old women who repulse them, and a debate between Lysistrata and an elderly Magistrate (one of the board of ten Probouloi) who has come to arrest her. When the occupation plot has eliminated official opposition, and the strike plot has made the young husbands capitulate to their wives, Athenian and Spartan ambassadors negotiate their differences and promise eternal friendship. Reconciliation of the semi-choruses prefigures reconciliation between the warring cities and symbolizes the end of bitter divisiveness between the sexes and citizens generally. Lysistrata's name, though it was borne by actual women, is appropriate to her dramatic roles both strategic and sexual: it means "Disbander of Armies," with the first element (Lysi-) also connoting the power of sexual desire to "loosen" a man's limbs.

The plot of Lysistrata is typical of Aristophanes' "heroic" plays (the others are Acharnians, Peace, Birds and Assemblywomen). By means of a fantastic scheme a hero(ine), who typifies a class of citizens who feel frustrated or victimized by the operations of contemporary society, manages to evade or alter the situation about which (s)he initially complains and proceeds to effect a triumph of wish-fulfillment over reality. Those powers human, natural or divine that would obstruct the scheme are either converted by argument or overcome by guile, magic or force. At the end there is a restoration of normality (typically portrayed in terms of an idealized civic past) and a celebration (typically involving food, wine, sex and festivity) in which only the hero(ine)'s supporters and converts participate, for those who do not accept the new order have been discredited and expelled.

Although the hero(ine) typically represents views likely to be held by members of a politically powerless class, whom the hero(ine) typifies, and although the scheme bypasses, undermines or discredits the powers currently enforcing the status quo, the hero(ine)'s goal is one likely to be shared by most spectators because the arguments (s)he uses to defend it appeal to their interests, to their sense of justice, and to their resentment of the powers that be. The powers that be are portrayed unsympathetically as self-interested, corrupt and misguided, and the status quo as unjustly burdensome for ordinary, decent people. In Lysistrata, the old politicians (represented by the Magistrate) and their supporters in the Assembly (represented by the Chorus of Old Men) are portrayed as prosecuting the war out of irrational anger and as making a profit at the expense of ordinary citizens and soldiers. Their claim that there is no alternative to war is exposed as false: conjugal love (or, more precisely, sex) can conquer all, and the ordinary citizens of all the combatant states feel much the same as the Athenians do. Once the evil old Magistrate is discredited and eliminated, peace and reconciliation can be easily achieved, and all will be happy once again.

Within this combination of a populist appeal and a utopian scenario, the harsh and intractable realities of life, politics and international aggression are transformed so that wives manage to overcome husbands, love conquers war, insignificant citizens manage to discredit powerful ones, Athens obtains a peace that allows her to keep her empire intact, and the Spartans turn out to be good friends after all. This transformation, impossible in the real world, Aristophanes makes quite plausible by constructing a logical, though fantastic, plot and by appealing to the spectators' wish for a better world—the world as it presumably was in the good old days before the war, when all would be happy and prosperous and where there would be no more violence. He also appeals to the feeling of average citizens that their wishes would be more likely to come true were there no authorities in the way, constantly imposing burdensome duties and reminding them of unpleasant realities.

The dreamlike achievement of regressive wish-fulfillment and Oedipal rebellion allowed a communal release of tensions. Insofar as the release was motivated by acceptable civic ideals (peace and solidarity) and achieved in humorous fantasy (wives determining policy), it was safe and festive, cohesive rather than divisive. But insofar as it was a valid expression of people's real war-weariness and an expression of social discontent that had no other public outlet, it was also a reminder, and a fair warning, to the people's leaders that public patience might not last indefinitely. As a vehicle for such popular expressions comedy, like tragedy in its own ways, allowed the people to look at their situation from vantage points not available in other communal assemblies; from those assemblies that determined military actions, women—and therefore the vantage point of the family—were excluded. In this role, comedy was a form of unofficial and experimental politics.[3]

At the same time, *Lysistrata* differs in important ways from earlier comic plays. The idea of making the comic savior-hero a woman was apparently new: although tragic and other mythical heroines were not uncommon, we know of no comic heroine before *Lysistrata*. That the heroine acts not alone (like the heroes of earlier comedies) but in concert with, and as the leader of, her whole class (citizen women both Athenian and foreign) seems to be a further novelty. Over and above sheer novelty, however, these ideas made political and dramatic sense: creating not a hero but a heroine solved some difficult problems confronting a poet with an appeal for peace in early 411. The volatile political atmosphere discouraged the usual finger-pointing, and an appeal for solidarity ruled out a hero representing any of the embattled factions. Somehow Aristophanes had to find a respectable citizen-hero who could make plausible arguments for reconciliation at home and abroad while at the same time standing outside and above the prevailing political turmoil and the military uncertainty. To make the hero a woman was an effective, and perhaps the only available, solution. Furthermore, to portray women as a united class provided an ideal model for the important theme of solidarity, which Aristophanes urged both for Athenians and for the Greek states generally. The women's concerted action in a just cause contrasts sharply with the factional and chaotic actions of the men, just as the old notion of a "race of women" (see Introduction, IV) neatly exemplifies a wished-for "race of Greeks" at peace with one another.

But the women of *Lysistrata* are no mere mouthpieces for male arguments, even though Aristophanes' appeal for peace and solidarity does echo actual political appeals at the time and is directed to the men in his audience: after all, it was only the men who were in a position to act on his advice. As the women are careful to point out, their real-life counterparts all had a vested interest in the war (fathers, sons, and husbands in the fight) and had sacrificed much; they represented every group and social class, and each combatant city; they had had nothing to do with bringing on the war in the first place; and though they stood outside its politics, they were integral to the polis: their importance in the home and in the cults of the gods entitled them to give sane advice to the men of their respective cities. And surely their comic complaints echo the complaints that actual women would indeed have been making at this time.[4] By using women as his heroic voices, Aristophanes could admonish and advise the Athenians from a nonpartisan direction (the private world), and in case the spectators should be offended they would have to admit that it was only a woman talking.

The utopian fantasy of *Lysistrata* also differs from the other comedies in being more practical. Its characters' actions are not fundamentally outside the realm of human possibility, nor do they alter their characteristic situations or adopt uncharacteristic ones. That women might occupy and barricade the Akropolis is of course highly unlikely in fifth-century Athens, but it is not unthinkable: after all, women, not men, normally had business on the Akropolis, which belonged to the goddess Athena and not to the male government, and the women are more or less in asylum there; the theme of helpless people taking refuge in sanctuaries from malevolent men was a familiar one in epic and tragedy. And tactical dereliction of domestic duties has always been a wife's chief weapon under patriarchal systems. By continuing the war the men (warrior husbands, politicians and their supporters) have threatened the survival of the polis, and the women stop them simply by withholding their services as wives and mothers and by transferring their skills as managers of the household and its finances temporarily to the Akropolis. Though Lysistrata protests women's exclusion from policy-making that affects women's lives, the women do not question their ordinary roles or seek in any way to change them; they merely want to force the men to listen to their good advice, then return to their ordinary lives, which the war has disrupted. Unlike the gynecocracy of *Assemblywomen*, where the women adopt exclusively masculine roles, usurp public functions reserved for men and effect fundamental and permanent changes in Athenian society, the women's rebellion in *Lysistrata* is temporary, since their aim is only to restore pre-war normality. The women do not take power from the men and become rulers, but only obstruct the men in order to safeguard the state's money until the men come to their senses; their conspiracy is unselfish and temporary and relies not on magical or supernatural mechanisms but only on the traditional skills, attributes and prerogatives peculiar to their gender: domestic management, care of kin, procreation.[5]

Both the practicality and the idealism of Lysistrata's scheme required Aristophanes to represent domestic life in a more sympathetic manner than was usual in drama. The extramarital outlets for husbands that in actual life were normally available (slaves and prostitutes of either sex), and which enabled husbands to neglect their wives if they so chose, are ignored in order to motivate the sexual tension on which the strike-plot turns. And in spite of the wives' stereotypical preoccupation with sex, in this play it is their husbands they long for, not lovers. Drawn from life, too, is the wives' complaint that war disrupts domestic life, the sphere after all where Athenian women were traditionally in charge and from which they drew their civic identity and had their safety. Although the household could be portrayed, as it often was in tragedy, as a place of dangerous disharmony or, as elsewhere in comedy, as a venue for selfish female conspiracies against men (e.g. in *Women at the Thesmophoria*), in *Lysistrata* the household and its women are shown to embody the stable core of Athenian life both civic and religious. Lysistrata's plan may be a conspiracy, but not the kind that the spectators would initially expect. It is a selfless conspiracy designed to save the men and the polis, and so the women and their typical roles are portrayed in a largely positive light that is unusual in comedy but continuous with such traditional figures as the Andromache of epic and the self-sacrificing heroines of Euripides' recent tragedies.[6]

The really fantastic idea in *Lysistrata* thus lies not in its portrayal of the women themselves but in its projection of their characteristic roles outside the domestic sphere. Aristophanes' comic mechanism is to assimilate the polis (Athens) to the individual household, and the aggregate of poleis (Greece) to a neighborhood. For in effect, Lysistrata converts the Akropolis into a household for all citizen women. Its exclusivity turns the tables on the men, who have neglected their wives and excluded them from the process of policy-making. And just as a wife might protect the household money from a spendthrift husband, so Lysistrata bars the Magistrate's access to the state treasuries. Fantastic, too, are the strength, independence and discipline displayed by the women versus the weakness, dependency and rapid capitulation of the men: a reversal of prevailing gender stereotypes and one that in Athenian terms could only reflect badly on the men. If this reversal, despite its humor, struck many men in the audience as threatening in principle (compare the dangerous female usurper Klytaimestra in Aeschylus' *Agamemnon*), the women's return to normality in the end would have been reassuring.

Except for Lysistrata, the play's characters are portrayed as conventional citizens and conform to the prevailing (male) stereotypes of gender, class and (in the case of the foreigners) ethnicity. The young wives (typified by Myrrhine) bear the brunt of Aristophanes' male-oriented jokes at the expense of women: as usual in comic satire of women, the wives are portrayed as frivolous, bibulous, ignorant of realities outside the home, obsessed with sex, untrustworthy and prone to making silly excuses for their misbehavior. The Spartan wife, Lampito, is an exception, being more courageous and politically astute than the Athenian wives: for the sake of the plot Lysistrata's chief foreign counterpart must be given a certain stature. For Lampito, the humor involves not frivolousness but rather ethnic jokes at the expense of Spartans. The wives' antagonists, the young warriors (typified by Myrrhine's husband, Kinesias), fare little better, as is also usual in comic portrayals of young men: they are just as obsessed with sex as the wives (and even less able to withstand deprivation)

and just as eager to return to a life of peace. It is important to note that
Aristophanes isolates his gender jokes within the strike plot involving wives
and young husbands, assigning the play's serious issues to the occupation-
plot involving older men and women; neither Lysistrata nor the older women
are made the butt of gender jokes. In addition, Lysistrata and the older women,
as part of their serious arguments for peace, invite male sympathy for the
plight of actual young wives and husbands in wartime, an appeal that is at
variance with their comic caricatures in the play but that allows Aristophanes to
have his cake and eat it too.

It is not the young warrior-husbands but the older men—the Magistrate
and the men's chorus—who are eager to continue the war and who oppose
the women's defiance on principle, and their characterization leaves no room
for spectator sympathy. Unlike the satire of husbands and wives, which is light
and innocuous, the satire of the Magistrate and the choristers is rough and
politically pointed. The old choristers are irascible veterans of earlier wars
who make a miserable living at the city's expense by serving on juries. Their
champion, the Magistrate, is a bureaucrat recently drawn out of retirement to
serve on an emergency board that had usurped some of the functions of the
citizen Assembly. Both the men's chorus and the Magistrate are motivated by
misogyny and greed, and their defeat at the hands of the women is intended to
be both just and humiliating. Their antagonists, the older women of the chorus
and Lysistrata's older helpers onstage, are indifferent to sexual temptation
(and thus more disciplined than the young wives); display the wisdom, forth-
rightness, independence and bold temper characteristic of their age group;
and boast of lifelong service in the city's most venerable religious institutions.[7]
Because they work for a righteous cause, Aristophanes portrays both older
women and wives as belonging to the respectable, perhaps even upper-class
stratum of Athenian society, and he associates them with the city's most
venerable religious cults, while the old men are clearly aligned with the vulgar
strata of jurymen and popular politicians, both targets of consistent abuse
from Aristophanes and other comic poets.[8]

Only Lysistrata is extraordinary. She is identified neither as a young housewife nor as an older woman. She is the master strategist, commander and
spokesman, while the other women are her agents. She understands and uses
her helpers' talents but does not herself share in them; in fact she pointedly
differentiates herself from the other women, especially the ludicrous young
wives. She champions not only the interests of her own sex but also the traditional values of all Greeks male and female, and she possesses a degree of
intelligence, will and eloquence that would have been considered extraordinary
in a citizen of either sex. In her possession of the most admired attributes of
power, wisdom and statesmanship, in her dual role as defender of home and

of polis, in her acquaintance with both domestic and martial arts, in her Pan-hellenic outlook, in her advocacy of internal solidarity, in her self-discipline and immunity to sexual temptation,[9] in her appeal to young and old and in her close connection with the Akropolis, Lysistrata finds her closest analogue in Athena herself.

The Akropolis-cult of Athena Polias, patron-goddess and citadel-protectress of Athens, was the city's oldest and most revered religious institution. Its priestess, who served for life, came always from the ancient and aristocratic family of the Eteoboutadai and had an official residence on the Akropolis, where she managed the cult and its female personnel, and where she dis-charged many ritual functions on behalf of the polis (including the guardian-ship of Athena's treasuries). Since Athena's temple on the Akropolis sym-bolized the ideal Athenian household, and her priestly personnel epitomized every household's female managers, the Polias priestess—the highest public position a woman could hold in Athens—was in effect the First Lady of the polis. She had a public visibility and authority unavailable to any other woman.[10]

In 411 the Polias priestess was Lysimache, who held office for sixty-four years and who appears to have been known, or thought, to be opposed to the war.[11] Since her name is very close to our heroine's (Lysimache means "Disbander of Battles," Lysistrata "Disbander of Armies")[12] and may be specifically alluded to in the play itself (in lines 572–73 Lysistrata says "all Greece will one day call us Disbanders of Battles [Lysimachas]"), it is not unlikely that Aristophanes intended to assimilate Lysistrata to Lysimache in order to invest his heroine with some of the priestess's authority, thus further strengthening her associ-ation with the goddess. We should not, however, imagine that Lysistrata represents Lysimache in any thoroughgoing way. The priestess, like the goddess, was but one associative element that went into the making of a unique heroine, who in the course of the play achieves a stature that no woman (Lysimache included) could ever actually have attained.[13] That said, the apparent com-parison of a comic heroine to an actual woman who was prominent and res-pected in civic-religious life suggests that (at least in Lysistrata) Aristophanes represents the views not merely of the theatrical construct "women" but of real women.

Still other elements from the world of cult and myth inform the plot of Lysistrata. Festive events in which women ritually exclude, defy or even replace the men figure prominently in the religious calendars of many Greek cities and, together with their associated myths, made a natural backdrop for comic plots involving women: Women at the Thesmophoria is actually set at the Thesmophoria festival, and in Assemblywomen we are told that the women's conspiracy was hatched at the Skira festival. In Lysistrata the formative mythic and ritual associations are broader and more complex, but four principal ones can be identified:

(1) Dionysos' maenads ("mad women"), who desert their homes and live together in the wild, following the god. In myths like the one treated in Euripides' play *Bakchai*, produced six years after *Lysistrata*, the women and the god (disguised as a mortal) combat a king, whom they kill or expel after dressing him in women's clothing; the Magistrate in our play is an obvious analogue.[14] Related to Dionysian maenadism proper were the many festivals of the Agrionia/Agriania type, where the maidens and wives banded together in rebellion against the men during a ritual period of social dissolution.[15]

(2) The Adonia, an unofficial ritual practiced by women, who go to their rooftops, plant quick-blooming and quick-withering plants, and mourn the death of Aphrodite's handsome young favorite, Adonis; in the play the Magistrate bitterly recalls how the Adonia counterpointed the dispatch of the disastrous expedition to Sicily. Interestingly, in antiquity *Lysistrata* seems to have been alternatively titled *Adoniazusae* ("women celebrating the Adonis festival").

(3) The myth of the Amazons, legendary women who behaved like, and lived without, men and who once seized the Pnyx (the hilltop where the Assembly met and the Thesmophoria was held) and then tried to occupy the Akropolis. They were defeated by the Athenian culture-hero Theseus in a battle frequently depicted on monuments; their graves lay around the Pnyx.[16]

(4) The festival of the New Fire on the island of Lemnos (at this time an Athenian colony): women and men gather separately; all fires are extinguished; a ship brings new fire; the sexes reunite. The festival's origin-myth explains that Aphrodite, angry at the women, afflicted them with a bad smell; their husbands abandoned them; the women massacred their husbands except for King Thoas, whose daughter Hypsipyle saved him by hiding him in a coffin or dressing him as Dionysos (i.e. in women's clothes); the women then ruled the island alone until Jason and his Argonauts arrived and married the women, with Jason marrying Hypsipyle.[17]

The pattern common to each of these mythic/ritual events is the takeover of the polis by "outsiders" (in this case women) during a liminal period marked by social dissolution, disorder, role-inversion (including cross-dressing) and the suspension of vital processes (principally sexuality, fertility, care of the young); the subsequent misrule leads to the reestablishment of (male) order and stability. In *Lysistrata*, the rebellious women show that the men are in the wrong: male warfare and misgovernance have caused the disorder represented by the women's rebellion.[18] The women master the men and thereby save the polis, just as women do when the individual household is disrupted or threatened.[19] But just as Jason each year replaces old King Thoas, who (like our

Magistrate) is feminized and ritually killed, male control is restored at the end—but in a better form: the men promise never to make the same mistakes again.

Finally, the prominence of Athena behind the heroine, and of the Akropolis behind the plot of *Lysistrata*, cannot have failed to remind the spectators of the foundation myth of Athens itself: Athena had challenged Poseidon for the city and won, only to support, in her uniquely gender-neutral way, the primacy of male institutions in the polis.[20] In 411 Aristophanes used such traditional myths and rituals as symbolic ingredients in a comic drama intended In large part to remind males of the crucial role women still played in the maintenance and success of those institutions.

## CHARACTERS

LYSISTRATA, *an Athenian woman*
KALONIKE, *Lysistrata's friend*
MYRRHINE, *an Athenian wife*
LAMPITO, *a Spartan wife*
MAGISTRATE, *one of the ten Probouloi*
OLD WOMEN (three), *allies of Lysistrata*
WIVES (four), *Lysistrata's co-conspirators*
KINESIAS, *Myrrhine's husband*
BABY, *son of Kinesias and Myrrhine*
SPARTAN HERALD
SPARTAN AMBASSADOR
ATHENIAN AMBASSADORS (two)

   Mute characters
ATHENIAN WOMEN
ISMENIA, *a Theban woman*
KORINTHIAN WOMAN
SPARTAN WOMEN
SKYTHIAN GIRL, *Lysistrata's slave*
MAGISTRATE'S SLAVES
SKYTHIAN POLICEMEN
OLD WOMEN, *allies of Lysistrata*
MANES, *Kinesias' slave*
SPARTAN DELEGATES
SPARTAN SLAVES, *with the Spartan delegation*
ATHENIAN DELEGATES

RECONCILIATION
DOORKEEPER

Chorus
OLD ATHENIAN MEN (twelve)
OLD ATHENIAN WOMEN (twelve)

## PROLOGUE

SCENE: *A neighborhood street in Athens, after dawn. The stage-building has a large central door and two smaller, flanking doors. From one of these Lysistrata emerges and looks expectantly up and down the street.*

LYSISTRATA: Now if someone had invited the women to a revel for Bakchos,[21] or to Pan's shrine,[22] or to Genetyllis's at Kolias,[23] they'd be jamming the streets with their tambourines.[24] But now there's not a single woman here.[25] [*The far door opens.*] Except for my own neighbor there. Good morning, Kalonike.[26]    5

KALONIKE: You too, Lysistrata.[27] What's bothering you? Don't frown, child.[28] Knitted brows are no good for your looks.

LYSISTRATA: But my heart's on fire, Kalonike, and I'm terribly annoyed about us women. You know, according to the men we're capable of all sorts of mischief—    10

KALONIKE: And so we are, by Zeus!

LYSISTRATA: but when they're told to meet here to discuss something that really matters, they're sleeping in and don't show up!

KALONIKE: Honey, they'll be along. For wives to get out of the house is a lot of trouble,[29] you know: we've got to look after the husband or wake up a slave    15 or put the baby to bed, or give it a bath or feed it a snack.

LYSISTRATA: Sure, but there's other business they ought to take more seriously than that stuff.

KALONIKE: Well, Lysistrata dear, what exactly *is* this business you're calling us women together for? What's the deal? Is it a big one?    20

LYSISTRATA: Big!

KALONIKE: Not hard as well?

LYSISTRATA: It's big *and* hard, by Zeus.

KALONIKE: Then how come we're not all here?

LYSISTRATA: That's not what I meant! If it were, we'd all have shown up fast   25
enough.[30] No, it's something I've been thinking hard *about*, kicking it around,
night after sleepless night.

KALONIKE: All those kicks must have made it really smart.

LYSISTRATA: Smart enough that the salvation of all Greece lies in the women's
hands!   30

KALONIKE: In the *women's* hands? That's hardly reassuring!

LYSISTRATA: It's true: our country's future depends on *us*: whether the
Peloponnesians[31] become extinct—

KALONIKE: Well, that would be just fine with me, by Zeus!

LYSISTRATA: and all the Boiotians get annihilated—   35

KALONIKE: Not *all* of them, though: please spare the eels![32]

LYSISTRATA: I won't say anything like that about the Athenians, but you know
what I *could* say. But if the women gather together here—the Boiotian
women, the Peloponnesian women and ourselves—together we'll be able to
rescue Greece!   40

KALONIKE: But what can mere *women* do that's intelligent or noble? We sit
around the house looking pretty, wearing saffron dresses and make-up and
Kimberic gowns[33] and canoe-sized slippers.[34]

LYSISTRATA: Exactly! That's exactly what I think will rescue Greece: our fancy
little dresses, our perfumes and our slippers, our rouge and our see-through   45
underwear!

KALONIKE: How do you mean? I'm lost.

LYSISTRATA: They'll guarantee that not a single one of the men who are still
alive will raise his spear against another—

KALONIKE: Then, by the Two Goddesses,[35] I'd better get my party dress dyed   50
saffron!

LYSISTRATA: nor hoist his shield—

KALONIKE: I'll wear a Kimberic gown!

LYSISTRATA: nor even pull a knife!

KALONIKE: I've got to buy some slippers!   55

LYSISTRATA: So shouldn't the women have gotten here by now?

KALONIKE: By now? My god, they should have taken wing and flown here ages ago!

LYSISTRATA: My friend, you'll see that they're typically Athenian: everything they do, they do too late. There isn't even a single woman here from the Paralia, nor from Salamis.[36]   60

KALONIKE: Oh, them: I just know they've been up since dawn, straddling their mounts.[37]

LYSISTRATA: And the women I reckoned would be here first, and counted on, the women from Acharnai, they're not here either.   65

KALONIKE: Well, Theogenes' wife, for one, was set to make a fast getaway. [Groups of women begin to enter from both sides.] But look, here come some of your women now!

LYSISTRATA: And here come some others, over there!

KALONIKE: Phew! Where are they from?   70

LYSISTRATA: From Dungstown.

KALONIKE: It seems they've got some sticking to their shoes.

MYRRHINE:[38] I hope we're not too late, Lysistrata. What do you say? Why don't you say something?

LYSISTRATA: Myrrhine, I've got no medal for anyone who shows up late for   75
important business.

MYRRHINE: Look, I couldn't find my girdle;[39] it was dark. But now we're here, so tell us what's so important.

LYSISTRATA: No, let's wait a little while, until the women from Boiotia and the Peloponnesos come.   80

MYRRHINE: That's a much better plan. And look, there's Lampito[40] coming now!

[Enter Lampito, accompanied by a group of other Spartan women, a Theban woman (Ismenia) and a Korinthian woman.][41]

LYSISTRATA: Greetings, my very dear Spartan Lampito! My darling, how dazzling is your beauty! What rosy cheeks, what firmness of physique! You could choke a bull![42]   85

LAMPITO:[43] Is true, I think, by Twain Gods.[44] Much exercise, much leaping to harden buttocks.

KALONIKE: And what a beautiful pair of boobs you've got!

LAMPITO: Hey, you feel me up like a sacrificial ox!

LYSISTRATA: And this other young lady here, where's *she* from?                    90

LAMPITO: By Twain Gods, she come as representative of Boiotia.

MYRRHINE: She's certainly like Boiotia, by Zeus, with all her lush bottomland.

KALONIKE: Yes indeed, her bush has been most elegantly pruned.[45]

LYSISTRATA: And who's this other girl?

LAMPITO: Lady of substance, by Twain Gods, from Korinth.                    95

KALONIKE: She's substantial all right, both frontside and backside.

LAMPITO: Who convenes this assembly of women here?

LYSISTRATA: I'm the one.

LAMPITO: Then please to tell what you want of us.

MYRRHINE: That's right, dear lady, speak up. What's this important business of    100
yours?

LYSISTRATA: I'm ready to tell you. But before I tell you, I want to ask you a small question; it won't take long.

MYRRHINE: Ask away.

LYSISTRATA: Don't you all pine for your children's fathers when they're off at    105
war? I'm sure that every one of you has a husband who's away.

MYRRHINE: My husband's been away five months, my dear, at the Thracian front; he's guarding Eukrates.[46]

KALONIKE: And mine's been at Pylos *seven* whole months.

LAMPITO: And mine, soon as he comes home from the regiment, is strapping    110
on the shield and flying off.

KALONIKE: Even *lovers* have disappeared without a trace,[47] and ever since the Milesians revolted from us, I haven't even seen a six-inch dildo, which might have been a consolation, however small.[48]

LYSISTRATA: Well, if I could devise a plan to end the war, would you be ready    115
to join me?

KALONIKE: By the Two Goddesses, I would, even if I had to pawn this dress and on the very same day—drink up the proceeds!

MYRRHINE: And I think I would even cut myself in two like a flounder and donate half to the cause!                                                           120

LAMPITO: And I would climb up to summit of Taÿgetos, if I'm able to see where peace may be from there.

LYSISTRATA: Here goes then; no need to beat around the bush. Ladies, if we're going to force the men to make peace, we're going to have to give up—

MYRRHINE: Give up what? Tell us.                                                     125

LYSISTRATA: You'll do it, then?

MYRRHINE: We'll do it, even if it means our death!

LYSISTRATA: All right. We're going to have to give up—cock.[49] Why are you turning away from me? Where are you going? Why are you all pursing your lips and shaking your heads? What means thine altered color and tearful      130 droppings? Will you do it or not? What are you waiting for?[50]

KALONIKE: Count me out; let the war drag on.

MYRRHINE: Me too, by Zeus; let the war drag on.

LYSISTRATA: This from you, Ms. Flounder? Weren't you saying just a moment ago that you'd cut yourself in half?                                            135

MYRRHINE: Anything else you want, anything at all! I'm even ready to walk through fire; *that* rather than give up cock. There's nothing like it, Lysistrata dear.

LYSISTRATA: And what about you?

KALONIKE: I'm ready to walk through fire too.                                        140

LYSISTRATA: Oh what a low and horny race are we! No wonder men write tragedies about us: we're nothing but Poseidon and a bucket.[51] Dear Spartan, if you alone would side with me we might still salvage the plan; give me your vote!

LAMPITO: By Twain Gods, is difficult for females to sleep alone without the        145 hard-on. But anyway, I assent; is need for peace.

LYSISTRATA: You're an absolute dear, and the only real woman here![52]

MYRRHINE: Well, what if we *did* abstain from, uh, what you say, which heaven forbid: would peace be likelier to come on account of *that*?

LYSISTRATA: Absolutely, by the Two Goddesses. If we sat around at home all         150
made up, and walked past them wearing only our see-through underwear
and with our pubes plucked in a neat triangle, and our husbands got hard
and hankered to ball us, but we didn't go near them and kept away, they'd
sue for peace, and pretty quick, you can count on that!

LAMPITO: Like Menelaos! Soon as he peek at Helen's bare melons, he throw his       155
sword away, I think.[53]

MYRRHINE. But what if our husbands pay us no attention?

LYSISTRATA: As Pherekrates said, skin the skinned dog.[54]

MYRRHINE: Facsimiles are nothing but poppycock. And what if they grab us
and drag us into the bedroom by force?[55]                                         160

LYSISTRATA: Hold onto the door.

MYRRHINE: And what if they beat us up?

LYSISTRATA: Submit, but disagreeably: men get no pleasure in sex when they
have to force you.[56] And make them suffer in other ways as well. Don't
worry, they'll soon give in. No husband can have a happy life if his wife          165
doesn't want him to.

MYRRHINE: Well, if the two of you agree to this, then we agree as well.

LAMPITO: And we shall bring our menfolk round to making everyway fair and
honest peace. But how do you keep Athenian rabble from acting like
lunatics?[57]                                                                      170

LYSISTRATA: Don't worry, we'll handle the persuasion on our side.

LAMPITO: Not so, as long as your battleships are afoot and your Goddess's
temple[58] have bottomless fund of money.

LYSISTRATA: In fact, that's also been well provided for: we're going to occupy
the Akropolis this very day. The older women[59] are assigned that part: while     175
we're working out our agreement down here, they'll occupy the Akropolis,
pretending to be up there for a sacrifice.

LAMPITO: Sounds perfect, like rest of your proposals.

LYSISTRATA: Then why not ratify them immediately by taking an oath,
Lampito, so that the terms will be binding?[60]                                    180

LAMPITO: Reveal an oath, then, and we all swear to it.

LYSISTRATA: Well said. Where's the Skythian girl?[61] [A slave-girl comes out of the *stage-building with a shield.*] What are you gawking at? Put that shield down in front of us—no, the other way—and someone give me the severings.

MYRRHINE: Lysistrata, what kind of oath are you planning to make us swear?     185

LYSISTRATA: What kind? The kind they say Aischylos once had people swear: slaughtering an animal over a shield.[62]

MYRRHINE: Lysistrata, you don't take an oath about peace over a shield!

LYSISTRATA: Then what kind of oath will it be?

MYRRHINE: What if we got a white stallion somewhere and cut a piece off     190
him?[63]

LYSISTRATA: White stallion? Get serious.

MYRRHINE: Well, how *are* we going to swear the oath?

LYSISTRATA: By Zeus, if you'd like to know, I can tell you. We put a big black wine-bowl hollow-up right here, we slaughter a magnum of Thasian wine     195
into it, and we swear not to pour any water into the bowl![64]

LAMPITO: Oh da, I cannot find words to praise that oath!

LYSISTRATA: Somebody go inside and fetch a bowl and a magnum. [*The slave-girl takes the shield inside and returns with a large wine-bowl and a large cup.*]

MYRRHINE: Dearest ladies, what a conglomeration of pottery!     200

KALONIKE: [*Grabbing at the bowl*]: Just touching this could make a person glad!

LYSISTRATA: Put it down! And join me in laying hands upon this boar. [*All the women put a hand on the magnum.*] Mistress Persuasion and Bowl of Fellowship, graciously receive this sacrifice from the women. [*She opens the magnum and pours wine into the bowl.*]     205

MYRRHINE: The blood's a good color and spurts out nicely.

LAMPITO: It smell good too, By Kastor!

KALONIKE: Ladies, let me be the first to take the oath!

MYRRHINE: Hold on, by Aphrodite! Not unless you draw the first lot![65]

LYSISTRATA: *All* of you lay your hands upon the bowl; you too, Lampito. Now     210
one of you, on behalf of you all, must repeat after me the terms of the oath, and the rest of you will then swear to abide by them. No man of any kind, lover or husband—

MYRRHINE: No man of any kind, lover or husband—

LYSISTRATA: shall approach me with a hard-on. I can't hear you!     215

MYRRHINE: shall approach me with a hard-on.

KALONIKE: Oh god, my knees are buckling, Lysistrata!

LYSISTRATA: At home in celibacy shall I pass my life—

MYRRHINE: At home in celibacy shall I pass my life—

LYSISTRATA: wearing a party-dress and makeup—     220

MYRRHINE: wearing a party-dress and makeup—

LYSISTRATA: so that my husband will get as hot as a volcano for me—

MYRRHINE: so that my husband will get as hot as a volcano for me—

LYSISTRATA: but never willingly shall I surrender to my husband.

MYRRHINE: but never willingly shall I surrender to my husband.     225

LYSISTRATA: If he should use force to force me against my will—

MYRRHINE: If he should use force to force me against my will—

LYSISTRATA: I will submit coldly and not move my hips.

MYRRHINE: I will submit coldly and not move my hips.

LYSISTRATA: I will not raise my oriental slippers toward the ceiling.     230

MYRRHINE: I will not raise my oriental slippers toward the ceiling.

LYSISTRATA: I won't crouch down like the lioness on a cheesegrater.[66]

MYRRHINE: I won't crouch down like the lioness on a cheesegrater.

LYSISTRATA: If I live up to these vows, may I drink from this bowl.

MYRRHINE: If I live up to these vows, may I drink from this bowl.     235

LYSISTRATA: But if I break them, may the bowl be full of water.

MYRRHINE: But if I break them, may the bowl be full of water.

LYSISTRATA: So swear you one and all?

ALL: So swear we all!

LYSISTRATA: All right, then, I'll consecrate the bowl. [She takes a long drink.]     240

KALONIKE: Only your share, my friend; let's make sure we're all on friendly terms right from the start.[67]

[*After they drink, a women's joyful cry is heard offstage.*]

**LAMPITO:** What's that hurrah?[68]

**LYSISTRATA:** It's just what I was telling you before: the women have occupied the Akropolis and the Goddess' temple. Now, Lampito: you take off and        245
arrange things in Sparta, but leave these women here with us as hostages.
[*Exit Lampito.*] Meanwhile, we'll go inside with the other women on the
Akropolis and bolt the gates behind us.

**MYRRHINE:** But don't you think the men will launch a concerted attack on us,
and very soon?        250

**LYSISTRATA:** I'm not worried about them. They can't come against us with
enough threats or fire to get these gates open, except on the terms we've
agreed on.

**MYRRHINE:** No they can't, by Aphrodite![69] Otherwise we women wouldn't
deserve to be called rascals you can't win a fight with!        255

[*All exit into the central door of the scene-building, which now represents the Akropolis.*]

## PARODOS

[*A semichorus composed of twelve old men, poorly dressed, slowly makes its way along one of the
wings into the orchestra. Each carries a pair of logs, an unlit torch and a bucket of live coals.*]

**MEN'S LEADER:** Onward, Drakes,[70] lead the way, even if your shoulder is sore;
you've got to keep toting that load of green olivewood, no matter how heavy
it is.

**MEN:** (*strophe*)
If you live long enough you'll get many surprises, yes sir!
Strymodoros: who in the world ever thought we'd hear        260
that women, the very creatures we've kept in our homes,
an obvious nuisance, now control the Sacred Image[71]
and occupy my Akropolis, and not only that,
they've locked the citadel gates with bolts and bars![72]

**MEN'S LEADER:** Let's hurry to the Akropolis, Philourgos, full speed ahead, so        265
we can lay these logs in a circle all around them, around all the women
who have instigated or abetted this business! We'll erect a single pyre and
condemn them all with a single vote, then throw them on top with our
own hands, starting with Lykon's wife![73]

**MEN:** (*antistrophe*)

> By Demeter, while I still live they'll never laugh at me!                    270
> Not even Kleomenes,[74] the first to occupy this place,
> left here intact. No, for all he breathed the Spartan spirit,
> he left without his weapons—surrendered to me![75]—
> with only a little bitty jacket on his back, starving,
> filthy, unshaven and unwashed for six whole years.                    275

**MEN'S LEADER:** That's the way I laid siege to that fellow—savagely! We kept watch on these gates in ranks seventeen deep. So: am I to stand by now and do nothing to put down the effrontery of these women, enemies of all the gods and of Euripides?[76] If so, take down my trophy that stands at Marathon![77]                    280

**MEN:** (*strophe*)

> I'm almost at the end of my trek;
> all that remains is the steep stretch
> up to the Akropolis; can't wait to get there!
> How in the world are we going to haul
> these loads up there without a donkey?                    285
> This pair of logs is utterly crushing my shoulder!
> But I've got to soldier on,
> and keep my fire alight.
> It mustn't go out on me before I've reached my goal.
> [*They blow into their buckets of coals.*]
> Ouch, ugh! The smoke!                    290

(*antistrophe*)

> How terribly, Lord Herakles, this smoke
> jumped from the bucket and attacked me!
> It bit both my eyes like a rabid bitch!
> And as for this fire, it's Lemnian[78]
> in every possible way; otherwise                    295
> it wouldn't have buried its teeth in my eyeballs that way!
> Hurry forth to the citadel,
> run to the Goddess's rescue!
> If this isn't the time to help her, Laches, when will that time be?
> [*They blow on their buckets of coals again.*]
> Ouch, ugh! The smoke!                    300

**MEN'S LEADER:** Praise the gods, this fire's awake and plenty lively too. Let's place our logs right here, then dip our torches into the buckets, and when they're lighted we'll charge the gates like rams. If the women don't unbolt

the gates when we invite their surrender, we'll set the portals afire and
smoke them into submission. Very well, let's put the logs down. Phew, that          305
smoke! Damn! Would any of the generals at Samos care to help us with this
wood? [*He laboriously wrestles his pair of logs to the ground.*] They've finally stopped
crushing my back! Now it's your job, bucket, to rouse your coals to flame and
thus supply me, first of all, with a lighted torch! Lady Victory,[79] be our ally,
help us win a trophy over the women on the Akropolis and their present          310
audacity!

[*As the men crouch down to light their torches the second semichorus enters on the run. It is
composed of twelve old women, nicely dressed and carrying pitchers of water on their heads.*]

WOMEN'S LEADER: I think I can see sparks and smoke, fellow women, as if a
fire were ablaze. We must hurry all the faster!

WOMEN: (*strophe*)
   Fly, fly, Nikodike,[80]
   before Kalyke and Kritylla are incinerated,          315
   blown from all directions
   by nasty winds and old men who mean death!
   I'm filled with dread: am I too late to help?
   I've just come from the well with my pitcher;[81]
   it was hard to fill by the light of dawn,          320
   in the throng and crash and clatter of pots,
   fighting the elbows of housemaids and branded slaves.[82]
   I hoisted it onto my head with zeal, and carry the water here
   to assist the women, my fellow citizens faced with burning.

(*antistrophe*)
   I've heard that some frantic old men          325
   are on the loose with three talents[83] of logs,
   like furnace-men at the public bathhouse.
   They're coming to the Akropolis, screaming
   the direst threats, that they mean to use their fire
   "to turn these abominable women into charcoal."          330
   Goddess, may I never see these women in flames;
   instead let them rescue Greece and her citizens from war and madness!
   O golden-crested Guardian of the citadel, that is why
   they occupy your shrine. I invite thee to be our ally, Tritogeneia,[84]
   defending it with water, should any man set it afire.          335

WOMEN'S LEADER: Hold on! Hey! What's this? Men! Awful, nasty men! No
gentlemen, no god-fearing men would ever be caught doing this!

MEN'S LEADER: This here's a complication we didn't count on facing: this swarm of women outside the gates is here to help the others!

WOMEN'S LEADER: Fear and trembling, eh? Don't tell me we seem a lot to handle: you haven't even seen the tiniest fraction of our forces yet!    340

MEN'S LEADER: Phaidrias, are we going to let these women go on jabbering like this? Why hasn't somebody busted a log over their heads?

WOMEN'S LEADER: Let's ground our pitchers then; if anyone attacks us they won't get in our way.    345

MEN'S LEADER: By Zeus, if someone had socked them in the mouth a couple of times, like Boupalos,[85] they wouldn't still be talking!

WOMEN'S LEADER: OK, here's my mouth; someone take a sock at it; I'll stand here and take it. But then I'm the bitch who gets to grab you by the balls!

MEN'S LEADER: If you don't shut up, I'll knock you right out of your old hide!    350

WOMEN'S LEADER: Come over here and just touch Stratyllis with the tip of your finger.

MEN'S LEADER: What if I give you the one-two punch? Got anything scary to counter with?

WOMEN'S LEADER: I'll rip out your lungs and your guts with my fangs.    355

MEN'S LEADER: There isn't a wiser poet than Euripides: no beast exists so shameless as women![86]

WOMEN'S LEADER: Let's pick up our pitchers of water, Rhodippe.

MEN'S LEADER: Why did you bring water here, you witch?

WOMEN'S LEADER: And why have you got fire, you tomb? To burn yourself up?    360

MEN'S LEADER: I'm here to build a pyre and burn up your friends.

WOMEN'S LEADER: And I've come to put it out with this.

MEN'S LEADER: You're going to put out my fire?

WOMEN'S LEADER: That's what you soon will see.

MEN'S LEADER: I think I might barbecue you with this torch of mine.    365

WOMEN'S LEADER: Got any soap with you? I'll give you a bath.

MEN'S LEADER: You give me a bath, you crone?

WOMEN'S LEADER: A bath fit for a bridegroom!

**MEN'S LEADER**: What insolence!

**WOMEN'S LEADER**: I'm a free woman![87]                                   370

**MEN'S LEADER**: I'll put a stop to your bellowing.

**WOMEN'S LEADER**: You're not on a jury now, you know.[88]

**MEN'S LEADER**: Torch her hair! [*The men advance.*]

**WOMEN'S LEADER**: Acheloos, do your thing![89] [*The women douse them.*]

**MEN'S LEADER**: Oh! Damn!                                                 375

**WOMEN'S LEADER**: It wasn't too hot, was it?

**MEN'S LEADER**: Hot? Stop it! What do you think you're doing?

**WOMEN'S LEADER**: I'm watering you, so you'll bloom.

**MEN'S LEADER**: But I'm already dried out from shivering!

**WOMEN'S LEADER**: You've got fire there; why not sit by it and get warm?    380

## EPISODE

[*Enter the Magistrate, an irascible old man, accompanied by two slaves carrying crowbars and four Skythian[90] policemen.*]

**MAGISTRATE**:[91] So the women's depravity bursts into flame again: beating drums, chanting "Sabazios!",[92] worshiping Adonis on the rooftops.[93] I heard it all once before while sitting in Assembly. Demostratos (bad luck to him!) was moving that we send an armada to Sicily,[94] while his wife was dancing and yelling "Poor young Adonis!"[95] Then Demostratos[96] moved that we sign    385
up some Zakynthian infantry, but his wife up on the roof was getting drunk and going "Beat your breast for Adonis!" But he just went on making his motions, that godforsaken, disgusting Baron Bluster! From women, I say, you get this kind of riotous extravagance![97]

**MEN'S LEADER** [*Pointing to the Chorus of Women*]: Save your breath till you hear    390
about their atrocities! They've committed every kind, even doused us with those pitchers. Now we get to shake water out of our clothes as if we'd peed in them!

**MAGISTRATE**: By the salty sea-god it serves us right! When we ourselves are accomplices in our wives' misbehavior and teach them profligacy, these are    395
the sort of schemes they bring to flower! Aren't we the ones who go to the

shops and say stuff like, "Goldsmith, about that necklace you made me: my wife was having a ball the other night, and now the prong's slipped out of its hole. Me, I've got to cruise over to Salamis.[98] So if you've got time, by all means visit her in the evening and fit a prong in her hole." Another husband      400
says this to a teenage shoemaker with a very grown-up cock, "Shoemaker, my wife's pinky-toe hurts. It seems the top-strap is cramping the bottom, where she's tender. So why don't you drop in on her some lunchtime and loosen it up so there's more play down there?" That's the sort of thing that's led to this, when I, a Magistrate, have lined up timber for oars and now come to get the      405
necessary funds, and find myself standing at the gate, locked out by women! But I'm not going to stand around. [To the two slaves] Bring the crowbars; I'll put a stop to their arrogance. What are you gaping at, you sorry fool? And where are you staring? I said crowbar, not wine bar![99] Come on, put those crowbars under the gates and start jimmying on that side; I'll help out on this      410
side.

LYSISTRATA [emerging from the gates]: Don't jimmy the gates; I'm coming out on my very own. Why do you need crowbars? It's not crowbars you need; it's rather brains and sense.

MAGISTRATE: Really! You witch! Where's a policeman? Grab her and tie both      415
hands behind her back! [One of the policemen advances on Lysistrata.]

LYSISTRATA: If he so much as touches me with his fingertip, by Artemis[100] he'll go home crying, public servant or not! [The policeman retreats.]

MAGISTRATE: What, are you scared? [To a second policeman] You there, help him out; grab her around the waist and tie her up, on the double!      420

[A large old woman emerges from the gates.]

FIRST OLD WOMAN: If you so much as lay a hand on her, by Pandrosos[101] I'll beat the shit out of you! [Both policemen retreat.]

MAGISTRATE: Beat the shit out of me! Where's another policeman? [A third policeman steps forward.] Tie her up first, the one with the dirty mouth!

[A second old woman emerges from the gates.]

SECOND OLD WOMAN: If you raise your fingertip to her, by our Lady of      425
Light[102] you'll be begging for an ice-pack! [The third archer retreats.]

MAGISTRATE: What's going on? Where's a policeman? [The fourth policeman steps forward.] Arrest her. I'll foil one of these sallies of yours!

[A third old woman emerges from the gates.]

THIRD OLD WOMAN: If you come near her, by Eastern Artemis I'll rip out your hair till it screams! [*The fourth policeman retreats.*]          430

MAGISTRATE: What a terrible setback! I'm out of policemen. But men must never, ever be worsted by women! Skythians, let's charge them *en masse*; form up ranks!

[*The four policemen prepare to charge.*]

LYSISTRATA: By the Two Goddesses, you'll soon discover that we also have four squadrons of fully armed combat-women,[103] waiting inside!          435

MAGISTRATE: Skythians, twist their arms behind their backs!

[*The policemen advance.*]

LYSISTRATA: [*Calling into the Akropolis like a military commander*]: Women of the reserve, come out double-time! Forward, you spawn of the marketplace,[104] you soup and vegetable mongers! Forward, you landladies, you hawkers of garlic and bread! [*Four squadrons of tough old market-women rush out of the*          440
*Akropolis and, together with the women already onstage, attack the four policemen.*] Tackle them! Hit them! Smash them! Call them names, the nastier the better! [*The policemen run away howling.*] That's enough! Withdraw! Don't strip the bodies!

[*The women of the reserve go back into the Akropolis.*]

MAGISTRATE: Terrible! What a calamity for my men!          445

LYSISTRATA: Well, what did you expect? Did you think you were going up against a bunch of slave-girls? Or did you think women lacked gall?

MAGISTRATE: They've got it aplenty, by Apollo, provided there's a wine-shop nearby.

MEN'S LEADER: You've little to show for all your talk, Magistrate of this country!          450
What's the point of fighting a battle of words with these beasts? Don't you comprehend the kind of bath they've given us just now—when we were still in our clothes, and without soap to boot?

WOMEN'S LEADER: Well, sir, you shouldn't lift your hand against your neighbors just anytime you feel like it. If you do, you're going to end up          455
with a black eye. I'd rather be sitting at home like a virtuous maiden, making no trouble for anyone here, stirring not a single blade of grass. But if anyone annoys me and rifles my nest, they'll find a wasp inside!

## ONSTAGE DEBATE

MEN: (*strophe*)
    Zeus, how in the world are we going to deal with these monsters?      460
    They've gone beyond what I can bear! Now it's time for a trial:
    together let's find out
    what they thought they were doing
    when they occupied Kranaos' citadel[105]
    and the great crag of the Akropolis,      465
    a restricted, holy place.

MEN'S LEADER: Question her and don't give in; cross-examine what she says.
It's scandalous to let this sort of behavior go unchallenged.[106]

MAGISTRATE: Here's the first thing I'd like to know, by Zeus: what do you mean
by barricading our Akropolis?      470

LYSISTRATA: To keep the money safe and to keep you from using it to finance
the war.

MAGISTRATE: So we're at war on account of the money?

LYSISTRATA: Yes, and the money's why everything else got messed up too.
Peisandros[107] and the others aiming to hold office were always fomenting      475
some kind of commotion so that they'd be able to steal it. So let them keep
fomenting to their hearts' content: they'll be withdrawing no more money
from this place.

MAGISTRATE: But what do you plan to do?

LYSISTRATA: Don't you see? We'll manage it for you!      480

MAGISTRATE: You'll manage the money?

LYSISTRATA: What's so strange in that? Don't we manage the household
finances for you already?[108]

MAGISTRATE: That's different!

LYSISTRATA: How so?      485

MAGISTRATE: These are war funds!

LYSISTRATA: But there shouldn't even be a war.

MAGISTRATE: How else are we to protect ourselves?

LYSISTRATA: We'll protect you.

MAGISTRATE: You?

LYSISTRATA: Yes, us.

MAGISTRATE: What brass!

LYSISTRATA: You'll be protected whether you like it or not!

MAGISTRATE: You're going too far!

LYSISTRATA: Angry, are you? We've got to do it anyway.          495

MAGISTRATE: By Demeter,[109] you've got no right!

LYSISTRATA: You must be saved, dear fellow.

MAGISTRATE: Even if I don't ask to be?

LYSISTRATA: All the more so!

MAGISTRATE: And where do you get off taking an interest in war and          500
peace?

LYSISTRATA: We'll tell you.

MAGISTRATE: Well, make it snappy, unless you want to get hurt.

LYSISTRATA: Listen then, and try to control your fists.

MAGISTRATE: I can't; I'm so angry I can't keep my hands to myself.[110]          505

FIRST OLD WOMAN: Then you're the one'll get hurt!

MAGISTRATE: Croak those curses at yourself, old bag! [*To Lysistrata*] Start
talking.

LYSISTRATA: Gladly.[111] All along, being proper women, we used to suffer in
silence no matter what you men did, because you wouldn't let us make a          510
sound. But you weren't exactly all we could ask for. No, we knew only too
well what you were up to, and too many times we'd hear in our homes
about a bad decision you'd made on some great issue of state. Then,
masking the pain in our hearts, we'd put on a smile and ask you, "How
did the Assembly go today? Any decision about a rider to the peace          515
treaty?" And my husband would say, "What's that to you? Shut up!" And
I'd shut up.

FIRST OLD WOMAN: I wouldn't have shut up!

MAGISTRATE: If you hadn't shut up you'd have got a beating!

LYSISTRATA: Well, that's why I *did* shut up. Later on we began to hear about          520
even worse decisions you'd made, and then we would ask, "Husband, how
come you're handling this so stupidly?" And right away he'd glare at me and
tell me to get back to my sewing if I didn't want major damage to my head:
"War shall be the business of menfolk," unquote.[112]

MAGISTRATE: He was right on the mark, by Zeus.          525

LYSISTRATA: How could he be right, you sorry fool, when we were forbidden
to offer advice even when your policy was *wrong?* But then—when we began
to hear you in the streets openly crying, "There isn't a man left in the land,"
and someone else saying, "No, by Zeus, not a one"—after *that* we women
decided to lose no more time and to band together to save Greece. What was          530
the point of waiting any longer? So, if you're ready to take your turn at
listening, we have some good advice, and if you shut up, as we used to, we
can put you back on the right track.

MAGISTRATE: *You* put *us*—outrageous! I won't stand for it!

LYSISTRATA: Shut up!          535

MAGISTRATE: *Me* shut up for *you?* A damned woman, with a veil on your face
too?[113] I'd rather die!

LYSISTRATA: If the veil's an obstacle, here, take mine, it's yours, put it on *your*
face [*she removes her veil and puts it on the Magistrate's head*], and then shut up!

FIRST OLD WOMAN: And take this sewing-basket too.          540

LYSISTRATA: Now hitch up your clothes and start sewing; chew some beans
while you work.[114] War shall be the business of womenfolk![115]

WOMEN'S LEADER: Come away from your pitchers, women: it's our turn to
pitch in with a little help for our friends!

WOMEN: (*antistrophe*)
    Oh yes! I'll dance with unflagging energy;          545
    the effort won't weary my knees.
    I'm ready to face anything
    with women courageous as these:
    they've got character, charm and guts,
    they've got intelligence and heart          550
    that's both patriotic and smart![116]

WOMEN'S LEADER: Now, most valiant of prickly mommies and spikey gran-
nies,[117] attack furiously and don't let up: you're still running with the wind!

LYSISTRATA: If Eros of the sweet soul and Cyprian Aphrodite imbue our thighs and breasts with desire, and infect the men with sensuous rigidity and club-cock, then I believe all Greece will one day call us Disbanders of Battles.[110]  555

MAGISTRATE: What's your plan?

LYSISTRATA: First of all, we can stop people going to the market fully armed and acting crazy.

FIRST OLD WOMAN: Paphian Aphrodite be praised!  560

LYSISTRATA: At this very moment, all around the market, in the pottery shops and the grocery stalls, they're walking around in arms like Korybantes![119]

MAGISTRATE: By Zeus, a man's got to act like a man!

LYSISTRATA: But it's totally ridiculous when he takes a shield with a Gorgon-blazon to buy sardines!  565

FIRST OLD WOMAN: Yes, by Zeus, I saw a long-haired fellow,[120] a cavalry captain, on horseback, getting porridge from an old women and sticking it into his brass hat. Another one, a Thracian, was shaking his shield and spear like Tereus;[121] he scared the fig-lady out of her wits and gulped down all the ripe ones!  570

MAGISTRATE: So how will you women be able to put a stop to such a compli-cated international mess, and sort it all out?

LYSISTRATA: Very easily.

MAGISTRATE: How? Show me.

[Lysistrata uses the contents of the basket which the Magistrate was given to illustrate her demonstration.][122]

LYSISTRATA: It's rather like a ball of yarn when it gets tangled up. We hold it  575 this way, and carefully wind out the strands on our spindles, now this way, now that way. That's how we'll wind up this war, if allowed, unsnarling it by sending embassies, now this way, now that way.

MAGISTRATE: You really think your way with wool and yarn balls and spindles can stop a terrible crisis? How brainless!  580

LYSISTRATA: I do think so, and if you had any brains you'd handle all the polis's business the way we handle our wool![123]

MAGISTRATE: Well, how then? I'm all ears.

LYSISTRATA: Imagine the polis as fleece just shorn. First, put it in a bath and wash out all the sheep-dung; spread it on a pallet and beat out the riff-raff  585 with a stick and pluck out the thorns; as for those who clump and knot themselves together to snag government positions, card them out and pluck off their heads.[124] Next, card the wool into a basket of unity and goodwill, mixing in everyone. The resident aliens and any other foreigner who's your friend, and anyone who owes money to the people's treasury, mix them in there too. And by Zeus, don't forget the cities that are colonies of this land: they're like flocks of your fleece, each one separated from the others. So take all these flocks and bring them together here, joining them all and making one big bobbin. And from this weave a fine new cloak for the people!                                    590

MAGISTRATE: Isn't it awful how these women go like this with their sticks and     595
like this with their bobbins, when they share none of the war's burdens!

LYSISTRATA: None? You monster! We bear more than our fair share, first of all by giving birth to sons and sending them off to the army—[125]

MAGISTRATE: Enough of that! Let's not open old wounds.

LYSISTRATA: Then, when we ought to be having fun and enjoying our bloom            600
of youth, we sleep alone because of the campaigns. And to say no more about our case,[126] it pains me to think of the maidens growing old in their rooms.[127]

MAGISTRATE: Men grow old too, don't they?

LYSISTRATA: That's quite a different story. When a man comes home he can quickly find a girl to marry, even if he's a greybeard. But a woman's prime is     605
brief; if she doesn't seize it no one wants to marry her, and she sits at home looking for good omens.[128]

MAGISTRATE: But any man who can still get a hard-on—[129]

LYSISTRATA: Why don't you just drop dead? Here's a grave-site, buy a coffin,
I'll start kneading you a honey cake.[130] [Taking off her garland] Use these as a     610
wreath.

FIRST OLD WOMAN [Handing him ribbons]: You can have these from me.

SECOND OLD WOMAN: And this garland from me.

LYSISTRATA: All set? Need anything else? Get on the boat, then. Charon is calling your name and you're holding him up![131]                                 615

MAGISTRATE: Isn't it shocking that I'm being treated like this?[132] By Zeus, I'm going straight to the other magistrates to display myself just as I am!

LYSISTRATA [As Magistrate exits with his slaves]: I hope you won't complain about the funeral we gave you. I tell you what: the day after tomorrow, first thing in the morning, we'll perform the third-day offerings at your grave! [The women     620
exit into the Akropolis.]

## CHORAL DEBATE

MEN'S LEADER: No free man should be asleep now! Let's strip for action, men, and meet this emergency! [*The men remove their jackets.*]

MEN: (*strophe a*)
    I think I smell much bigger trouble in this,
    a definite whiff of Hippias' tyranny![133]                    625
    I'm terrified that certain men from Sparta
    have gathered at the house of Kleisthenes[134]
    and scheme to stir up our godforsaken women
    to seize the Treasury and my jury-pay,
    my very livelihood.[135]                                    630

MEN'S LEADER: It's shocking, you know, that they're lecturing the citizens now, and running their mouths—mere women!—about brazen shields. And to top it all off they're trying to make peace between us and the men of Sparta, who are no more trustworthy than a starving wolf. Actually, this plot they weave against us, gentlemen, aims at tyranny! Well, they'll never   635 tyrannize over me: from now on I'll be on my guard, I'll "carry my sword in a myrtle-branch"[136] and go to market fully armed right up beside Aristogeiton.[137] I'll stand beside him like this [*assuming the posture of Harmdios' statue*]: that way I'll be ready to smack this godforsaken old hag right in the jaw! [*He advances on the Women's Leader with fist raised.*]

WOMEN'S LEADER: Just try it, and your own mommy won't recognize you when you get home! Come on, fellow hags, let's start by putting our jackets on the ground. [*The women remove their jackets.*]

WOMEN: (*antistrophe a*)
    Citizens of Athens, we want to start
    by offering the polis some good advice,                         645
    and rightly, for she raised me in splendid luxury.[138]
    As soon as I turned seven I was an Arrephoros;[139]
    then I was a Grinder;[140] when I was ten I shed
    my saffron robe for the Foundress[141] at the Brauronia.[142]
    And once, when I was a beautiful girl, I carried the Basket,        650
    wearing a necklace of dried figs.[143]

WOMEN'S LEADER: Thus I owe it to the polis to offer some good advice. And even if I *was* born a woman, don't hold it against me if I manage to suggest something better than what we've got now. I have a stake in our community: my contribution is men. You miserable geezers have no stake, since you've   655 squandered your paternal inheritance, won in the Persian Wars, and now pay no taxes in return. On the contrary, we're all headed for bankruptcy on account of you! Have you anything to grunt in rebuttal? Any more trouble from you and I'll clobber you with this rawhide boot right in the jaw! [*She raises her foot at the Men's Leader.*]     660

**MEN'S LEADER**: (*strophe b*)
    This behavior of theirs amounts to extreme hubris,[144]
    and I do believe it's getting aggravated.
    No man with any balls can let it pass.

**MEN'S LEADER**: Let's doff our shirts,[145] 'cause a man's gotta smell like a man from the word go and shouldn't be all wrapped up like souvlaki.     665
[*The men remove their shirts.*]

**MEN**:
    Come on, Whitefeet![146]
    We went against Leipsydrion[147]
    when we still were something;
    now we've got to rejuvenate, grow wings
    all over, shake off these old skins of ours!     670

**MEN'S LEADER**:[148] If any man among us gives these women the tiniest thing to grab onto, there's no limit to what their nimble hands will do. Why, they'll even be building frigates and launching naval attacks, cruising against us like Artemisia.[149] And if they turn to horsemanship, you can scratch our cavalry: there's nothing like a woman when it comes to mounting and riding; even     675
riding hard she won't slip off.[150] Just look at the Amazons in Mikon's painting, riding chargers in battle against men.[151] Our duty is clear: grab each woman's neck and lock it in the wooden stocks! [*He moves toward the Women's Leader.*]

**WOMEN**: (*antistrophe b*)
    By the Two Goddesses, if you fire me up I'll come at you like a wild sow     680
    and clip you bare,
    and this very day you'll go bleating to your friends for help!

**WOMEN'S LEADER**: Quickly, women, let's also take off our tunics;[152] a woman's gotta smell like a woman, mad enough to bite! [*The women remove their shirts.*]

**WOMEN**:
    All right now, someone attack me!     685
    He'll eat no more garlic
    and chew no more beans.
    If you so much as curse at me, I'll boil over with such rage,
    I'll be the beetle-midwife to your eagle's eggs.[153]

WOMEN'S LEADER: You men don't worry me a bit, not while my Lampito's          690
around and my Ismenia, the noble Theban girl. You'll have no power to do
anything about us, not even if you pass seven decrees: that's how much
everyone hates you, you good-for-nothing, and especially our neighbors.
Why, just yesterday I threw a party for the girls in honor of Hekate,[154] and
I invited my friend from next door, a fine girl who's very special to me: an          695
eel from Boiotia.[155] But they said she couldn't come because of your decrees.
And you'll never stop passing these decrees until someone grabs you by the
leg and throws you away and breaks your neck! [She makes a grab for the Men's
Leader's leg.]

## EPISODE

[Lysistrata comes out of the Akropolis and begins to pace.]

WOMEN'S LEADER:[156]

O mistress of this venture and strategem,          700
why com'st thou from thy halls so dour of mien?

LYSISTRATA:

The deeds of ignoble women and the female heart
do make me pace dispirited to and fro.

WOMEN'S LEADER:

What say'st thou? What say'st thou?

LYSISTRATA:

'Tis true, too true!          705

WOMEN'S LEADER:

What dire thing? Pray tell it to thy friends.

LYSISTRATA:

'Twere shame to say and grief to leave unsaid.

WOMEN'S LEADER:

Hide not from me the damage we have taken.

LYSISTRATA:

The story in briefest compass: we need to fuck![157]

WOMEN'S LEADER:

Ah, Zeus!          710

LYSISTRATA:

Why rend the air for Zeus? You see our plight. The truth is, I can't keep the wives away from their husbands any longer; they're running off in all directions. The first one I caught was over there by Pan's Grotto,[158] digging at her hole, and another was trying to escape by clambering down a pulley-cable. And yesterday another one mounted a sparrow[159] and was    715 about to fly off to Orsilochos' house[160] when I pulled her off by her hair. They're coming up with every kind of excuse to go home.

[*A wife comes out of the Akropolis, looks around, and begins to run offstage.*]

LYSISTRATA: Hey you! What's your hurry?

FIRST WIFE: I want to go home. I've got some Milesian wool in the house, and the moths are chomping it all up.    720

LYSISTRATA: Moths! Get back inside.

FIRST WIFE: By the Two Goddesses, I'll be right back; just let me spread it on the bed!

LYSISTRATA: You won't be spreading anything, nor be going anywhere.

FIRST WIFE: So I'm supposed to let my wool go to waste?    725

LYSISTRATA: If that's what it takes. [*As the first wife walks back toward Lysistrata a second runs out of the Akropolis.*]

SECOND WIFE: Oh my god, my god, the flax! I forgot to shuck it when I left the house!

LYSISTRATA. Here's another one off to shuck her flax. March right back here.    730

SECOND WIFE: By our Lady of Light, I'll be back in a flash; just let me do a little shucking.

LYSISTRATA: No! No shucking! If you start doing this, some other wife will want to do the same. [*While the second wife walks back toward Lysistrata a third runs out of the Akropolis, holding her bulging belly.*]    735

THIRD WIFE: O Lady of Childbirth, hold back the baby till I can get to a more profane spot![161]

LYSISTRATA: What are you raving about?

THIRD WIFE: I'm about to deliver a child!

LYSISTRATA: But you weren't pregnant yesterday.    740

THIRD WIFE: But today I am. Please, Lysistrata, send me home to the midwife, and right away!

LYSISTRATA: What's the story? [*She feels the wife's belly.*] What's this? It's hard.

THIRD WIFE: It's a boy.

LYSISTRATA [*knocking on it*]: By Aphrodite, it's obvious you've got something          745
metallic and hollow in there. Let's have a look. [*She lifts up the wife's dress,
exposing a large bronze helmet.*] Ridiculous girl! You're big with the sacred
helmet, not with child![162]

THIRD WIFE: But I *am* with child, by Zeus!

LYSISTRATA: Then what were you doing with this?          750

THIRD WIFE: Well, if I began to deliver here in the citadel, I could get into the
helmet and have my baby there, like a pigeon.

LYSISTRATA: What kind of story is that? Excuses! It's obvious what's going on.
You'll have to stay here til your—helmet has its naming-day.

THIRD WIFE: But I can't even *sleep* on the Akropolis, ever since I saw the snake          755
that guards the temple.

FOURTH WIFE: And what about poor me—listening to the owls go *woo woo* all
night is killing me!

LYSISTRATA: You nutty girls, enough of your horror stories! I guess you do
miss your husbands; but do you think they don't miss *you*? They're spending          760
some very rough nights, I assure you. Just be patient, good ladies, and put up
with this, just a little bit longer. There's an oracle predicting victory for us, if
we stick together. Here's the oracle right here. [*She produces a scroll.*][163]

THIRD WIFE: Tell us what it says.

LYSISTRATA: Be quiet, then.          765
Yea, when the swallows hole up in a single home,
fleeing the hoopoes[164] and leaving the penis alone,
then are their problems solved, what's high is low:
so says high-thundering Zeus—

THIRD WIFE: You mean *we'll* be lying on top?          770

LYSISTRATA: But:
if the swallows begin to argue and fly away
down from the citadel holy, all will say,
no bird more disgustingly horny lives today!

THIRD WIFE: A pretty explicit oracle. Ye gods!                                    775

LYSISTRATA: So let's hear no more talk of caving in. Let's go inside.
Dear comrades, it would be a real shame if we betrayed the oracle.
[*All enter the Akropolis.*]


## CHORAL SONGS

MEN: (*strophe*)
I want to tell you all a tale
that once I heard when but a lad.
In olden times there lived a young man,                                          780
his name was Melanion.[165]
He fled from marriage until
he got to the wilderness.
And he lived in the mountains
and he had a dog,                                                               785
and he wove traps and hunted rabbits,
but never went home again
because of his hatred.
That's how much *he* loathed women.
And, being wise, *we* loathe them just                                         790
as much as Melanion did.

MEN'S LEADER: How about a kiss, old bag?

WOMEN'S LEADER: Try it, and you've eaten your last onion!

MEN'S LEADER: How about I haul off and kick you? [*He kicks up his leg.*]

WOMEN'S LEADER [*laughing*]: That's quite a bush you've got down there!        795

MEN'S LEADER:
Well, Myronides too was rough down there,
and hairy-assed to all his enemies;
so too was Phormion.[166]

WOMEN: (*antistrophe*)
I also want to tell you all a tale,
a reply to your Melanion.                                                       800
There once was a drifter named Timon,[167]
who fenced himself off with impregnable thorns,
as implacable as a Fury.

So this Timon too
left home because of his hatred                                      805
"and lived in the mountains,"
constantly cursing and railing
against the wickedness of men.
That's how much *he* loathed *you*,
wicked men, ever and always.                                         810
But he was a dear friend to women.

**WOMEN'S LEADER**: How would you like a punch in the mouth?

**MEN'S LEADER**: No way! You're really scaring me!

**WOMEN'S LEADER**: Then how about a good swift kick?

**MEN'S LEADER**: If you do you'll be flashing your twat!        815

**WOMEN'S LEADER**:
Even so you'll never see
any hair down there on me:
I may be getting antiquated
but I keep myself well depilated.[168]

[*The Women's Chorus picks up their and the men's discarded clothing and both semichoruses withdraw from the center of the orchestra to sit along its edges; during the ensuing episode the women put their clothing back on.*]


## EPISODE

[*Lysistrata appears on the roof of the stage-building, which represents the Akropolis ramparts, and walks to and fro, looking carefully in all directions; suddenly she stops and peers into the distance.*]

**LYSISTRATA**: All right! Yes! Ladies, come here, quick!        820

[*Myrrhine and several other wives join Lysistrata.*]

**WIFE**: What is it? What's all the shouting?

**LYSISTRATA**: A man! I see a man coming this way, stricken, in the grip of Aphrodite's mysterious powers. Lady Aphrodite, mistress of Cyprus and Kythera and Paphos, . . . make thy journey straight and upright!

**WIFE**: Where is he, whoever he is?                            825

**LYSISTRATA**: He's by Chloe's shrine.

WIFE: By Zeus, I see him now! But who is he?

LYSISTRATA: Take a good look. Anyone recognize him?

MYRRHINE: Oh God, I do. He's my own husband Kinesias!

LYSISTRATA: All right, it's your job to roast him, to torture him, to bamboozle    830
him, to love him and not to love him, and to give him anything he wants—
except what you swore over the bowl not to.[169]

MYRRHINE: Don't you worry, I'll do it!

LYSISTRATA: Great! I'll stick around here and help you bamboozle him and
roast him. Now everyone get out of sight!                                        835

[*All the wives go back inside except Lysistrata. Enter Kinesias, wearing a huge erect phallus and accompanied by a male slave holding a baby. He is in obvious pain.*]

KINESIAS [*to himself*]: Oh, oh, evil fate! I've got terrible spasms and cramps. It's
like I'm being broken on the rack!

LYSISTRATA [*Leaning down from the ramparts*]: Who's that who's standing up
within our defense perimeter?

KINESIAS: Me.                                                                    840

LYSISTRATA: A man?

KINESIAS [*brandishing his phallus*]: Of course a man!

LYSISTRATA: In that case please depart.

KINESIAS: And who are you to throw me out?

LYSISTRATA: The daytime guard.                                                   845

KINESIAS: Then in the gods' name call Myrrhine out here to me.

LYSISTRATA: Listen to him, "call Myrrhine"! And who might you be?

KINESIAS: Her husband, Kinesias, from Paionidai.[170]

LYSISTRATA: Well, hello, dear chum! Among us your name is hardly unknown
or without celebrity. Your wife always has you on her lips; she'll be eating an   850
egg or an apple and she'll say, "This one's for Kinesias."[171]

KINESIAS: Oh gods!

LYSISTRATA: Yes, by Aphrodite. And whenever the conversation turns to men,
your wife speaks up forthwith and says, "Compared to Kinesias, everything
else is trash!"                                                                  855

KINESIAS: Come on now, call her out!

LYSISTRATA: Well? Got anything for me?

KINESIAS [*Indicating his phallus*]: Indeed I do, if you want it. [*Lysistrata looks away.*] What about this? [*He tosses her a purse.*] It's all I've got, and you're welcome to it.[172]                                                                              860

LYSISTRATA: OK then, I'll go in and call her for you. [*She leaves the ramparts.*]

KINESIAS: Make it quick, now! [*Alone*] I've had no joy or pleasure in my life since the day Myrrhine left the house. I go into the house and feel agony; everything looks empty to me; I get no pleasure from the food I eat. Because I'm horny!                                                                                                  865

MYRRHINE: [*Still out of sight, speaking to Lysistrata*]: I love that man, I love him! But he doesn't want my love. Please don't make me go out to him!

KINESIAS: Myrrhinikins, dearest, why are you doing this? Get down here!

MYRRHINE: [*Appearing at the ramparts*]: By Zeus I'm not going down there!

KINESIAS: You won't come down even when I ask you, Myrrhine?                           870

MYRRHINE: You're asking me, but you don't want me at all.

KINESIAS: Me not want you? Why, I'm desolate!

MYRRHINE: I'm leaving.

KINESIAS: No, wait! At least listen to the baby! [*He grabs the baby from the slave and holds it up towards Myrrhine.*] Come on you, yell for mommy!                                  875

BABY: Mommy! Mommy! Mommy!

KINESIAS [*To Myrrhine*]: Hey, what's wrong with you? Don't you feel sorry for the baby, unwashed and unsuckled for six days now?

MYRRHINE: Him I feel sorry for. Too bad his father doesn't care about him!

KINESIAS: Get down here, you screwy woman, and see to your child!                           880

MYRRHINE: How momentous is motherhood! I've got no choice but to go down there. [*She leaves the ramparts. Kinesias returns the baby to the slave.*]

KINESIAS: "Absence really does make the heart grow fonder!"[173] She seems much younger than I remember, and she has a sexier look in her eyes. She acted prickly and very stuck-up too, but that just makes me want her even         885
more!

[*Myrrhine enters from the Akropolis gates and goes over to the baby, ignoring Kinesias.*]

**MYRRHINE**: Poor sweetie pie, with such a lousy father, let me give you a kiss, mommy's little dearest!

**KINESIAS** [*To Myrrhine's back*]: What do you think you're doing, you naughty girl, listening to those other women and giving me a hard time and hurting     890
yourself as well? [*He puts a hand on her shoulder.*]

**MYRRHINE** [*Wheeling around*]: Don't you lay your hands on me!

**KINESIAS**: You know you've let our house, your things and mine, become an utter mess?

**MYRRHINE**: It doesn't bother me.     895

**KINESIAS**: It doesn't bother you that the hens are pulling your woollens apart?

**MYRRHINE**: Not a bit.

**KINESIAS**: And what a long time it's been since you've celebrated Aphrodite's holy mysteries.[174] Won't you come home?

**MYRRHINE**: Not me, by Zeus; I'm going nowhere until you men agree to a     900
settlement and stop the war.

**KINESIAS**: Well, if that's what's decided, then that's what we'll do.

**MYRRHINE**: Well, if that's what's decided, I'll be going home. But for the time being I've sworn to stay here.

**KINESIAS**: But at least lie down here with me; it's been so long.     905

**MYRRHINE**: No way. But I'm not saying I don't love you.

**KINESIAS**: Love me? So why won't you lie down, Myrrhine?

**MYRRHINE**: Right here in front of the baby? You must be joking!

**KINESIAS**: Zeus no! Boy, take him home. [*Exit slave.*] There you are, the kid's out of our way. Now, why don't you just lie down?     910

**MYRRHINE**: Lie down where, you silly man?

**KINESIAS**: [*Looking around*]: Where? Pan's Grotto[175] will do fine.

**MYRRHINE**: But I need to be pure before I can go back up to the Akropolis.[176]

**KINESIAS**: Very easily done: just wash off in the Klepsydra.[177]

**MYRRHINE**: You're telling me, dear, that I should go back on the oath I swore?     915

KINESIAS: Don't worry about any oath; let me take the consequences.[178]

MYRRHINE: All right then, I'll get us a bed.

KINESIAS: No, don't; the ground's OK for us.

MYRRHINE: Apollo no! I wouldn't dream of laying you on the ground, no matter what kind of man you are. [Myrrhine goes into one of the flanking doors, which represents Pan's Grotto.] 920

KINESIAS: She really loves me, that's quite obvious!

MYRRHINE: [returning with a cot]: There you are! Lie right down while I undress. [Kinesias lies on the cot.] But wait, I forgot, what is it, yes, a mattress! Got to get one. 925

KINESIAS: A mattress? Not for me, thanks.

MYRRHINE: By Artemis, it's shabby on cords.

KINESIAS: Well, give me a kiss.

MYRRHINE [kissing him]: There. [She returns to the Grotto.]

KINESIAS: Oh lordy! Get the mattress quick! 930

MYRRHINE [returning with a mattress]: There we are! Lie back down and I'll get my clothes off. But wait, what is it, a pillow, you haven't got a pillow!

KINESIAS: I don't need a pillow!

MYRRHINE: I do. [She returns to the Grotto.]

KINESIAS: Is this cock of mine supposed to be Herakles waiting for his dinner?[179] 935

MYRRHINE [returning with a pillow]: Lift up now, upsy daisy. There, is that everything?

KINESIAS: Everything I need. Come here, my little treasure!

MYRRHINE: Just getting my breastband off. But remember: don't break your promise about a peace settlement. 940

KINESIAS: May lightning strike me, by Zeus!

MYRRHINE: You don't have a blanket.

KINESIAS: It's not a blanket I want—I want to fuck!

MYRRHINE: That's just what you're going to get. I'll be back in a flash. [She returns to the Grotto.] 945

KINESIAS: That woman drives me nuts with all her bedding!

MYRRHINE [*returning with a blanket*]: Get up.

KINESIAS [*pointing to his phallus*]: I've already got it up! [*Myrrhine carefully arranges the blanket while Kinesias fidgets.*]                                                     950

MYRRHINE: Want some scent?

KINESIAS: Apollo no, none for me.

MYRRHINE: But I will, by Aphrodite, whether you like it or not.

KINESIAS [*as Myrrhine returns to the Grotto*]: Then let the scent flow! Lord Zeus!

MYRRHINE [*returning with a round bottle of perfume*]: Hold out your hand. Take      955
some and rub it in.

KINESIAS: I don't like this scent, by Apollo; it takes a long time warming up and
it doesn't smell like conjugal pleasures.

MYRRHINE: Oh silly me, I brought the Rhodian brand![180]

KINESIAS: No, wait, I like it! Let it go, you screwy woman!                          960

MYRRHINE: Nonsense! [*She returns to the Grotto.*]

KINESIAS: Goddamn the man who first decocted scent!

MYRRHINE [*returning with a long, cylindrical bottle*]: Here, try this tube.

KINESIAS [*pointing to his phallus*]: Got one already! Now lie down, you slut, and
don't bring me anything more.                                                         965

MYRRHINE: By Artemis I will. Just getting my shoes off. But remember, darling,
you're going to vote for peace. [*At this, Kinesias averts his eyes from Myrrhine and
fiddles with the blanket; Myrrhine dashes off into the Akropolis.*]

KINESIAS: I'll give it serious consideration. [*He looks up again, only to find Myrrhine
gone.*] The woman's destroyed me, annihilated me! Not only that: she's              970
pumped me up and dropped me flat!
[*During the ensuing duet both semichoruses return to the center of the orchestra; the women
carry the shirts that the men had removed earlier.*][181]
    Now what shall I do? Whom shall I screw?
    I'm cheated of the sexiest girl I knew!
    How will I raise and rear this orphaned cock?
    Is Fox Dog[182] out there anywhere?                           975
    I need to rent a practical nurse!

MEN'S LEADER:

> Yea, frightful agony, thou wretch,
> dost rack the soul of one so sore bediddled.
> Sure I do feel for thee, alack!
> What kidney could bear it,                                    980
> what soul, what balls,
> what loins, what crotch,
> thus stretched on the rack
> and deprived of a morning fuck?[183]

KINESIAS:

> Ah, Zeus! The cramps attack anew!                             985

MEN'S LEADER:

> And this is what she's done to you,
> the detestable, revolting shrew!

WOMEN'S LEADER:

> No, she's totally sweet and dear!

MEN'S LEADER:

> Sweet, you say! She's wicked, wicked!

KINESIAS:

> You're right: wicked is what she is!                          990
> O Zeus, Zeus, raise up a great tornado,
> with lightning bolts and all,
> to sweep her up like a heap of grain
> and twirl her into the sky,
> and then let go and let her fall                              995
> back down to earth again,
> and let her point of impact be
> this dick of mine right here!

## EPISODE

[Enter a Spartan herald, both arms hidden beneath a long travelling cloak and pushing it out in front.]

HERALD [to Kinesias]: Where be the Senate of Athens or the Prytanies? Have some news to tell them.                                                    1000

KINESIAS: And what might you be? Are you human? Or a Konisalos?[184]

HERALD: Am Herald, young'un, by the Twain, come from Sparta about settlement.

KINESIAS: And that's why you've come hiding a spear in your clothes?

HERALD: Not I, by Zeus, no spear!                                                                                      1005

KINESIAS: Why twist away from me? And why hold your coat out in front of you? You've got a swollen groin from the long ride, maybe?

HERALD: By Kastor, this guy crazy! [He accidently reveals his erect phallus.]

KINESIAS: Hey, that's a hard-on, you rascal!

HERALD: No, by Zeus, is not! Don't be silly!                                                              1010

KINESIAS: Then what do you call that?

HERALD: Is Spartan walking-stick.

KINESIAS [pointing to his own phallus]: Then this is a Spartan walking-stick too. Listen, I know what's up; you can level with me. How are things going in Sparta?                                                                                              1015

HERALD: All Sparta rise, also allies. All have hard-on. Need Pellana.[185]

KINESIAS: What caused this calamity to hit you? Was it Pan?[186]

HERALD: Oh no. Was Lampito started it, yes, and then other women in Sparta, they all start together like in footrace, keep men away from their hair-pies.                                                                                              1020

KINESIAS: So how are you faring?

HERALD: Hard! Walk around town bent over, like men carrying oil-lamp in wind. The women won't permit even to touch the pussy till all of us unanimously agree to make peace treaty with rest of Greeks.

KINESIAS: So this business is a global conspiracy by all the women! Now I get it!     1025
OK, get back to Sparta as quick as you can and arrange to send ambassadors here with full powers to negotiate a treaty. And I'll arrange for our Council to choose their own ambassadors; this cock of mine will be Exhibit A.

HERALD: I fly away. You offer capital advice. [He exits by the way he entered; Kinesias exits in the opposite direction.]                                                                                  1030

MEN'S LEADER:
   A woman's harder to conquer than any beast,
   than fire, and no panther is quite so ferocious.

WOMEN'S LEADER:
    You understand that, but then you still resist us?
    It's possible, you rascal, to have our lasting friendship.     1035

MEN'S LEADER:
    I'll never cease to loathe women!

WOMEN'S LEADER:
    Well, whenever you like. But meanwhile I'll not stand
    for you to be undressed like that. Just look how ridiculous you are!
    I'm coming over to put your shirt back on.

[*She walks over and replaces his shirt, and the other women each follow suit for one of the men.*]

MEN'S LEADER:
    By god, that's no mean thing you've done for us.     1040
    And now I'm sorry I got mad and took it off.

WOMEN'S LEADER:
    And now you look like a man again, not so ridiculous.
    And if you weren't so hostile I'd have removed
    that bug in your eye, that's still in there, I see.

MEN'S LEADER:
    So *that's* what's been driving me nuts! Here, take my ring;     1045
    please dig it out of my eye, then show it to me;
    by god, it's been biting my eye for quite some time.

WOMEN'S LEADER:
    All right, I will, though you're a grumpy man.
    Great gods, what a humongous gnat you've got in there!
    There, take a look. Isn't it positively Trikorysian?[187]     1050

MEN'S LEADER:
    By god, you've helped me; that thing's been digging wells,
    and now it's out my eyes are streaming tears.

WOMEN'S LEADER:
    Then I'll wipe them away, though you're a genuine rascal,
    and kiss you.

MEN'S LEADER:
                    Don't kiss me!     1055

WOMEN'S LEADER:

I'll kiss you whether you like it or not!

[*She does so, and the other women follow suit as before.*]

WOMEN'S LEADER:

The worst of luck to you! You're born sweet-talkers.
The ancient adage gets it in a nutshell:
"Can't live with the pests or without 'em either."
But now I'll make peace, and promise nevermore          1060
to mistreat you or to take mistreatment from you.
Let's get together, then, and start our song.

[*The semichoruses become one and for the remainder of the play perform as a single chorus.*]

CHORUS: (strophe)

We don't intend to say anything
the least bit slanderous about
any citizen,[188] you gentlemen out there,          1065
but quite the opposite: to say and do
only what's nice, because the troubles
you've got already are more than enough.

So let every man and woman[189] tell us
if they need to have a little cash,          1070
say two or three minas;[190] we've got it at home
and we've got some purses for it too.
And if peace should ever break out,
everyone that we lent money to
can forget to repay—if they got anything!          1075

(antistrophe)

We're getting set to entertain
some visitors from Karystos today;[191]
they're fine and handsome gentlemen.
There'll be a special soup, and that piglet
of mine, I've sacrificed it on the grill,          1080
and it's turning out to be fine and tender meat.
So come on over to my house today:
get up early and take a bath,
and bathe the kids, and walk right in.
You needn't ask anyone's permission,          1085
just go straight on inside like it was yours,
because the door will be locked!

**EPISODE**

[*The Spartan Ambassadors enter, wearing short cloaks that barely conceal conspicuous bulges. They are accompanied by slaves.*]

CHORUS-LEADER: Hey! Here come ambassadors from Sparta, dragging long beards and wearing something around their waists that looks like a pigpen. [*To the Spartans.*] Gentlemen of Sparta: first, our greetings! Then tell us how    1090 you all are doing?

SPARTAN AMBASSADOR: No use to waste a lot of time describing. Is best to show how we're doing. [*The Spartans open their cloaks to reveal erect phalli.*]

CHORUS-LEADER: Gosh! Your problem's grown very hard, and it seems to be even more inflamed than before.    1095

SPARTAN AMBASSADOR: Unspeakable! What can one say? We wish for someone to come, make peace for us on any terms he likes.

[*Athenian Ambassadors enter from the opposite direction, with cloaks bulging.*]

CHORUS-LEADER: Look, I see a party of native sons approaching, like men wrestling, holding their clothes away from their bellies like that! Looks like a bad case of prickly heat.[192]    1100

FIRST ATHENIAN AMBASSADOR [*To the Chorus-Leader*]: Who can tell us where Lysistrata is? The men are here, and we're . . . as you see. [*They reveal their own erect phalli.*]

CHORUS-LEADER: Their syndrome seems to be the same as theirs. These spasms: do they seize you in the wee hours?    1105

FIRST ATHENIAN AMBASSADOR: Yes, and what's worse, we're worn totally raw by being in this condition! If someone doesn't get us a treaty pretty soon, there's no way we won't be fucking Kleisthenes![193]

CHORUS-LEADER: If you've got any sense, you'll cover up there: you don't want one of the Herm-Dockers to see you like this.[194]    1110

FIRST ATHENIAN AMBASSADOR: By god, that's good advice. [*The Athenians rearrange their cloaks to cover their phalli.*]

SPARTAN AMBASSADOR: By the Twain Gods, yes indeed. Come, put cloaks back on! [*The Spartans follow suit.*]

FIRST ATHENIAN AMBASSADOR: Greetings, Spartans! We've had an awful    1115 time.

**SPARTAN AMBASSADOR**: Dear colleague, we've had a fearful time, if those men saw us fiddling with ourselves.

**FIRST ATHENIAN AMBASSADOR**: Come on, then, Spartans, let's talk details. The reason for your visit?                                                                                    1120

**SPARTAN AMBASSADOR**: Are ambassadors, for settlement.

**FIRST ATHENIAN AMBASSADOR**: That's very good; us too. So why not invite Lysistrata to our meeting, since she's the only one who can settle our differences?[195]

**SPARTAN AMBASSADOR**: Sure, by the Twain Gods, Lysistrata, and Lysistratos                 1125
too if ye like![196]

[*Lysistrata emerges from the Akropolis gate.*]

**FIRST ATHENIAN AMBASSADOR**: It looks as if we don't have to invite her: she must have heard us, for here she comes herself.

**CHORUS-LEADER**: Hail, manliest of all women![197] Now is your time: be forceful and flexible, high-class and vulgar, haughty and sweet, a woman           1130
for all seasons; because the head men of Greece, caught by your charms, have gathered together with all their mutual complaints and are turning them over to you for settlement.

**LYSISTRATA**: Well, it's an easy thing to do if you get them when they're hot for it and not testing each other for weaknesses. I'll soon know how ready they          1135
are. Where's Reconciliation? [*A naked girl*[198] *comes out of the Akropolis.*] Take hold of the Spartans first and bring them here; don't handle them with a rough or mean hand, or crudely, the way our husbands used to handle us, but use a wife's touch, like home sweet home. [*The Spartan ambassador refuses to give his hand.*] If he won't give you his hand, lead him by his weenie. [*The Spartan*           1140
*ambassador complies, and she leads him and his colleagues to Lysistrata, where they stand to her left.*] Now go and fetch those Athenians too; take hold of whatever they give you and bring them here. [*Reconciliation escorts the Athenians to Lysistrata's right.*] Spartans, move in closer to me, and you Athenians too; I want you to listen to what I have to say. I am a woman, but still I've got a mind: I'm pretty          1145
intelligent in my own right, and because I've listened many a time to the conversations of my father and the older men I'm pretty well educated too.[199] Now that you're a captive audience I'm ready to give you the tongue-lashing you deserve—both of you.[200] Don't both of you sprinkle altars from the same cup like kinsmen, at the Olympic Games, at Thermopylai, at Delphi,           1150
and so many other places I could mention if I had to make a long list? Yet with plenty of enemies available with their barbarian armies, it's *Greek* men

and Greek cities you're determined to destroy! That's the first point I wanted to make.

FIRST ATHENIAN AMBASSADOR [Gazing at Reconciliation]: My cock is bursting    1155
out of its skin and killing me!

LYSISTRATA: Next I'm going to turn to you, Spartans. Don't you remember the
time when Perikleidas the Spartan came here on bended knee and sat at
Athenian altars, white-faced in his scarlet uniform, begging for a military
contingent? That time when Messenia was up in arms against you and the    1160
god was shaking you with an earthquake? And Kimon came with four
thousand infantrymen and rescued all Lakedaimon? And after that sort of
treatment from the Athenians, you're now out to ravage their country,
who've treated you so well?[201]

FIRST ATHENIAN AMBASSADOR: By Zeus they *are* guilty, Lysistrata!    1165

SPARTAN AMBASSADOR: We're guilty—[looking at Reconciliation] but what an
unspeakably fine ass!

LYSISTRATA: Do you Athenians think I'm going to let *you* off? Don't you
remember the time when you were dressed in slaves' rags and the Spartans
came in force and wiped out many Thessalian fighters, many friends and    1170
allies of Hippias? That day when they were the only ones helping you to
drive him out? How they liberated you, and replaced your slaves' rags with a
warm cloak, as suits a free people?[202]

SPARTAN AMBASSADOR [still gazing at Reconciliation]: I never saw such a classy
woman!    1175

FIRST ATHENIAN AMBASSADOR: I've never seen a lovelier cunt!

LYSISTRATA: So after so many good deeds done, why are you at war? Why not
stop this terrible behavior? Why not make peace? Come on, what's in the
way?

[During the following negotiations Reconciliation's body serves as a map of Greece.][203]

SPARTAN AMBASSADOR: We are ready, if they ready to return to us this    1180
abutment.[204]

LYSISTRATA: Which one, sir?

SPARTAN AMBASSADOR: Back Door[205] here, that we for a long time count on
having, and grope for.

FIRST ATHENIAN AMBASSADOR: By Poseidon, that you won't get!    1185

**LYSISTRATA**: Give it to them, good sir.

**FIRST ATHENIAN AMBASSADOR**: Then who will we be able to harrass?

**LYSISTRATA**: Just ask for some other place in return for that one.

**FIRST ATHENIAN AMBASSADOR**: Well, let's see now. First of all give us
Echinous here and the Malian Gulf behind it and both Legs.[206]                1190

**SPARTAN AMBASSADOR**: By Twain Gods, we will not give everything, dear fellow!

**LYSISTRATA**: Let it go, both of you: don't be squabbling about legs.

**FIRST ATHENIAN AMBASSADOR**: Now I'm ready to strip down and do some
ploughing!

**SPARTAN AMBASSADOR**: Me first, by Twain Gods: before one ploughs one        1195
spreads manure!

**LYSISTRATA**: You may do that when you've ratified the settlement. If, after due
deliberation, you do decide to settle, go back and confer with your allies.

**FIRST ATHENIAN AMBASSADOR**: Allies, dear lady? We're too hard up for that!
Won't our allies, all of them, come to the same decision we have, namely, to    1200
fuck?

**SPARTAN AMBASSADOR**: Ours will, by Twain Gods!

**FIRST ATHENIAN AMBASSADOR**: And so will the Karystians, by Zeus!

**LYSISTRATA**: You make a strong case. For the time being see to it you remain
pure,[207] so that we women can host you on the Akropolis with what we          1205
brought in our boxes. There you may exchange pledges of mutual trust, and
after that each of you may reclaim his wife and go home.[208]

**FIRST ATHENIAN AMBASSADOR**: What are we waiting for?

**SPARTAN AMBASSADOR** [To Lysistrata]: Lead on wherever you wish.

**FIRST ATHENIAN AMBASSADOR**: By Zeus yes, as quick as you can!               1210

[Lysistrata escorts Reconciliation inside, followed by the Spartan and Athenian ambassadors; the
Spartans' slaves sit down outside the door, which is attended by a doorkeeper.]

**CHORUS**:[209] (strophe)
    Intricate tapestries,
    nice clothes and fine gowns
    and gold jewellery: all that I own
    is yours for the asking

for your sons and for your daughter too,                                    1215
when she's picked to march with the basket.[210]
I declare my home open to everyone
to take anything you want.
Nothing is sealed up so tight
that you won't be able to break the seals                                    1220
and take away what you find inside.
But you won't see anything
unless your eyes are sharper than mine.

(antistrophe)

If anyone's out of bread
but has slaves and lots of little kids to feed,                              1225
you can get flour from my house:
puny grains, but a pound of them
grow up to be a loaf
that looks very hearty.
Any of you poor people are welcome                                           1230
to come to my house with sacks and bags
to carry the flour away; my houseboy will load them up.
A warning though: don't knock at my door—
beware of the watchdog there!


## EPISODE

FIRST ATHENIAN AMBASSADOR [still inside, knocking at the door and yelling to the    1235
doorkeeper]: Open the door, you! [He bursts through the door, sending the doorkeeper
tumbling down the steps. He wears a garland and carries a torch, as from a drinking-party.]
You should have got out of the way. [Other Athenians emerge, similarly equipped. To
the slaves] You there, why are you sitting around? Want me to singe you with
this torch? What a stale routine! I refuse to do it. [Encouragement from the         1240
spectators.] Well, if it's absolutely necessary we'll go the extra mile, to do you
all a favor. [He begins to chase the slaves with his torch.]

SECOND ATHENIAN AMBASSADOR [joining the First]: And we'll help you go
that extra mile! [To the slaves] Get lost! You'll cry for your hair if you don't!

FIRST ATHENIAN AMBASSADOR: Yes, get lost, so the Spartans can come out           1245
after their banquet without being bothered. [The slaves are chased off.]

SECOND ATHENIAN AMBASSADOR: I've never been at a better party! The

Spartans were really great guys, and we made wonderful company ourselves over the drinks.

FIRST ATHENIAN AMBASSADOR: Stands to reason: when we're sober we're not ourselves. If the Athenians will take my advice, from now on we'll do all our ambassadorial business drunk. As it is, whenever we go to Sparta sober, we start right in looking for ways to stir up trouble. When they say something we don't hear it, and when they don't say something we're convinced that they did say it, and we each return with completely different reports. But this time everything turned out fine. When somebody sang the Telamon Song when he should have been singing the Kleitagora Song,[211] everybody would applaud and even swear up and down what a fine choice it was. [Some of the slaves approach the door again.] Hey, those slaves are back! Get lost, you whip-fodder! [They chase the slaves away.]                    1250

1255

1260

SECOND ATHENIAN AMBASSADOR: Yes, by Zeus, here they come out of the door. [The Spartan ambassadors file out; their leader carries bagpipes.]

SPARTAN AMBASSADOR [to the stage-piper or to a piper who accompanies the Spartans]: Take pipes, my good man, and I dance two-step and sing nice song for Athenians and ourselves.                    1265

FIRST ATHENIAN AMBASSADOR: God yes, take the pipes: I love to watch you people dance!

SPARTAN AMBASSADOR:
Memory, speed to this lad
your own Muse, who knows
about us and the Athenians,                    1270
about that day at Artemision[212]
when they spread sail like gods
against the armada
and whipped the Medes,
while Leonidas led us,[213]                    1275
like wild boars we were, yes,
gnashing our tusks, our jaws running
streams of foam, and our legs too.
The enemy, the Persians,
outnumbered the sand on the shore.                    1280
Goddess of the Wilds, Virgin Beast-Killer,[214]
come this way, this way to the treaty,
and keep us together for a long long while.

Now let friendship in abundance
attend our agreement always,                                    1285
and may we ever abandon
foxy strategems.
Come this way, this way,
Virgin Huntress!

[*Lysistrata comes out of the Akropolis, followed by the Athenian and Spartan wives.*]

LYSISTRATA[215]: Well! Now that everything else has been wrapped up so nicely,     1290
it's time for you Spartans to reclaim these wives of yours; and you Athenians,
these here. Let's have husband stand by wife and wife by husband; then to
celebrate our great good fortune let's have a dance for the gods. And let's be
sure never again to make the same mistakes! [*The couples descend into the orchestra
to dance to the Ambassador's song; around them dance the members of the chorus, who are*     1295
*also paired in couples.*]

Bring on the dance, include the Graces,[216]
and invite Artemis,
and her twin brother, the benign Healer,[217]
and the Nysian whose eyes flash                                 1300
bacchic among his maenads,[218]
and Zeus alight with flame
and the thriving Lady his consort;[219]
and invite the divine powers
we would have as witnesses                                      1305
to remember always
this humane peace,
which the goddess Kypris[220] has fashioned.

CHORUS:

Alalai, yay Paian!
Shake a leg, iai!                                              1310
Dance to victory, iai!
Evoi evoi, evai evai!

LYSISTRATA: Now, my dear Spartan, you give us some music: a new song to
match the last one!

SPARTAN AMBASSADOR:

Come back again from fair Taygetos,                            1315
Spartan Muse, and distinguish this occasion
with a hymn to the God of Amyklai[221]
and Athena of the Brazen House[222]

and Tyndareos' fine sons,[223]
who gallop beside the Eurotas.                                      1320
Ho there, hop!
Hey there, jump!
Let's sing a hymn to Sparta,
home of dance divine
and stomping feet,                                                  1325
where by the Eurotas' banks
young girls frisk like fillies,
raising dust-clouds underfoot
and tossing their tresses
like maenads waving their wands and playing,                        1330
with Leda's daughter pre-eminent,
their chorus-leader pure and pretty.[224]

[*To the chorus*] Come on now, hold your hair in your hand, get your feet hopping like a deer and start making some noise to spur the dance! And sing for the goddess who's won a total victory, Athena of the Brazen House!

[*All exit dancing, the chorus singing a traditional hymn to Athena.*]

# WOMEN AT THE THESMOPHORIA

❧

# INTRODUCTION

## 1. *The Play*

In the prologue, the tragic poet Euripides (who was at this time about seventy years old), accompanied by his Kinsman (whose name we are never told), visits the young tragic poet Agathon to seek his help in a crisis. Agathon is portrayed as effeminate: he is clean-shaven, has a high-pitched voice, wears women's clothes and enjoys the passive role in sex. Under hostile questioning by the conventionally masculine Kinsman, Agathon reveals that his effeminacy not only expresses his own nature and his preference for the luxurious clothing of old-time Ionian poets, but also has a practical purpose: by dressing and acting like a woman he can better create female roles for his plays.[1] Now we learn the reason for Euripides' visit: the matrons of Athens are about to decree a death sentence on him because his scandalous heroines have opened husbands' eyes to the hitherto secret misbehavior of wives. This decree is to be enacted at the festival of Thesmophoria, which in actual life was exclusively run by citizen matrons and off-limits to men. In the play, the matrons plan to use their festive assembly to usurp the juridical function of the male Assembly and thus condemn Euripides to death. Euripides asks Agathon to infiltrate the Thesmophoria as a woman and plead his case. When Agathon refuses, the Kinsman reluctantly volunteers for the job. Shaven and disguised as a woman, the Kinsman attends the festival and delivers a defense speech that outrages rather than mollifies the matrons: Euripides, he argues, failed to reveal even the tiniest fraction of the whole shocking truth about women, a claim which he proceeds to document graphically. The women become suspicious, and with the help of another Athenian effeminate, Kleisthenes, soon expose the Kinsman as a male intruder and sentence him to death. But the Kinsman (in parody of Euripides' play *Telephos*) seizes a hostage (which turns out to be a

93

wineskin disguised as a baby girl) and takes refuge at an altar, where he is guarded first by Kritylla, a tough old woman, and then by a barbaric archer-policeman. Euripides tries to rescue the Kinsman by reenacting rescue scenes from his own recent plays (*Palamedes, Helen* and *Andromeda*), but these fail to deceive Kritylla. Finally, Euripides disguises himself as an old bawd, distracts the policeman with a sexy young prostitute and escapes with the Kinsman, having promised the women that he will never again portray them unfavorably.

Like *Lysistrata, Women at the Thesmophoria* was produced in 411 (almost certainly at the Dionysia, some three months later than *Lysistrata*) and depicts a conspiracy of citizen wives provoked by a grievance against men and ends with reconciliation between the genders. But there the major similarities end. Unlike *Lysistrata, Women at the Thesmophoria* makes practically no reference to the current political and military situation: focusing almost entirely on the worlds of art and festival, it is one of Aristophanes' least politically engaged plays. And while reversal of gender-roles is essential to the humor of both plays, in *Lysistrata* it is the wives who infiltrate male space and temporarily occupy male gender roles,[2] whereas in *Women at the Thesmophoria* both sexes transgress gender boundaries, especially the men: all the play's characters, except for the barbaric slave-policeman who appears late in the play, are either women with power over men or men who at some point impersonate women.

The two plays differ also in their portrayal of women's characters. *Lysistrata* had featured as an admirable heroine whose conspiracy was unselfish and sympathetic: under Athena's aegis Lysistrata saves all of Greece from its misguided men by forcing them to resolve their differences and negotiate a lasting peace. The young wives, it is true, are given stereotypically feminine foibles and weaknesses, but they overcome these, so that the heroine may remind the Athenians how essential to the safety and well-being of the polis were the women's roles as spouses, mothers and managers of the household. In the end, the women of *Lysistrata* seem superior to the men both in their civic priorities and in their ethical dispositions. *Women at the Thesmophoria*, by contrast, has no heroine, virtually ignores the Athenians' darkening military and political situation[3] and portrays the matrons in at best a very suspect light: save for wanting Euripides and the Kinsman dead, they have no ambition higher than that of continuing to live the life of the stereotypical Athenian wife—a category that in this play Aristophanes exploits to the fullest. In fact, *Women at the Thesmophoria* contains more jokes about wives' mis-behavior than *Lysistrata* and *Assemblywomen* combined. Drinking and adultery get the most attention, but domestic theft and baby-swapping are thrown in for good measure. The women are made the butts of both Euripidean "slander" and comic satire.

Although the matrons resent Euripides' portrayals and the Kinsman's speech, and although we never *see* them seriously misbehaving—drinking wine at their festival being only a minor dereliction—they never actually refute or even deny Euripides' or the Kinsman's charges; in fact, the particulars of the oath they swear at the beginning of their assembly virtually confirm the worst male suspicions. And so the matrons turn out to be not righteously indignant victims of slander but deceivers of their husbands angrily conspiring to avoid exposure. By contrast with the other two "women's" plays, *Women at the Thesmophoria* nowhere invites the audience to feel the slightest admiration, or even sympathy, for women either as individuals or as a gender.

The differences between the two plays do not mean that Aristophanes had suddenly changed his mind about women; rather, he emphasized positive female stereotypes in *Lysistrata* and negative ones in *Women at the Thesmophoria* because each play has a different thematic focus. In *Lysistrata* Aristophanes focused on what he saw as perverse civic and military policies in the public world of men. In order to discredit these, he compared the polis (which was male-run) unfavorably with the traditional, stable world of the private household (which was female-run), and that comparison required a favorable—or at least a benign—portrayal of the wives. By overcoming their stereotyped weaknesses, the wives live up to their *ideal* roles as defenders of the household and therefore of the polis. In *Women at the Thesmophoria* Aristophanes focuses instead on husbands' anxiety about the private conduct of wives, as an element in a larger exploration of the nature of fictive illusion.[4] In a society like fifth-century Athens, where the honor and even the survival of a man's household depended on the unassailable propriety of its women,[5] male suspicions about female misconduct were inevitable and always easy to inflame. Was the wives' *apparent* propriety a mere facade that concealed *secret* misbehavior, and if so, how could the men find out? The deceitful and even scandalous behavior of mythical wives in tragedies by Euripides offered a peek through the window, but were Euripides' portrayals true to life, as some men were all too willing to believe, or outright slander, as the wives (at least officially) claim?

In *Women at the Thesmophoria* Aristophanes explores the often ludicrous plasticity of the social construct known as gender roles and the public media by which a society seeks to define it; in particular, he inquires into the relative capacity of the chief dramatic media—the male-written genres of comedy and tragedy—to capture and reveal its elusive reality.[6] In the end, the play satirizes not so much women as male attempts to understand them. This is a play about male fantasies, and it makes no attempt to incorporate a vision of women separate from those fantasies.

## 2. Gender Transgression and Thesmophoria

In this play Aristophanes sets his women in the context of one of the oldest and most widespread women's festivals in Greece. At Athens, Thesmophoria was one segment of a series of interlocking women's festivals, held in the autumn sowing-season, that variously celebrated the ancient association of women with agriculture and with fertility generally.[7] During its three days the matrons (lawfully married citizen women) of Athens abandoned their homes and lived by themselves in a sacred precinct, all other categories of women, and all men, being strictly excluded. During the festival the matrons constituted their own society, which their husbands had to finance and which had its own "leaders" (archousai), two being elected by the matrons of each deme (local community), for a total of about 300 "leaders." There the matrons enacted immemorially ancient rituals, including the uttering of ritual obscenity and the performance of sacrificial slaughter, which was normally the exclusive prerogative of men.[8] Since the purpose of the ritual could not have been more important for the entire community—to ensure the continuity of plant and animal life through the winter to come—the men had no choice but to stay at home while their wives met in assembly: a reversal of the normal pattern. Thus the Thesmophoria provided Aristophanes with a ready-made setting for a gender-satire featuring role reversal.

In the play, the women decide to use the second (middle) day of the festival, when "we have the most free time," for a special assembly (372–79) to be held on the Pnyx Hill (658), where the Athenian assembly (composed exclusively of adult citizen men) normally met, so that they transgress not only gender *roles* but also gender *boundaries*, much like the wives of *Lysistrata*, who leave their homes, occupy the Akropolis, and debar the men, or the women of *Assembly-women*, who pack the assembly in disguise. But was the holding of a women's assembly on the Pnyx Hill a comic fantasy, or was the Thesmophoria itself normally held there, in which case this "transgression" was already a feature of the festival?

There is no (other) testimony for the location of the Thesmophorion and little archaeological support for a suitable separate structure on the Pnyx, which in any case would be a surprising venue for such an ancient cult. Since one element of the play's fantasy is the women's imitation of male political assemblies, the women may merely be *calling* their meeting-place the Pnyx, while everyone knew that in real life the women met elsewhere: if so, they most likely met in the Eleusinion, located on the Akropolis slope abutting the SW Agora and the principal precinct of Demeter and Kore in Athens.

But there are some reasons to prefer the Pnyx as the real-life venue for the Thesmophoria. The Eleusinion is never explicitly referred to as, or said to contain, a Thesmophorion, nor do its archaeological remains provide room enough for all the matrons of Athens to meet in assembly. If the Thesmophoria festival was held there, at most only the 300-odd "leaders" could have attended, and the idea of an assembly of "the demos of women" paralleling the men's would be mere comic fantasy. But if that was the case, it is strange that Aristophanes did not highlight this fantastic idea, as he did with the women's transgressions of male space in *Lysistrata* and *Assemblywomen*. As it is, the play takes the matrons' assembly and its location on the Pnyx for granted: true, the assembly is a special initiative, but it is assumed that it takes place as part of the festival without a change of venue, and if the Pnyx was an abnormal location, we would expect to hear at least something about how its takeover was managed.

There are two other pieces of suggestive, if not decisive, evidence in favor of the Pnyx. An inscription shows that on the only attested occasion when the Athenian assembly met during the Thesmophoria, it met in the theater, not on the Pnyx—presumably because the women were meeting there.[9] This inscription dates from 122 BCE, nearly 300 years later than our play. But if the Thesmophoria was held on the Pnyx in the second century, there is no reason why it should not have been held there in the fifth century too. Second, a cult-statue from Mylasa in Karia (from the third century BCE) stipulates that the rites of Demeter Thesmophoros should be carried out "as the women have decreed" (*hos edoxe tais gynaixi*), using the standard formula for assembly decisions.[10] While Karia was far from Athens, the Thesmophorian assembly there was apparently no comic fantasy.

On balance, then, Aristophanes seems to have chosen an actual occasion for ritual female "transgression" as the basis for his fantasy about the matrons of Athens enacting legislation against a tragic poet. Moreover, the occasion he chose was distinct from other female rituals in being more closely associated with the continuity of the polis: unlike the cults of ritual rebellion (separation from and violation of communal controls) with which the women of *Lysistrata* and *Assemblywomen* are aligned, the Thesmophoria dramatizes the roles that women played in the *maintenance* of the community; hence its orderly and pseudo-civic protocols. Naturally, Aristophanes emphasizes (and exaggerates) the parallels between the matrons' assembly and the assemblies familiar to his male audience, and is not much interested in other details of the Thesmophorian ritual, if indeed he even knew what they were. Nevertheless, the myths and procedures associated with the Thesmophorian festival are thematically relevant to the general theme of gender transgression and thus to an understanding of Aristophanes' comic fantasy.

The principal deities of Thesmophoria were the archetypal mother Demeter, goddess of both cereal crops and human fertility, and her daughter Kore (also known as Pherephatta or Persephone). Their myth told how Hades, god of the underworld, kidnapped and raped Kore and forced her to be his queen, and of Demeter's angry search for her raped daughter, her blighting of the land in retaliation and her final compromise with Hades: Demeter would provide crops for half the year but withhold them during the other half, when Kore lived with her infernal husband. This myth provided a coherent explanation of the festival's rituals, mysteries and sexual symbolism; of the power, solidarity and self-sufficiency of its celebrants; and of its pervasive atmosphere of hostility toward men.[11]

The sexual polarities and inversions of Thesmophoria reflected the social tensions surrounding procreative sexuality itself. On the one hand, the matrons demonstrated intimacy with the awesome secrets of life and death: they handled snakes, phalloi and other sexual symbols, slaughtered animals, indulged in ritual obscenity and abuse, and perhaps even flagellation. On the other hand, the matrons were expected to be pure and pious: they abstained from sex during the festival and for a preparatory period before it, and during the festival they wore the plainest garments and sat, fasting, on mats made from antaphrodisiac plants. The exclusion of men was absolute: legends told of the repulse, capture or even castration of male intruders, for any contact with men would pollute the matrons and imperil the efficacy of their fertility-magic. In the end, purity and sexuality were perceived as polar aspects of the same complex: like the sex-strike in Lysistrata, the pointedly asexual aspect of the Thesmophoria "focuses attention on the idea of productive sexual union by a paradoxical temporary insistence upon its opposite."[12] At the same time, the wives' dual aspect of purity and sexuality opens a satirical avenue for the comic poet to play with the tension between positive norms of chastity and negative stereotypes of licentiousness. As in the festival and its myth, the play ends on a positive note of reconciliation and a return to normality.

Although Aristophanes chose Thesmophoria as an appropriate dramatic venue for a women's assembly and a confrontation between the genders, he avoids satirizing its ritual activities per se, choosing only a few superficial details as the basis for a comic fantasy: the female festive community parodies the male civic polis and the women's assembly parodies the men's assembly, including the ability to condemn an enemy. The play is set on the second day of Thesmophoria, a gloomy fast in which the women reverted to "the ancient way of life"—appropriate to the irritability and spirit of vengefulness with which they attack Euripides.[13] The capture of a male spy (the Kinsman) recalls not merely Euripides' play Telephos but also episodes from Thesmophorian legends,[14] much as the fate of the Magistrate in Lysistrata recalls the mythical victims of Dionysos' maenads.[15] And Euripides, in his attempts to rescue the

Kinsman from death and in his final compromise with the women, lightly suggests Demeter herself.

### 3. Genre Transgression and the Theater

Euripides' reputation as a "misogynist"—in the sense that in his plays he portrayed women as being capable of what Athenian audiences would consider the worst sorts of misbehavior—is first attested in the plays of 411.[16] This reputation was evidently based both on the unprecedented intensity and vividness of Euripides' female characters and on the predilection of so many of them for criminal misconduct: in the extant plays alone there are seven heroines who commit or plot murder (Medeia, Phaidra in *Hippolytos*, Hermione in *Andromache*, Hekabe, Elektra, Kreousa in *Ion*, Agave in *Bakchai*), and the adulterous schemes of two heroines from lost plays (Phaidra in the first *Hippolytos* and Stheneboia in *Bellerophon* and *Stheneboia*) are known to have outraged Athenian standards of propriety.[17] It is true that these characters were already present in the traditional heroic myths and that other tragic poets had created dangerous female characters too (for example, Aischylos' Klytaimestra, in his *Oresteia*, and Sophokles' Elektra). But Euripides frequently embellished the myths, making bad characters (male and female) even worse; invited the audience at least to empathize with bad characters; and in his general use of language, characterization, "realism" and romantic sensationalism made the old mythical plots and characters seem closer to everyday experience than was customary in tragedy. In Aristophanes' *Frogs* Euripides boasts that he created roles "for slaves no less than wives, mothers, maidens and old women" in order to be "democratic," to which Aischylos (the spokesman for tradition) replies that such novelty deserves the death penalty (948–50).

Thus Euripides' portrayal of women could be thought relevant to the women who inhabited the spectators' own households. The negative responses seem to have been various. Artistic traditionalists thought such portrayals simply too sordid for tragedy: in *Frogs* Aischylos says to Euripides, "I never used to create cheap whores (*pornas*) like Phaidra and Stheneboia, nor can anybody point to any love-struck woman I ever created" (1043–44). Conservative Athenian men, who frowned on any public reference to respectable women whether for praise or blame,[18] will have thought that Euripides' portrayals hit too close to home: his *femmes fatales* might compromise the respectable public image of Athenian womanhood, and worse, might make men wonder about the propriety of their *own* wives. The Aischylos of *Frogs* claims that characters like Euripides' Phaidra and Stheneboia "have moved noble spouses of noble men to drink poison out of shame" (1050–51), implying either that such spouses thought the honor of their gender irretrievably besmirched or that they had been emboldened to commit adultery, then committed suicide when spurned or detected. The women in our play, who are supposed to represent the respectable matrons of Athens, voice the same complaints, and (comically) add that, because their husbands have become more watchful and suspicious, they no longer enjoy the same freedoms as before (implying that Euripides' portrayals were not entirely false).[19]

But do Aristophanes' matrons really reflect the attitudes of their actual counterparts, or was this too merely a comic fantasy? Aristophanes is certainly being funny when he has the wives try to silence Euripides for revealing their secrets, but the idea would not have been *very* funny had it not been based on an actual public perception of Euripides' art, nor would Aischylos' charges in *Frogs* have sounded very cogent. If women did attend performances of tragedy,[20] they will have witnessed Euripides' shocking portrayals for themselves; if not, they would certainly have heard about them at secondhand and/or read them (*Frogs* 52–53 shows that texts of Euripides' plays were in circulation). In either case, it would be surprising if Euripides' controversial women elicited no reaction from their real-life counterparts. Needless to say, any women who had been angered by Euripides' portrayals would have been made even angrier if she watched *Women at the Thesmophoria*.

The creation of convincing female portrayals demanded authorial empathy on the part of a tragedian, and Aristophanes' comic idea was to take the idea of empathy literally: like the effeminate Agathon, who represents the second generation of tragedy in the Euripidean mode, Euripides had literally turned himself into a woman in order to create his "realistic" female roles. That is why they are not only believable but true, and why the wives try not to refute Euripides but to silence him. If the wives *qua* celebrants of Thesmophoria cross gender-boundaries to attack Euripides, it is because Euripides *qua* tragic poet has done the same to them.

Thus Euripides has crossed not only gender boundaries but also genre boundaries. Even mythical drama, if it seems believable in terms of life as lived by the spectators, can be called topical, but realism and topicality were traditionally hallmarks not of tragedy but of comedy.[21] In *Women at the Thesmophoria* Aristophanes decided to put Euripidean "realism" to the test of real life, or at any rate, real life as fabricated by comedy: can the Kinsman bring off his role as a matron at the Thesmophoria, and when that fails, can Euripides rescue the Kinsman by restaging his escape scenes? In the end, Euripidean tragedy is exposed as being just as artificial as the female costumes worn by Agathon, Euripides and the Kinsman, and just as inadequate in the face of real-life danger and real-life "women." Meanwhile, comedy reveals its own superiority at depicting the real world: the Kinsman's speech on the misbehavior of women is more "realistic" (according to the motive stereotypes) than Euripides' plays, and, when Euripides' own stratagems have failed, he is forced to resort to a comic gimmick to rescue himself and the Kinsman. We feel that the comic poet has exposed and punished Euripides' genre-transgression just as effectively as the women his gender-transgression. On the dramatic stage as in the women's world, normality is restored: Euripides will continue to write plays, but not about "real" women, and the rebellious matrons will go back to being (or at least seeming to be) model wives.

Comedy's onstage representative is the earthy and irrepressible Kinsman, who is unintentionally thrust into the alien worlds of tragic mimesis and women's festival, and whose reactions guide our laughter at Euripides, Agathon, the women and the archer-policeman. Alongside the Kinsman's plain language, forthright honesty, conventional attitudes and sheer masculinity—in short, his comic manhood—the language, characters and plot-contrivances of Euripidean tragedy are constantly exposed as precious and artificial, pale imitations of true feminine artificiality.[22] Euripides' disguising of the Kinsman may be adequate for the purposes of tragic illusion but it cannot fool the women, who are past masters of illusion and deception. Nor do the rescue-stratagems, which had been so successful on the tragic stage, prove effective before an audience of the tough Kritylla and the barbaric policeman; against *him* a real dancing-girl (not a disguised man or a tragic "heroine") must ultimately be deployed. It would seem that Euripidean realism is effective only when the audience suspends its disbelief and cooperates with the artifice. Not so comedy: "as the tragedies are falling apart under the assault of the non-believers, the comedy is succeeding brilliantly."[23] Comedy, while (like the Kinsman) it maintains its own generic integrity, can incorporate tragedy and also (at least in the case of Euripides) go it one better.

In the end, Euripides promises the wives that he will never again reveal their secrets in his plays. But the husbands will not be left in the dark: as the Kinsman's defense-speech has graphically shown, Euripides had never revealed even the smallest fraction of what the wives were *really* up to. Revelation of *those* secrets is after all the prerogative not of effeminate tragic illusion but of manly comic satire.

## CHARACTERS

KINSMAN of Euripides
EURIPIDES, the tragic poet
SLAVE of Agathon

AGATHON, *the tragic poet*
KRITYLLA, *a Thesmophorian priestess*
MIKA *assembly speaker*
WOMAN *assembly speaker*
KLEISTHENES, *an effeminate Athenian*
MARSHAL
POLICEMAN
ECHO, *an elderly goddess*
CHORUS *of Athenian women*

   Mute characters
PHILISTE *and other Athenian women*
MANIA, *nurse of Mika, and other servants of the women*
ELAPHION, *a dancing girl*
TEREDON, *a boy piper*


## PROLOGUE

SCENE: *A street in Athens, after dawn on a late October morning. Two elderly men, one hurrying and the other lagging, enter along the parodos and make their way toward the stage.*

KINSMAN [*stopping and clutching his side*]: Zeus! Will the swallow-time of spring ever come? This guy's going to kill me, plodding along since daybreak like a mill-ox. [*Calling loudly to Euripides' hurrying back.*] Might it be possible, before I puke out my guts, to find out where you're taking me, Euripides?

EURIPIDES: No; no need to hear the whole of what you presently will see.    5

KINSMAN: What? Say again? I don't need to hear . . .

EURIPIDES: No, not what you're going to see.

KINSMAN: And I don't need to see . . .

EURIPIDES: No, not what you should hear.

KINSMAN: What are you telling me? It's pretty subtle. Do you say I shouldn't    10
either hear or see?

EURIPIDES: These two are by nature mutually distinct.

KINSMAN: How "distinct"?

EURIPIDES: The way they were sundered in time afore. Aether,[24] you see, when
in primordial time he began to separate from Earth and with her begat    15

within himself living things astir, first fashioned for sight the eye, counter-image of the solar disc, and for hearing drilled that funnel, the ear.

KINSMAN: On account of this funnel, then, I'm not to hear or see? By Zeus, I'm delighted to have this additional lesson! Deep colloquies are such a dandy thing!                                                                                                20

EURIPIDES: You could learn many other such lessons from me.

KINSMAN: As a matter of fact I'd love another fine lesson: learning how to be lame in both legs.

EURIPIDES [crossly]: Come along here and pay attention.

KINSMAN: OK, OK.                                                                                                25

[They mount the stage and move toward the central door of the stage-building.]

EURIPIDES: Do you see that little door?

KINSMAN: By Herakles, I think I do!

EURIPIDES: Be quiet now.

KINSMAN: Quiet about the little door?

EURIPIDES: Listen.                                                                                                30

KINSMAN: I'm listening and being quiet about the door.

EURIPIDES: This happens to be the dwelling of the renowned tragic poet, Agathon.[25]

KINSMAN: What Agathon do you mean?

EURIPIDES: There is an Agathon . . .                                                                                                35

KINSMAN: You mean the suntanned one, strong guy?[26]

EURIPIDES: No, a different one. You've never seen him?

KINSMAN: The one with the full beard?[27]

EURIPIDES: You've never seen him?

KINSMAN: By Zeus, never, as far as I can recall.                                                                                                40

EURIPIDES: Well, you must have fucked him, though you might not know it.[28]
[The door of Agathon's house begins to open.] But let's hunker out of the way: one of his slaves is coming out the door with brazier and myrtle-sprigs, probably off to a make a sacrifice for success in poetic composition.

[*They crouch down to one side of the door. Enter Agathon's slave, a beardless and effeminate young man; holding the smoking brazier and a sprig of myrtle, he begins to sing in Agathonian fashion.*][29]

SLAVE:

> Let the folk keep holy silence,                                45
> gating the mouth, for here sojourns
> the holy company of Muses
> within the suzerain's halls,
> fashioning song.
> Aether windless hold thy breath                                50
> and whelming brine thy boom,
> gray—

KINSMAN [*fidgeting*]: Blah![30]

EURIPIDES [*listening attentively*]: Shhh! What's he say?

SLAVE:

> Lie down, feathered tribes, in rest,                           55
> paws of wild beasts run not
> through the timber—

KINSMAN: Blah blah blah!

SLAVE:

> For that craftsman of poesy, Agathon
> our helmsman, prepares—                                        60

KINSMAN: to get fucked?

SLAVE [*looking around*]: Who uttered that?

KINSMAN [*in a fruity voice*]: Windless Aether.

SLAVE [*satisfied*]:—prepares to position
> the keel-braces of his inchoate drama.
> He's warping fresh strakes for his verses;                     65
> some he planes down, others he couples,
> minting aphorisms, swapping meanings,
> channeling wax and rounding the mold
> and funneling metal—                                           70

KINSMAN: and giving blow jobs.

SLAVE [*looking around*]: What savage draws nigh the portals?

KINSMAN [*mimicking the Slave*]:
  One who's ready, for you
  and your craftsman of poesy too,                                    75
  to fashion and mold
  and funnel this cock of mine
  into your back portals.[31]

SLAVE [*spinning around and glaring at the Kinsman*]: I can't imagine what a rapist you
  were when you were a boy, old man.                                  80

EURIPIDES [*to the Slave*]: My good fellow, forget about him! Just summon
  Agathon here to me; it's urgent.

SLAVE: Supplicate not; the master shall soon emerge. In fact he's beginning to
  fashion a song, and in wintertime he's hard put to bend his riffs without
  coming outside into the sun.[32]                                    85

EURIPIDES: And what am I supposed to do?

SLAVE: Wait around; he's coming out. [*Exit Slave.*]

EURIPIDES: O Zeus, what meanest thou to do to me today?

KINSMAN: I would like to know what's going on here. What's all this
  groaning? What's the trouble? You shouldn't be hiding anything from me:    90
  I'm your kinsman.

EURIPIDES: Some rather nasty trouble's been cooked up for me.

KINSMAN: What kind?

EURIPIDES: This very day it will be adjudged: shall Euripides live or shall he
  die?                                                                95

KINSMAN: How could that be? The courts aren't in session today and the
  Council isn't sitting. It's the middle day of Thesmophorial![33]

EURIPIDES: And that's *exactly* why I think I'm done for. The women, you see,
  have devised a plot against me, and in the sanctuary of the Thesmophoroi[34]
  they're going to call an assembly[35] and vote for my destruction.    100

KINSMAN: Whatever for?

EURIPIDES: Because I write tragedies about them and slander them.[36]

KINSMAN: Well, it would serve you right, by Poseidon! But what's your
  strategy against the women?

EURIPIDES: To persuade the tragic producer Agathon to attend the            105
  Thesmophoria.

KINSMAN [*after a pause*]: To do what? Tell me.

EURIPIDES: To go to the women's assembly and say whatever's necessary on my behalf!

KINSMAN: Openly or in disguise?                                                                110

EURIPIDES [*impatiently*]: In disguise, dressed up like a woman.

KINSMAN: A pretty cute bit; just your style. You guys take the cake for craftiness!

EURIPIDES: Shh!

KINSMAN: What?                                                                                  115

EURIPIDES: Agathon's coming out.

[*Agathon, reclining on a chaise longue, is wheeled out of the house on the ekkyklema; he is a languid, beardless young man, dressed in sexually ambivalent fashion and surrounded by feminine paraphernalia.*]

KINSMAN: Where is he?

EURIPIDES [*Puzzled*]: Where? There, the man who's being rolled out!

KINSMAN: I must be blind; I can't see any *man* there at all, only the whore Kyrene!                                                                                    120

[*Agathon begins to tune up his voice.*]

EURIPIDES: Shh! He's getting ready to sing an aria.

KINSMAN: Is that ant-tracks[37] or some kind of vocalizing?

AGATHON [*singing the parts both of a chorus of Trojan maidens and their leader*]:[38]

        [*as leader*]
Maidens, receive the torch of the Nether Twain[39]
and in your freedom dance with ancestral cries!                                                125

        [*as chorus*]
For which deity hold we our revel?
O say! I'm a very soft touch
when it comes to adoring the gods.

        [*as leader*]
Come now, Muses,[40] venerate
him who draws arrows golden,                                                                    130
Phoibos, who based our country's vales
in the land of the Simois.[41]

[*as chorus*]
Take joy in our song most fair,
Phoibos, the first to accept the holy gift
of our musical tribute.                                            135

[*as leader*]
Hymn too the maiden born
in the oak-engendering mountains,
Artemis of the wild.[42]

[*as chorus*]
In turn I invoke in praise
the holy spawn of Leto,                                            140
Artemis untried in bed!

[*as leader*]
Yes Leto, and the chords of the Asian lyre,
beating nicely against the beat,
with the Phrygian Graces nodding time!

[*as chorus*]
I venerate Lady Leto                                               145
and the kithara, mother of hymns,
renowned for its masculine clangor.

[*as leader*]
Because of thee, kithara, and by virtue
of thy startling vociferation
did the light of joy whisk                                         150
from the eyes of the gods.
Wherefore glorify Lord Phoibos!

[*as chorus*]
Hail, happy scion of Leto!

KINSMAN: Holy Genetyllides,[43] what a pretty song! How feministic and deep-
kissed and tongue-tickled! Just hearing it brought a tingle to my very butt![44]    155
And you, young lad—if that's what you are—I want to ask you a question
out of Aischylos' *Lykourgos Trilogy*:[45] Whence comes this femme? What's its
homeland? What its dress? What this confoundment of nature? What does
the lute have to chat about with the party dress? Or the lyre with the hairnet?
Here's a bottle of aftershave—and a brassiere! How un—fitting! And what's    160
this community of mirror and sword? And you yourself, child: are you being
raised male? Then where's your dick? Your suit? Your Spartan shoes? All

right, say you're a woman. Then where are your tits? Well? Why don't you
answer? Must I find you out from your song, since you yourself refuse to
speak?                                                                    165

AGATHON: Old man, old man! I hear thy envious mockery, yet feel no pain
thereat. My clothing always matches my thoughts. To be a poet a man must
suit his fashions to the requirements of his plays. If, say, he's writing plays
about women, his body must partake of women's ways.

KINSMAN: So, if you're writing about Phaidra, you straddle your boyfriend?[46]   170

AGATHON: If one writes of manly matters, that element of the body is at hand.
But qualities we do not have must be sought by mimicry.

KINSMAN: Well, let me know when you're writing about satyrs:[47] I'll get
behind you with my hard-on and show you how.

AGATHON: Besides, 'tis uncultivated for a poet to look loutish and shaggy.     175
Observe that the renowned Ibykos and Anakreon of Teos and Alkaios,[48]
who seasoned their harmonies like chefs, used to wear bonnets and disport
themselves in Ionian style. [The Kinsman scratches his head in puzzlement.] And
Phrynichos[49]—you must have heard of him—was both beautiful and
beautifully dressed. And that's why his plays are also beautiful. For as we     180
are made, so must we compose.

KINSMAN: That must be why the revolting Philokles writes so revoltingly, and
the base Xenokles so basely, or the frigid Theognis so frigidly!

AGATHON: By absolute necessity. And recognizing this, I doctored myself.

KINSMAN [alarmed]: How, for heaven's sake?                                     185

EURIPIDES: Stop your barking! I was the same way at his age, when I began to
write.

KINSMAN: God, I don't envy you your rearing!

EURIPIDES [to Agathon]: All right, let me tell you why I've come.

AGATHON: Do say.                                                               190

EURIPIDES: Agathon, the wise man knows how to say much in a few well-
trimmed words. Smitten by fresh misfortune, I am come a suppliant to thy
door.

AGATHON: What is thy need?

EURIPIDES: The women at the Thesmophoria are preparing to destroy me this     195
very day, because I slander them.

AGATHON: What way, then, can we be of aid to thee?

EURIPIDES: *Every* way! If you sit in on the women's meeting covertly—since you'll pass as a woman—and rebut their accusations against me, you'll surely be my salvation. For you alone could speak in a manner worthy of me.    200

AGATHON: Then why don't you go and make your own defense?

EURIPIDES: I'll tell you. First, I'm well known. Second, I'm an old grey-beard. You, by contrast, are good-looking, pale, clean-shaven, soft, presentable, and you sound like a woman.

AGATHON: Euripides—    205

EURIPIDES: Well?

AGATHON: —you yourself once wrote, "You love life, son: you think your father doesn't?"[50]

EURIPIDES: I did.

AGATHON: Then hope not that I shall bear thy trouble for thee. I'd have to be    210 crazy![51] No, you yourself must see to your own affairs. Misfortune should by rights be confronted not with tricky contrivances but in a spirit of submission.

KINSMAN: You certainly got your wide asshole, you faggot, not with words but in the "spirit of submission"!    215

EURIPIDES: What is it that makes you afraid to go to *that* particular place?

AGATHON: I would perish more wretchedly than you!

EURIPIDES: Why?

AGATHON: Why, you ask? I'd look to be stealing the nocturnal doings of women and absconding with the female Kypris.[52]    220

KINSMAN: "Stealing" he says! Getting fucked is more like it, by Zeus! Still, his excuse is pretty plausible.

EURIPIDES [*to Agathon*]: Well, then? Will you do it?

AGATHON: Don't count on it.

EURIPIDES [*with one forearm over his eyes*]: Thrice-wretched me, oh, thus to    225 perish!

KINSMAN: Euripides! Dearest fellow! Kinsman! Don't give up on yourself!

EURIPIDES [*sobbing*]: But what will I *do*?

KINSMAN: Well, tell this guy to go to hell, and put me to use however you want.

EURIPIDES [dropping his forearm]: Well, now! You've signed yourself over to me,    230
so take off your clothes.[53]

KINSMAN [complying]: OK, they're on the ground. But what do you mean to do
to me?

EURIPIDES [pointing to the Kinsman's beard]: To shave this off, and [pointing to the
Kinsman's lower trunk] singe you down below.    235

KINSMAN [visibly shaken]: Well, if that's your decision, go ahead; if I say no I
shouldn't have promised my services in the first place.

EURIPIDES: Agathon, you've always got razors with you; how about lending us
one?

AGATHON: Take one yourself—they're right there in the razor-case.    240

EURIPIDES: You're a true gentleman. [After opening a large box which sits by Agathon's
chaise and selecting a long razor and a strop, he takes a small chair from under Agathon's
dressing-table and turns to the Kinsman.] Sit down. [Stropping the razor] Blow out
your cheek. The right one. [He shaves off the beard on the Kinsman's right cheek.]

KINSMAN [whimpering]: Oh no!    245

EURIPIDES [crossly]: What's this bellyaching? If you don't quiet down I'll have
to stick a peg in your mouth! [He prepares to shave the other cheek.]

KINSMAN [getting up and running away]: Ayeeee!

EURIPIDES: Hey! Where are you running off to?

KINSMAN: To the shrine of the Venerable Goddesses![54] 'Cause, by Demeter, I'm    250
not about to sit here getting cut up!

EURIPIDES: Then won't you look ridiculous, walking around with one side of
your face shaved!

KINSMAN: I don't care!

EURIPIDES: In the name of heaven, don't let me down! Come back here!    255

KINSMAN [walking resignedly back and resuming his seat]: What a fix I'm in!

EURIPIDES: Now hold still and tilt your head back. [He shaves the other cheek.]
Don't squirm!

KINSMAN [squealing through closed lips]: Mmmmmmmm.

EURIPIDES: What are you mmmmmmmm-ing for? It's done, and you look        260
fine!

KINSMAN: Damn it all, when I rejoin my regiment I'll literally be a leatherneck!

EURIPIDES: Don't worry about it: you'll be so good-looking! [*Taking a mirror
from Agathon's box*] Want to see yourself?

KINSMAN: OK, if you like. [*He takes the mirror and peers into it.*]        265

EURIPIDES: You see yourself?

KINSMAN [*horrified*]: God no! I see Kleisthenes![55]

EURIPIDES: Get up now. I've got to singe you, so bend over.[56]

KINSMAN: Oh me oh my, I'm going to be a roast pig![57]

EURIPIDES [*calling to the open door of Agathon's house*]: Somebody bring out a torch        270
or a lamp! [*A slave brings out a lighted torch and hands it to Euripides. To the Kinsman*]
Bend over. Now watch out for the tip of your dick.

KINSMAN: I'll watch out, by Zeus—[*Euripides applies the torch to his backside*]
except that I'm on fire! Oh no, no! [*To the audience*] Water! Water, neighbors,
before somebody *else's* asshole catches fire!        275

EURIPIDES: Be brave!

KINSMAN: How am I supposed to be brave when I'm being turbo-vulcanized?

EURIPIDES: There's nothing much left; you've suffered through the worst part.

KINSMAN: Phew! [*Running his hand along his backside and then looking at it*] Oh, the
soot! All around my crotch I'm charred!        280

EURIPIDES [*pointing to the audience*]: Don't worry, somebody *else* will sponge it
off.

KINSMAN: Anyone tries to wipe my ass for me, he'll be sorry!

EURIPIDES: Agathon, since you refuse to offer yourself, at least loan us a dress
for this fellow here, and a brassiere; you can't deny you've got them.        285

AGATHON: Take them and use them; I don't mind.

KINSMAN [*rummaging through Agathon's box*]: Which one should I take?

EURIPIDES [*joining him*]: Hmm. This party dress here; try it on first.

KINSMAN: By Aphrodite,[58] it smells good—like little pricks. Help me belt it up.

EURIPIDES: Now pass me the brassiere.        290

AGATHON: Here.

KINSMAN: Come on, arrange the pleats around my legs.

EURIPIDES: We need a hairnet and a hat.

AGATHON: Even better, this wig I wear at night!

EURIPIDES: By god, that's just the thing!                                              295

KINSMAN [putting it on and primping]: Well, how do I look?

EURIPIDES: Perfect! [To Agathon] Let's have a wrap.

AGATHON: There's one on the couch here.

EURIPIDES: He needs pumps.

AGATHON [removing his own]: Take mine.                                              300

KINSMAN: Will they fit me? [Puts them on.] You obviously like a loose fit.

AGATHON: Settle that for yourself; now you have what you need. [He claps his hands.] Someone roll me back inside, on the double!

[The ekkyklema rolls back inside the house, the door closing behind it.]

EURIPIDES: Our gentleman here is a real lady, at least in looks. But when you talk, be sure your voice sounds feminine, and be convincing!                      305

KINSMAN: I'll try.[59]

EURIPIDES: Off with you now! [He begins to walk off toward the wings.]

KINSMAN [following him]: Apollo, no![60] First you've got to promise me—

EURIPIDES: Promise what?

KINSMAN: that you'll use any and all means to help save me if anything bad          310
befalls me.

EURIPIDES: I swear then by Aether, Abode of Zeus![61]

KINSMAN [disdainfully]: Why not swear instead by Hippokrates' apartment
building?

EURIPIDES: I swear then by all the gods bar none!                                   315

KINSMAN: Well then, remember that thy heart hath sworn and not merely thy
tongue, and I didn't get the promise only from your tongue![62]

EURIPIDES: Will you please get going! There's the signal for the assembly over
at the Thesmophorion! As for me, I'm off.

[*Euripides exits through the wings. Stage-hands transform the scene-building to represent the Assembly Room of the Thesmophorion and set up a dais and chairs at center-stage. Meanwhile, women (the Herald, Mika, Second Woman, Mania holding Mika's baby) enter from one wing and move toward the chairs. The Kinsman heads for center-stage too, talking in falsetto to an imaginary maid.*][63]

KINSMAN:[64] Come along this way, Thraitta. Oh Thraitta, look! The torches are      320
burning, and such a lot of smoke rises toward the sanctuary! Thesmophorian
Goddesses, surpassingly lovely, grant that good luck attend me both coming
here and going home again! Thraitta, put down the box and take out the
cake, so I can make an offering to the Twain Goddesses. [*Miming an offering*]
Demeter, reverend Mistress mine, and Pherephatta,[65] grant me plenty for      325
plenty of sacrifices to you, and if not, grant at least that I get away with this!
And may my daughter Pussy[66] meet a man who's rich but childishly stupid,
and may my son Dick have a mind and a heart![67] [*Reaching the chairs at center-
stage*] Now where do I find a good seat for hearing everything the speakers say?
You go away from here, Thraitta; no slaves are allowed to listen to the      330
speeches.

[*The Kinsman takes a seat among the women, who begin to chatter excitedly.*][68]


## PARODOS

[*The Chorus, carrying torches,*[69] *enter the orchestra; as they arrange themselves, the priestess in charge of the assembly mounts the dais in front to the stage-building.*]

KRITYLLA:[70] Observe ritual silence; ritual silence please! Offer your prayers
to the Twain Thesmophorian Goddesses, to Wealth, to Kalligeneia, to
Kourotrophos, to Hermes and to the Graces,[71] that this assembly and today's
convocation be conducted in the finest and most excellent manner, a great      335
benefit to the Athenian polis and fortunate for us ourselves. And may victory
in the debate go to her whose actions and whose counsel best serve the
sovereign people of the Athenians and the sovereign people of the women.[72]
Be this your prayer, and for yourselves all good things. Ié Paion, ié Paion, ié
Paion! Let's have a grand time!      340

CHORUS:
    We say amen to that and ask
    the race of gods to signal
    their pleasure at our prayers.
    Zeus of the grand name and you,
    god of the golden lyre      345

who live on holy Delos,[73]
and you, almighty Maiden
with the gleaming eyes and golden spearpoint,[74]
who dwell in a polis you fought for,[75]
come this way!                                                          350
And you, goddess of many names,
slayer of beasts,
seed of Leto with the golden eyes,[76]
and you, august master Poseidon,
who rule the brine,                                                    355
quit now the fishy deep
so lashable to frenzy,
and you, daughters of marine Nereus,
and you nymphs who range the mountains!
May Apollo's golden lyre resound                                        360
in harmony with our prayers,
and may we well-born women of Athens
hold a faultless meeting!

KRITYLLA:[77] Pray to the Olympian gods and to the Olympian goddesses, to the
Pythian gods and Pythian goddesses, to the Delian gods and Delian god-          365
desses, and to the other gods as well. If anyone conspires in any way to harm
the people of the women; or negotiates secretly with Euripides and the
Medes[78] in any way to the women's harm; or contemplates either becoming a
tyrant or abetting a tyrant's installation; or denounces a woman who has
passed off another's child as her own;[79] or is a mistress' go-between slave        370
who spills the beans to the master or when sent with a message delivers it
wrong; or is a lover who deceives a woman with lies or reneges on promised
gifts; or is an old woman who gives gifts to a young lover;[80] or is a courtesan
who takes gifts from her lover and then betrays him; or is a barman or
barmaid who sells short pints or litres:[81] put a curse on every such person,      375
that they perish wretchedly and their families along with them! As for the
rest of you, ask the gods to give you every blessing!

CHORUS:
Our prayers are like yours:
that what we pray for will be fully accomplished
for the polis and for the people as well;                               380
and that she who advises best, deserving
to prevail, will prevail.
But she who deceives us
and breaks her solemn oaths for profit;

or tries to substitute decrees for laws;                                              385
or reveals our secrets to our enemies;
or to make money invites the Medes in,
to our harm: all such are impious
and culpable in the city's eyes.[82]
O Zeus all-powerful, ratify these prayers,                                            390
array the gods on our side,
although we are but women!

## EPISODE

KRITYLLA: Attention, everyone! The Women's Assembly—Archikleia
presiding, Lysilla being secretary, Sostrate proposing[83]—has passed the
following motion: an Assembly will be held on the morning of the second           395
day of Thesmophoria, when we have the most free time,[84] its principal
agendum being deliberation about the punishment of Euripides, who in the
view of us all is a criminal. Now who wishes to speak to this question?[85]

MIKA [rising from her chair and approaching the platform]: I do.

KRITYLLA [handing her a garland]: Put this on first, then speak.                   400

CHORUS-LEADER: Quiet! Silence! Pay attention, because she's clearing her
throat just as the politicians do. It's likely she'll deliver a long speech.

MIKA [assuming an oratorical posture]: By the Twain, I have not risen to speak,
fellow women, out of any personal ambition; no, but because I have for a
long time unhappily endured seeing you dragged through the mire by             405
Euripides,[86] that son of a woman who sells wild herbs[87] and whose own
reputation is everyway and everywhere bad. With what evil has this fellow
not besmirched us? Where, on any occasion where there are spectators,
tragic actors and choruses, has he spared us his disparagement, that we are
lover-bangers, nymphos, wine-oglers, disloyal, chattery, unwholesome, the         410
bane of men's lives? It's gotten so that as soon as our men get home from
the grandstand they start right in giving us suspicious looks and searching
the house for a concealed lover. We can no longer do anything that we used
to do before, so terrible are the things this man has taught our husbands
about us.[88] So if a wife so much as weaves a garland, she's suspected of having   415
a lover, and if she drops some utensil as she moves around the house, the
husband asks, "Who's the pot being broken for? 'Tis sure in honor of our
Korinthian guest!"[89] A girl gets sick, and right away her brother says, "This
maiden's hue doth please me not at all!"[90] There's more. A childless wife

wants to pass off another's baby as her own and can't even get away with that,    420
because now our husbands plant themselves nearby. He's slandered us to the
old men too, who used to marry young girls; now no old man wants to get
married because of the line, "The elderly bridegroom takes himself a boss."[91]
Then, because of this man, men put locks and bolts on their women's doors
to guard them, and not only that, they raise Molossic hounds as scarecrows    425
to repel lovers. Even that stuff might be forgiven. But not when we're no
longer allowed even to do what used to be our own jobs: keeping household
inventory and removing supplies on our own, flour, oil, wine,[92] because our
husbands now carry the housekeys with them—complicated, nasty things
with triple teeth, imported from Sparta. Before, we had no trouble opening    430
the door just by getting a signet ring made for three obols.[93] But now their
household spy, Euripides, has taught them to use little seals made of complex
wormholes, which they carry around fastened to their clothes. Accordingly,
I propose that one way or another we brew up some kind of destruction
for this man, either poisons or some particular technique whereby he gets    435
destroyed. This then is the argument of my speech; the rest I will enter into
the draft of my resolution with the Secretary's assistance. [*She returns the garland
to Kritylla and returns to her chair.*]

CHORUS:
　　I've never heard a woman
　　more intricate of mind    440
　　or more impressive as a speaker.
　　Everything she says is right.
　　She's reviewed all sides of the case;
　　she's considered everything intelligently;
　　she's sagaciously found a whole spectrum    445
　　of well-chosen arguments.
　　So if Xenokles, Karkinos' son,[94]
　　should vie with her at speaking,
　　I think that all of you would find him
　　absolutely overmatched.    450

[*Another woman rises from her chair, takes the garland from the Herald and mounts the
platform.*]

WOMAN: I take my turn before you to make but a few remarks, since I have
little to add to the previous speaker's cogent indictment. But I do want to
share with you my own personal sufferings. My husband died in Cyprus,
leaving me with five small children that I've had a struggle to feed by
weaving garlands in the myrtle-market. Still, until recently I managed to    455
make do, but now this man who composes poetry in the tragedy-market[95]

has persuaded the men that gods don't exist, so that my sales are down more
than 50%.[96] I therefore urge and advise all women to punish this man for his
many crimes, for wild are his attacks upon us, since he himself was raised
among wild herbs.[97] But I must be going to the market: some men have          460
ordered twenty garlands. [*She steps down, hands her garland to the Herald and exits.*]

CHORUS:
>    This second courageous testimony
>    turns out to be even classier than the first!
>    The stuff she prattled about wasn't irrelevant,
>    owned good sense and close-woven thought,                                   465
>    wasn't silly but altogether convincing!
>    For this outrage the man must pay us the penalty
>    in no uncertain terms!

[*The Kinsman rises from his chair, takes the garland from Kritylla and mounts the platform.*]

KINSMAN:[98] That you are so enraged at Euripides, ladies, when he slanders you
this way, is hardly surprising, nor that your bile is aboil. Why, let me have no   470
profit in my children if I myself don't hate the man; I'd have to be crazy not
to! Still, we should permit open discussion: we're by ourselves and no one
will divulge what we say. Why do we bring the man up on these charges and
get so angry with him for telling two or three things he knows we do, out of
the thousands of other things we actually do? I myself—not to mention anyone     475
else—have a lot of awful things on my conscience. I'll tell you maybe the
worst. I'd been married only three days, and my husband was sleeping beside
me. But I had a boyfriend, who'd deflowered me when I was seven and still
had the hots for me. He came scratching at the door and I knew right away
who it was. I start to steal downstairs, and my husband asks, "Why are you       480
going downstairs?" "Why? My stomach's paining me, husband, and aching.
So I'm going to the toilet." "Go on then." And he starts grinding up juniper
berries, dillweed and sage,[99] while I oil the door-hinges and go out to meet
my lover. Then I bend over, holding onto the laurel tree by Apollo's Pillar,[100]
and get my humping. You see, Euripides never said anything about that.           485
Nor does he talk about how we get banged by slaves and mule-grooms when
no other man's available, nor how, whenever we spend the night getting
thoroughly balled by somebody, we chew garlic in the morning so the
husband won't smell anything when he gets home from guard duty and
suspect that we've been doing something nasty. That, you see, he's never         490
spoken about. If he abuses Phaidra,[101] what do we care? Nor has he ever told
the one about how the wife showed her husband her robe to look at against
the light, so her lover can scamper all muffled up out of the house; he's never

told about that. And I know another wife who pretended to be in labor for
ten days, until she could buy a baby.[102] Meanwhile her husband was running      495
all over town buying medicine to quicken birth, while an old woman
brought it in a pot—the baby, I mean—with a honeycomb in its mouth so
it wouldn't cry. Then the old woman gives the signal and the wife yells, "Out
you go, out, husband: this time I seem to be giving birth!"[103] The baby, you
see, had kicked the pot's belly! He ran from the room in joy, she pulled the      500
comb out of its mouth, and it started bawling. Then the dirty old woman
who'd brought the baby runs out to the husband, smiling and saying,
"You've got a lion, sir, a lion, the very image of yourself, sir, with everything
a perfect match, little weenie too, shaped like an acorn!"[104] Aren't these the
bad things we do? [*The women gasp in astonishment.*] By Artemis, we do too! And      505
then we get mad at Euripides, though we suffer less than our deeds deserve!
[*He hands the garland to Kritylla and returns to his seat.*]

CHORUS:
   This is really astonishing!
   Where was *she* dug up?
   What land brought forth                                                         510
   a woman so audacious?
   I'd never have imagined
   she'd unscrupulously say
   this kind of thing among us
   so openly and brazenly—                                                         515
   what unheard-of nerve!
   Now I've seen it all;
   the old proverb is true:
   you've got to look under every rock,
   or you might be bitten by a politician.[105]                                    520

CHORUS-LEADER: No, there's nothing worse in every way than women born
   shameless[106]—save the rest of women![107]

MIKA [*standing up*]: No, by Aglauros![108] Women, you're not thinking straight;
   you've been bewitched, or something else is wrong with you, if you let this
   pest get away with slandering all of us so outrageously! [*Surveying the specta-*      525
   *tors.*] Is there anyone out there who'll . . . well, if not [*appealing to the women*],
   we ourselves, with our slave-girls, will get a hot coal somewhere and singe
   the hair off this woman's pussy—that'll teach her never again to badmouth
   her fellow women!

KINSMAN [*standing and backing up against the platform*]: No, ladies, please, not my      530
   pussy! If all of us who are citizen women are allowed to speak freely,[109] and if

I merely spoke on Euripides' behalf what I know to be fair, is that a reason why you should punish me by depilation?

MIKA: So you shouldn't be punished? You, the only woman with the effrontery to contradict us about a man who's done us such wrong by purposely finding stories where a woman turns out bad, by creating Melanippes[110] and Phaidras.[111] But he's never created a Penelope,[112] because she was a woman famous for her virtue.                                                                                 535

KINSMAN: Well, I can tell you why: you can't cite me a single Penelope among all the women now alive; absolutely all of us are Phaidras!                                          540

MIKA: Women, hear how the hussy insults us all, again and again!

KINSMAN: By god, I haven't yet told everything I know: you want to hear more?

MIKA: You can't have anything else to say: you've poured out every drop of what you know.                                                                                                            545

KINSMAN: Not even the ten-thousandth part of what we do. For example, I haven't mentioned, you know, how we use bath-scrapers as scoops to siphon off grain—

MIKA: You should be whipped for that remark!

KINSMAN: —or how we give cutlets from the Apatouria Feast[113] to our go-     550
betweens and then say the cat took them—

MIKA: Oh me oh my, what nonsense!

KINSMAN: —or how another woman bashed her husband with an axe, I haven't mentioned that; or how another woman drugged her husband and made him insane; or how one time an Acharnian woman buried under the     555
tub—

MIKA: I hope you die!

KINSMAN: —her own father—

MIKA: Must we listen to this?

KINSMAN: —or how your slave-girl had a baby boy and you passed it off as your     560
own, and gave your own baby girl to the slave?

MIKA: By the Twain, you won't get away with saying this—I'll pluck out your short and curlies with my own hands!

KINSMAN: Don't you lay a hand on me!

MIKA [*marching menacingly toward him*]: Just watch me!                                    565

KINSMAN [*rolling up his sleeves*]: Just watch me!

MIKA [*removing her jacket*]: Hold my jacket, Philiste.

KINSMAN: So much as touch me and by Artemis I'll—

MIKA: You'll what?

KINSMAN: That sesame-cake you gulped down, I'll make you shit it out!          570

KRITYLLA: Stop abusing each other! A woman is running toward the meeting
in a hurry. Before this gets to be a brawl I want you quiet, so we can hear
what she has to say in an orderly fashion.

[*Enter Kleisthenes, a beardless and effeminately dressed man.*][114]

KLEISTHENES: Dear women, my kindred in lifestyle, my devotion to you is
evident from my clean jowls. For I am crazy about women and represent          575
your interests always.[115] This time, I've heard of a grave business concerning
you that's being chattered about in the marketplace, and I am here to apprise
you of it and to inform you, so that you may consider and take steps to
forestall a great and terrible trouble that threatens to befall you while your
guard's down.                                                                  580

KRITYLLA: What is it, my boy?—and I may fittingly call you boy, since your
jowls are not armored with a beard.

KLEISTHENES: I'm told that Euripides has sent a kinsman of his, an old man,
up here this very day.

KRITYLLA: To do what, and for what reason?                                      585

KLEISTHENES: To be a spy, eavesdropping on whatever you women discuss
and plan to do.

KRITYLLA: And just how could a man go unnoticed in the women's
assembly?

KLEISTHENES: Euripides singed him and plucked him, and decked him out         590
exactly like a woman.

KINSMAN [*rising from his seat*]: Do you believe what he says? What man would
be fool enough to stand still for a plucking? I for one doubt it, ye Two
Honorable Goddesses!

KLEISTHENES: Rubbish! I wouldn't have come here with this news if I hadn't     595
heard it from knowledgeable sources.

KRITYLLA: It's a terrible business that's reported. Well, women, we mustn't sit around doing nothing! We've got to look for this man and find out where he's been sitting unnoticed in his disguise. [*To Kleisthenes*] And you, our representative, help us in the search: you'll double our debt of gratitude to you!    600

KLEISTHENES [*to Mika*]: Let's see, you first: who are you?

KINSMAN [*aside*]: How do I get out of here?

MIKA: You want to know who I am? I'm Kleonymos' wife.[116]

KLEISTHENES: Do all of you recognize this woman?    605

KRITYLLA: Yes, we know her; question the others.

KLEISTHENES: Then you've all got to be questioned!

KINSMAN [*aside*]: What terrible luck!

KLEISTHENES: This one: who is she? The one with the baby?

MIKA: She's my wet nurse.    610

KINSMAN [*aside*]: I'm done for! [*He begins to sneak away toward the stage-door.*]

KLEISTHENES [*to the KINSMAN*]: You there! Where are you going? Stay where you are! [*The Kinsman begins to writhe uncomfortably.*] What's the matter?

KINSMAN: Let me go piss. [*Kleisthenes offers his arm.*] You're a pretty rude fellow!    615

KLEISTHENES: All right, then, go ahead; I'll wait for you here. [*The Kinsman enters the stage building.*]

KRITYLLA: Yes, wait for her, and watch her closely. She's the only woman, sir, that we don't recognize.

KLEISTHENES [*to the door*]: You're certainly taking a long time to piss!    620

KINSMAN [*from within*]: Yes, my good man, I am: I'm retaining water; ate cress-seeds yesterday.

KLEISTHENES: Cress-seeds? Come out here, I want to talk to you!

[*The Kinsman comes out, and Kleisthenes takes him by the arm.*]

KINSMAN [*shaking off Kleisthenes' hand*]: Why are you pulling me about when I'm not feeling well?    625

KLEISTHENES: Tell me, who is your husband?

KINSMAN: You want to know who my husband is? Well, you know him; guy from Kothokidai?[117]

KLEISTHENES: Guy? Who?

KINSMAN: He's a guy, who once, a guy who was the son of a guy—    630

KLEISTHENES: I think you're babbling. Have you been here before?

KINSMAN: Sure, every year.

KLEISTHENES: And who's your roommate here?

KINSMAN: Mine? A gal.

KLEISTHENES: Damn it all, you're making no sense!    635

MIKA [to Kleisthenes]: Step aside; I'll give this gal a good grilling about last year's festivities. Come on, stand well away, so you won't overhear what a man mustn't know about. [To the Kinsman] Now, you: tell me which of the holy things was revealed to us first.

KINSMAN: Let's see now, what was the first thing? We had a drink.    640

MIKA: And what was the second?

KINSMAN: We drank a toast.[118]

MIKA: Somebody told you! And what was the third?

KINSMAN: Xenylla asked for a potty because there wasn't a urinal.[119]

MIKA: Wrong! Come here, Kleisthenes: this is the man you're after!    645

KLEISTHENES: Well, what do I do now?

MIKA: Strip him: his story's fishy. [Kleisthenes removes the Kinsman's dress; the Kinsman hides his phallus between his legs.]

KINSMAN: So you'd actually strip a mother of nine?

KLEISTHENES: Get that brassiere off, quickly.    650

KINSMAN: You shamelessness, you!

[Kleisthenes removes the brassiere.]

MIKA: She's really stocky and looks strong. And by Zeus, her tits aren't like ours!

KINSMAN: That's because I'm sterile—never been pregnant.

MIKA: Really! Just now you were the mother of nine!    655

KLEISTHENES: Stand up straight! Where are you hiding your cock down there?

MIKA [running behind the Kinsman]: Here it is! Its head is sticking out—nice color, too, deary!

KLEISTHENES [joining Mika]: Where?

[The Kinsman pulls his phallus from between his legs.]

MIKA: Now it's gone back in front!                                                      660

[Kleisthenes runs to the front, and the Kinsman pushes the phallus back between his legs.]

KLEISTHENES: It's not up here!

MIKA: No, it's back here again!

KLEISTHENES: That's some isthmus you've got there, buddy! You drag your cock back and forth more than the Korinthians drag their ships!

MIKA: What a degenerate! That's why he spoke up for Euripides and insulted     665
us!

KINSMAN: I'm done for! What a mess I've tumbled into!

MIKA [to Kleisthenes]: All right, what now?

KLEISTHENES: Put him under close guard, and see that he doesn't escape. I'll go and report this to the authorities.                                                   670

[Exit Kleisthenes; the Herald and other women enter the stage house (i.e. the sanctuary); Mika and Mania, holding the baby, stand guard over the Kinsman.]

CHORUS-LEADER: Well, after this our job is to light these torches, take off our jackets and gird up right manfully to find out if any other man has managed to get in here; to go over every inch of the Pnyx;[120] to search the tents and alleyways of our encampment. So forward march! First launch your feet lightly and inspect everything thoroughly and silently. Just don't take too     675
long: now is the time for decisive action! I'll lead the foray: on the run now, as quick as we can, all around the area!

CHORUS [as they dance about the orchestra searching]:
Move out then! If still another man
lurks about the place without our knowledge,
track him down and search him out!                                               680

Cast your eyes in all directions,
up and down, here and there;
give everything a good examination!

If we catch him in such sacrilege,
he'll be punished, and more than that:　　　　　　　　685
to other men he'll be an example
of violence, injustice and impiety!
He'll have to admit the gods clearly exist;
he'll be a lesson to all other men
to revere the gods and justly perform　　　　　　　690
what divine and human law require,
taking care to do what's good.

And here's what happens if they don't:
any man caught in an impious act
will burn and rage in rabid insanity,　　　　　　　695
his every act a manifest proof
for women and mortals to see
that lawlessness and sacrilege
are punished on the spot by god!

CHORUS-LEADER: Well, we seem to have given everything a thorough　　　700
inspection. In any case, there's no sign of any other man lurking
hereabouts.

[*The Kinsman suddenly grabs Mika's baby and runs with it to the altar in the orchestra.*][121]

MIKA: Hey! Hey! Where do you think you're going? Stop, you! Stop! Oh my
god! He's gone and snatched the baby right from the tit!

KINSMAN: Scream away! You'll never feed it again if you don't let me go! Nay,　　705
right here and now, smitten to his crimson veins by this bodkin midst the
thigh-bones, shall he begore the altar!

MIKA: Heavens me! [*To the chorus*] Women, help! Raise a great war-cry and rout
the foeman, nor overlook me bereft of mine only child!

CHORUS:
　　Ah! Ah! August Fates, what novel horror do I behold?　　　　　　710

CHORUS-LEADER: The whole world is full of impudence and brass! What a
deed he's done this time, fellow women, what a deed!

KINSMAN: A deed that'll knock the stuffing out of your arrogance!

CHORUS-LEADER: Isn't this an awful business, and worse than awful?

MIKA: Awful indeed! He's gone and snatched my baby from me!　　　　715

CHORUS:
> What can we say of a deed like this,
> when deeds like this cause him no shame?

KINSMAN: And you've yet to see my worst!

CHORUS:
> Well, wherever you came from,
> you won't be getting back there so easily                          720
> and boasting that you did such a deed,
> then gave us the slip. No, you'll get yours!

KINSMAN: I pray to god that never ever happens!

CHORUS:
> Who, I say, who of the immortal gods
> would come to the aid of a wrongdoer?                              725

KINSMAN: Your point is moot anyway. [*Holding up the baby.*] I'll never give up
this baby girl!

CHORUS:
> But mayhap soon, by the Twain Goddesses,
> your outrage will bring you no joy,
> nor the unholy speech you utter                                    730
> at your godless work:
> for we shall pay you back
> for all this, as is fitting.
> Your luck has suddenly turned around
> and aims disaster at you!                                          735

CHORUS-LEADER [*to Mika and Mania*]: Come on, you should take these torches
and fetch some wood, and then burn the bastard down and incinerate him at
once!

MIKA: Let's go get the firewood, Mania![122] [*To the Kinsman*] In a minute
I'll turn you into a shower of sparks! [*Mika and Mania go into the*           740
*scene-building.*]

KINSMAN: Light me up and burn me down! [*To the baby*] And you, get this
Cretan swaddling off. For your death, child, blame but a single woman: your
mother! [*He removes the swaddling.*] What's this? The baby girl's turned into a
skin full of wine, and wearing Persian booties to boot![123] Women, ye over-       745
heated dipsomaniacs, never passing up a chance to wangle a drink, a great

boon to bartenders but a bane to us—not to mention our dishes and our woollens!

[*Mika and Mania reenter with arms full of firewood.*]

MIKA: Pile them up nice and high, Mania. [*They begin to lay the wood around the altar.*]   750

KINSMAN: Go ahead, pile them. But tell me one thing [*pointing to the baby*]: do you claim to have given birth to this?

MIKA: Carried it all nine months myself.

KINSMAN: You carried it?

MIKA: I swear by Artemis!   755

KINSMAN: How big was it? [*He holds up the wineskin.*] A magnum, perhaps?

MIKA: How dare you? You've undressed my child—disgusting!—a tiny baby!

KINSMAN: Tiny? It is pretty small, by Zeus. How many years old? Three Wine-Jug Festivals or four?[124]

MIKA: That's about right, plus a Dionysia. Give her back to me.   760

KINSMAN [*laying his hand on the altar*]: No, by Apollo here![125]

MIKA: We'll have to incinerate you, then.

KINSMAN: By all means. Incinerate away. [*He produces a long knife.*] But this little girl will get sacrificed on the spot!

MIKA: Don't do it, I beseech you! Do what you want with me, but spare her!   765

KINSMAN: You've a good mother's instincts. But nonetheless this girl's going to get her throat cut.

MIKA: Ah, my baby! Give me the slaughter-bowl, Mania, so I can at least catch my own child's blood! [*Mika passes her the bowl.*]

KINSMAN: Hold it under there—I'll do you this one favor. [*The Kinsman slashes the wineskin with a sacrificer's stroke, letting the wine flow into the bowl.*]   770

MIKA: Damn you to hell! You're hateful and cruel!

KINSMAN [*holding up the empty wineskin*]: The hide here goes to the priestess.[126]

[*Enter Kritylla.*]

KRITYLLA: What goes to the priestess?

KINSMAN: This—catch! [*Tosses the skin to Kritylla.*]    775

KRITYLLA: Poor, poor Mika! Who's ungirled you? Who's drained out your only lass?

MIKA: This criminal here! But since you're here, stand guard over him, so I can get hold of Kleisthenes and tell the authorities what this man has done. [*Mika and Mania exit through the wings, leaving Kritylla in charge of the Kinsman.*][127]    780

KINSMAN: Now what's my plan for saving myself? What move? What scheme? The man who got me involved in this mess in the first place is nowhere to be seen. Let's see—whom could I send to him with a message? [*He ponders.*] I know! The way it was done in *Palamedes*![128] I'll write my message on oar-blades too, and throw them into the sea! But I haven't got those oar-blades here. Where could I get some? [*He looks around at the scenery.*] Aha! What if instead of oar-blades I wrote on these votive tablets and then tossed them in all directions! [*He plucks several tablets off the wall of the scene-building.*] That's much better! They're wooden too, just like oar-blades! [*He picks up the tablets and the knife.*]    785    790

> Hands of mine,
> now's the time
> to put your hand
> to the work of my salvation!

[*carving on the tablets*]

> Tablets of planed board,    795
> accept the knife's scratchings,
> harbingers of my troubles!
> Damn! This R is a troublemaker!
> There we go, there we go!
> What a scratch!    800

[*tossing the tablets in all directions*]

> Be off then, travel every road,
> this way and that.
> You've got to come quickly!

[*He sits down to wait for Euripides.*]


## PARABASIS[129]


CHORUS-LEADER [*to the spectators*]: Well, let's step forward and sing our own praises![130] We'd better, because every single man blames the female race for a    805
host of evils, claiming that we're entirely bad for humanity and the source of

all ills: disputes, quarrels, bitter factionalism, distress, war. But really, if we're
that bad, why do you marry us? If we're really so bad, why do you forbid us
to leave the house or even get caught peeking out the window?[131] Why do
you want to keep such a careful eye on something so bad? If the little woman      810
goes out somewhere and you find her outdoors, you have an apoplectic fit
instead of toasting the gods and giving thanks, which you would do if you'd
really found the bane of your household missing and couldn't find her
anywhere in the house. If we fall asleep at a friend's house, tired out from
enjoying ourselves,[132] every husband makes the rounds of the couches      815
looking for what's bad for him. If we peek out of our bedroom windows
you all try to get a good look at what's bad; and if we duck back in from
embarrassment, you're even more eager to catch a glimpse of what's bad
when it peeks again. Thus it's pretty clear that we're far superior to you,
and I've got a way to prove it. Here's a test to see which sex is worse, for we      820
say you are and you say we are. Let's look at the question, then, by juxtaposing
any man and any woman and comparing their names. Take Charminos: he's
worse than Nausimache[133]—it goes without saying. And then Kleophon is of
course worse in every way than Salabakcho.[134] And it's been a long time since
any of you has even tried to measure up to Aristomache—I mean the one at      825
Marathon—and Stratonike.[135] Well? Which of last year's Councillors, who
handed over his powers to someone else, is better than Euboule?[136] Not even
Anytos would say that! And so we claim to be much better than men. You'll
never see a woman drive up to the Akropolis in a chariot after stealing about
50 talents from the public treasury! The most a woman will filch is a cup of      830
flour from her husband, and then she'll pay him back the same day.[137]
[Indicating the spectators] We could point out many men here who do these very
things and worse, who are more likely than we are to be potbellies, muggers,
spongers, slave-drivers! And when it comes to their patrimony, they're less
able to preserve it than we are.[138] We've still got our looms and weaving rods,      835
our wool-baskets and parasols. Contrast these husbands of ours: most have let
their spear-shafts disappear from their houses, points and all, and many
others have cast from their shoulders, in the heat of battle, their parasols![139]
Yes, we women have plenty of justified complaints to lodge against our
husbands, one of which is most monstrous. If a woman bears a son who's      840
useful to the polis—a taxiarch or a commander—she ought to be honored in
some way and to be given front-row seating at the Stenia and the Skira and
any other festivals we women might celebrate.[140] But if a woman bears a son
who's a coward and a rascal—a bad trierarch or an incompetent pilot—she
ought to sit behind the hero's mother with her hair cropped off. By what      845
logic, o polis, should Hyperbolos' mother,[141] dressed in white and wearing
her hair long, get to sit near Lamachos'[142] mother and make loans?[143] If she

lends money at interest, no borrower in the world should pay her back but
should grab her money by force and tell her, "You're a fine one to be
charging points after discharging such a disappointing son!"    850

## EPISODE

KINSMAN: I've gone cross-eyed looking for him! But he's never come. What
could be keeping him? No doubt he's ashamed that his *Palamedes* was a flop.
So: which of his plays could I use to entice him? I've got it! I'll do a take-off
on his recent *Helen*:[144] I'm certainly *dressed* for that role! [*He puts on a veil.*]

KRITYLLA: What are you cooking up *now*? Why are you rubbernecking    855
around? You'll see one hell of a Helen if you don't behave yourself till a cop
gets here!

KINSMAN [*singing as Helen*]:[145]
    These are the fair-maidened currents of the Nile,
    that in lieu of heavenly distillment floods the flats
    of bright Egypt for a people much given to laxatives.    860

KRITYLLA: By Hekate Torch-Bearer, you're a villain!

KINSMAN:
    The land of my fathers is not without a name:
    'tis Sparta, and my sire is Tyndareus.

KRITYLLA: He's your father, you disaster? More likely it was Phrynondas.[146]

KINSMAN:    865
    And Helen was I named.

KRITYLLA: You're turning into a woman *again*, before you've been punished
for your first drag show?

KINSMAN:
    Many a soul on my account by Scamander's
    streams hath perished.    870

KRITYLLA: You should have been one of them!

KINSMAN:
    And I am here, but my own ill-starrèd husband,
    Menelaos, has never come for me. So why
    do I still live?

KRITYLLA: Because the vultures are lazy!                                                                875

KINSMAN:
    Yet something, as 'twere, tickles at my heart:
    deceive me not, o Zeus, in my nascent hope!

[*Enter Euripides, disguised as Menelaos.*]

EURIPIDES:
    Who, wielding power in this doughty manse,
    would welcome strangers sore beset in the briny
    deep midst tempest and shipwrecks?                                                                  880

KINSMAN:
    These are the halls of Proteus.

KRITYLLA: *Proteus, you sorry wretch?* [*To Euripides*] By the Twain Goddesses,
    he's lying: Proteas[147] has been dead for ten years!

EURIPIDES:
    What land have we put into with our hull?

KINSMAN:                                                                                                885
    Egypt.

EURIPIDES:
    Ah wretched, to have made for such a port!

KRITYLLA: Do you believe the ravings of this awful man, condemned to an
    awful death? This is the Thesmophorion!

EURIPIDES:
    Is lord Proteus within, or out of doors?                                                            890

KRITYLLA: You've got to be still seasick, stranger, if you ask if Proteas is within
    or out of doors, when you just heard that he's dead!

EURIPIDES:
    Alas, he is dead! Where was he duly entombed?

KINSMAN:
    This is his very tomb whereon I sit.

KRITYLLA: Well, die and go to hell—and you will die for daring to call this altar          895
    a tomb!

EURIPIDES:
    Why dost thou sit upon this sepulchral seat,
    veiled in a shroud, strange lady?

KINSMAN:

> Against my will am I to serve the bed
> of Proteus' son in marriage.                                          900

KRITYLLA: You villain, why do you keep lying to the stranger? This criminal
came here to the women's meeting, stranger, to snatch their baubles!

KINSMAN:

> Bark thou at my person, pelt me with abuse!

EURIPIDES:

> Strange lady, what old woman vilifies thee?

KINSMAN:

> 'Tis Proteus' daughter, Theonoe.                                     905

KRITYLLA: No, by the Twain Goddesses, I'm Kritylla, daughter of Antitheos,
from Gargettos![148] [To the Kinsman] And you're a villain!

KINSMAN:

> Say what you will, for never shall I wed
> your brother and so betray Menelaos, my husband
> at Troy.                                                              910

[Euripides approaches the Kinsman.]

EURIPIDES:

> What said'st thou, lady? Return my pupils' gaze!

KINSMAN:

> I feel shame—for the violation of my jowls.

EURIPIDES:

> What can this be? A speechlessness holds me fast!
> [He removes the Kinsman's veil.]
> O gods, what sight do I see? Who art thou, lady?

KINSMAN:

> And who art thou? The same thought strikes us both.                  915

EURIPIDES:

> Are you Greek, or a native woman?

KINSMAN:

> Greek. But I now would learn your story.

EURIPIDES:

> I cannot help but see Helen in you, lady!

KINSMAN:
And I Menelaos in you—to judge from your rags!

EURIPIDES:
You have recognized aright the unluckiest of men!                                    920

[Euripides embraces the Kinsman.]

KINSMAN:
O timely come into your own wife's charms![149]
O hold me, hold me, husband, in your arms!
Come, let me kiss you! Take, oh take, oh take
me away posthaste!

[Euripides takes the Kinsman by the hand and begins to lead him from the altar.]

KRITYLLA [blocking their path]: By the Twain Goddesses, whoever tries to take            925
you away is going to be sorry, after he gets pummeled with this torch!

EURIPIDES:
Wouldst thou prevent me my very own wife, the daughter
of Tyndareus, to take to Sparta?

KRITYLLA: Oh my, you strike me as being a villain yourself, and some kind
of ally of this other one! No wonder you kept acting like Egyptians![150] But            930
this man is going to pay the price: here comes the marshal and a policeman.

EURIPIDES: This is bad. I've got to mosey on out of here.

[He moves to the wings.]

KINSMAN: But what about me? What am I going to do?

EURIPIDES: Stay calm. I'll never desert you, as long as I draw breath, or until I
exhaust my vast supply of stratagems! [Exit Euripides.]                               935

KINSMAN: Well, this particular fishing-line didn't catch much!

[Enter Marshal and a Policeman armed with a whip, bow and quiver.]

MARSHAL: So this is the villain that Kleisthenes told us about! [To the Kinsman] You!
What are you skulking for? [To the Policeman] Archer, take him inside and bind
him on the plank,[151] then set him up right here and keep an eye on him. Don't
let anybody get near him. If anybody tries to, take your whip and hit him!            940

KRITYLLA: Do that, by god, because just a minute ago a man did try to make off
with him—a sail-stitcher!

KINSMAN: [*kneeling before the Marshal*]: Marshal, by this right hand of yours—
which you're so fond of cupping in the direction of anyone who might put
silver in it—do me a small favor even though I'm condemned to death!    945

MARSHAL: What favor?

KINSMAN: Tell the policeman he's got to strip me naked before he ties me to
the plank: I'm an old man and I don't want to be left dressed in scarves and
petticoats when the crows eat me—they'd laugh!

MARSHAL: The Council has decreed that you must die wearing these,[152] so that    950
everyone who sees you will know what kind of criminal you are!

KINSMAN: Aieee! O dresses, what ye have wrought! There's no chance I'll be
saved now!

[*The Policeman takes the Kinsman inside; Kritylla and the Marshal exit.*]

## CHORAL INTERLUDE

CHORUS-LEADER: All right, now, let's do a cheerful dance, as is the women's
custom here, when in the holy season we celebrate our solemn mysteries    955
for the Twain Goddesses—the very ones Pauson,[153] too, honors by fasting,
as he joins in our prayer to them that from year to year many more such
celebrations may come his way!

CHORUS:
Let's start our number: go light on your feet,
form up a circle and all join hands;    960
everyone mark the beat of our holy dance
with an agile foot!
Let every dancer arrange herself
so she can look this way and that,
as you celebrate in song and dance    965
the race of Olympian gods.
Let everyone lift her voice,
transported by the dance!

If people expect that we, as women,
will in this sanctuary utter abuse against men,    970
they are wrong![154]
But now we should rather halt
the graceful steps of our circle-dance
and go on to our next number!

Step out singing for the God with the Lyre[155]                               975
and for Artemis with her Quiver,
the Chaste Lady.
Hail, Thou who work from afar,[156]
and grant us victory![157]
It's right that we also sing for Hera,                                        980
fulfiller of marriages,
who takes part in all our dances
and holds the passkey to wedlock.
We ask Hermes the Shepherd
and Pan and his Nymphs                                                        985
to smile heartily and enjoy
this dancing of ours![158]
So begin the spirited double-time
in the cause of dancing well:
let's get into it, ladies,                                                    990
in the customary fashion—
we're fasting anyway!

All right now, jump,
return with a solid beat,
take the song in full voice!                                                  995
Lord Bakchos crowned with ivy
please personally lead our dance:
we will hymn you in revels
that love the dance!

Noisy Dionysos,                                                              1000
son of Zeus and Semele,
who enjoy the charming songs
of Nymphs as you ramble
over the mountains—
*evoi evoi evoi!*—                                                           1005
striking up the dances
all night long!
And all around you their cries
echo on Kithairon,
and the mountains shady with dark leaves                                     1010
and the rocky valleys resound.
And all round you ivy tendrils
twine in lovely bloom!

## EPISODE

[*Enter Policeman,[159] dragging the Kinsman, who is now clamped to a plank, feet-first. He props the Kinsman up against the altar.*]

POLICEMAN: There, now: you can do your bellyachin' to the open air!

KINSMAN: Officer, I beseech you—                                           1015

POLICEMAN: Don't seech me!

KINSMAN: Loosen the clamps!

POLICEMAN: No, but I'll do this. [*He tightens them.*]

KINSMAN: Owww! Hey, you're tightening them!

POLICEMAN: Want me to keep going?                                          1020

KINSMAN: Owww! Ahhh! God damn you!

POLICEMAN: Shut up, you damn geezer! Well, I'm gonna go get a mat, so I can get comfortable while I guard you. [*He goes inside.*]

KINSMAN: This is the reward I get for befriending Euripides! [*Peering into the distance, as if catching sight of something.*] Hey, my gods! Savior Zeus, hope is not    1025
dead! It looks like the man's not given up: he's sending me a signal by zipping by in the Perseus outfit! I'm supposed to be Andromeda![160] I'm certainly chained up like her! And he's obviously on his way to rescue me! Otherwise he wouldn't have shot by!
[*As Andromeda, singing*]
    Dear maidens, dear,                                            1030
    how might I escape
    unseen by the cop?
    Dost hear me,
    thou who from the caverns
    singest in answer                                               1035
    to my cries?
    Permit, allow me
    to go home to my wife!
    Pitiless he who enchained me,
    most sorely tested of mortal men!                               1040
    I got free of a rotten old hag
    only to die anyway!

For this barbarian guard,
my long-time watcher,
has hung me out,                                                    1045
doomed and friendless,
as food for vultures!
You see, 'tis not to dance,
nor yet with girls my age
to wield the voting-funnel[161]                                     1050
that I am here;
nay rather enchained
in tight bondage
am I set out as fodder
for the monster Glauketes![162]                                     1055
Mourn me, ladies, with a hymn
not of marriage but of jail,
for wretched do I suffer wretchedly
—alas alack, woe is me!—
horrid sufferings too                                               1060
at the hands of kin, and wrongly,
tho I implored a man,
igniting tearfullest Stygian groans
—ai ai!—
the man who first shaved me,                                        1065
who put on me this dress
and sent me on this errand
to this sanctuary
of the women!
O force of destiny,                                                 1070
engendered by a god!
O me accursed!
Who would not behold my suffering,
in its drastic evils, as unenviable?
Ah, would that a fiery bolt from heaven above                       1075
would obliterate the barbarian!
No more is it agreeable to look upon the sun's deathless flame,
for I am hung up,
damned by the gods to cut-throat grief,
bound for a flashing trip to the grave!                             1080

[Enter Echo.]

ECHO:[163]

>Greetings, dear girl; but may the gods obliterate
>your father Kepheus for exposing you out there!

KINSMAN:

>And who are you, who takest pity on my suffering?

ECHO:

>Echo, a comedienne who sings back what she hears,
>who just last year, in this very place, personally assisted Euripides in the          1085
>contest. But now, child, you must play your part: to wail piteously!

KINSMAN: And you'll wail in response!

ECHO: I'll take care of that. But now, you start the script.

KINSMAN:

>O holy night,
>how long is thy chariot's course                                          1090
>as thou drivest o'er the stellar back
>of holy Aether[164]
>through Olympos most august!

ECHO:

>Through Olympos!

KINSMAN:

>Why o why has Andromeda had                                              1095
>so much more than her share of ills?

ECHO:

>Share of ills!

KINSMAN:

>Unhappy in my death!

ECHO:

>Unhappy in my death!

KINSMAN:

>You're killing me, old bag, with your jabbering!                          1100

ECHO:

>Jabbering!

KINSMAN:

>God, your interruptions are annoying—too much!

ECHO:
> Too much!

KINSMAN:
> Dear fellow, please let me finish my song, thank you very much!
> Stop!                                                                          1105

ECHO:
> Stop!

KINSMAN:
> Go to hell!

ECHO:
> Go to hell!

KINSMAN:
> What's wrong with you?

ECHO:
> What's wrong with you?                                                          1110

KINSMAN:
> You're babbling!

ECHO:
> You're babbling!

KINSMAN:
> Suffer!

ECHO:
> Suffer!

KINSMAN:
> Drop dead!                                                                      1115

ECHO:
> Drop dead!

POLICEMAN [*returning with a mat, which he places on a bench near the altar; to the
Kinsman*]: Hey, you, what's all this talking?

ECHO: All this talking?

POLICEMAN: I'll call the Marshals!                                                1120

ECHO: I'll call the Marshals!

POLICEMAN: What's going on?

ECHO: What's going on?

POLICEMAN: Where's that noise coming from?

ECHO: Noise coming from!                                                    1125

POLICEMAN [to the Kinsman]: Are you making all this racket?

ECHO: This racket?

POLICEMAN: You're gonna be sorry!

ECHO: Gonna be sorry!

POLICEMAN: You laughin' at me?                                              1130

ECHO: Laughin' at me?

KINSMAN: God no, it's this woman, over here!

ECHO: Over here!

POLICEMAN [looking around]: Where is the bitch?

ECHO: The bitch!                                                            1135

KINSMAN: She's getting away!

POLICEMAN [running about]: Where ya goin'?

ECHO: Where ya goin'?

POLICEMAN: You won't get away with it!

ECHO: Get away with it!                                                     1140

POLICEMAN: Still yappin'?

ECHO: Yappin?

POLICEMAN: Grab the bitch!

ECHO: Grab the bitch!

POLICEMAN: Yackety, confounded woman!                                       1145

[Euripides, still disguised as Perseus, reappears on the crane and flies about the stage.]

EURIPIDES:
    Ye gods, to what barbaric land am I come
    on sandal swift? For through the empyrean
    cutting a swath I aim my wingèd foot
    to Argos, and the cargo that I carry
    is the Gorgon's head![165]                                             1150

POLICEMAN: Say what? You got the head of Gorgos, the secretary?[166]

EURIPIDES:
'Tis the Gorgon's, I say once more.

POLICEMAN: George's, yeah, that's what I said.

EURIPIDES: [*alighting from the crane onto the stage*]:
Oho, what crag is this I see? What maiden                    1155
fair as a goddess moored like a boat thereto?

KINSMAN:
O stranger, pity my misfortune cruel!
O free me from my bonds!

POLICEMAN: You, button your lip! You slimeball, you've got the nerve to blab
when you're about to be a *dead* maiden?                     1160

EURIPIDES:
O maiden, 'tis with pity I see you hang there!

POLICEMAN: That's no maiden! That's a dirty old man, a crook and a creep!

EURIPIDES: Rubbish, you vulgarian! This is Kepheus' child, Andromeda.

POLICEMAN: [*pointing to the Kinsman's phallus*]: Lookit that figgie:[167] it don't
look little, do it now?                                       1165

EURIPIDES: Give me her hand, that I might clasp the lass! [*The Policeman steps
between them.*] Please, Skythian: all human flesh is weak. In my case, love for
this girl has seized me.

POLICEMAN: I don't envy you. But I tell you, if his asshole was turned around
this way I wouldn't say nothin' if you was to screw it.       1170

EURIPIDES: Why don't you let me untie her, officer, that I may couch her in the
nuptial bower?

POLICEMAN: If you're so hot to bugger the old guy, why don't you drill a hole
in the backside of that there plank and buttfuck him that way?

EURIPIDES: Gods no, I'd rather untie the chains. [*He approaches the Kinsman.*]  1175

POLICEMAN [*blocking his way*]: Try it—if you wanna get whipped.

EURIPIDES: I shall do it anyway!

POLICEMAN [*drawing his sword*]: I'd have to chop off yer head with this here
scimitar.

EURIPIDES [aside]:
    Ah me, what action, what clever logic now?         1180
    All wit is lost upon this savage lout.
    For work a novel ruse upon a clod
    and thou hast worked in vain. No, I must find
    a different stratagem, one suitable for him.

[Exit Euripides.]

POLICEMAN [to the Kinsman]: Lousy fox, the monkey-tricks he tried to pull on    1185
me!

KINSMAN [calling after Euripides]: Remember, Perseus, what a wretched state
you're leaving me in!

POLICEMAN: So you're still hungry for a taste of the whip, are ya?

[The Policeman administers a few strokes with his whip, then stretches out on his mat and
sleeps.]


## CHORAL INTERLUDE

CHORUS:[168]
    Pallas Athena, the dancers' friend,         1190
    heed our customary invitation
    to the dance!
    Maiden girl unwedlocked,
    guardian of our country,
    sole manifest sovereign         1195
    who is called keeper of the keys!
    Show yourself, you
    who loathe tyrants,
    as is fitting.[169]
    The country's female people         1200
    summon you: please come,
    bringing peace, comrade of festivity!
    Come, gracious happy sovereigns,[170]
    to your own precinct,
    where torchlight reveals         1205
    your divine rites,
    an immortal sight
    forbidden to men!

O come, we pray,
potent goddesses                                                    1210
of the Thesmophoria!
If ever before you answered our call,
come now at our invitation,
we beseech you, here to us!

## EPISODE

[*Enter Euripides, undisguised and carrying a small harp and a travel-bag, with Elaphion, a dancing girl, and Teredon, a boy piper.*][171]

EURIPIDES [*to the Chorus*]: Ladies, if you want to make a permanent peace treaty with me, now's the time. I'll stipulate that in the future none of you women will ever again be slandered in any way by me. I'm making that my official offer.

CHORUS-LEADER: And what is your purpose in making this offer?

EURIPIDES: That one on the plank there is my kinsman. If I can take him away    1220 with me, you'll never hear another insult. But if you refuse, whatever you've been doing behind your husbands' backs while they're away at the front, I'll denounce to them when they return.

CHORUS-LEADER: We're happy to honor our part in this deal. But you've got to make your own deal with this barbarian [*indicating the Policeman*].                  1225

EURIPIDES: I'm ready for that job![172] [*He takes an old woman's dress out of his travel-bag, puts it on and veils his face.*] And your job, Elaphion, is to remember to do what I told you on the way over here. All right, the first thing is to walk back and forth swinging your haunches. [*She does so.*] And you, Teredon, accompany her on your pipes with a Persian dance-tune. [*He does so, while*    1230 *Euripides plays his harp.*]

POLICEMAN [*awakening and sitting up on his bench*]: What's all the noise for? Some partiers waking me up.

EURIPIDES: The girl wants to rehearse, officer. She's on her way to dance for some gentlemen.                                                               1235

POLICEMAN: Let her dance and rehearse; I won't stop her. She's pretty nimble: like a bug on a rug!

EURIPIDES: [*to Elaphion*]: All right, girl, take off your dress and sit on the cop's lap. [*She does so, with her back to the Policeman.*] Now stick out your feet so I can take off your shoes.                                                                                          1240

POLICEMAN: Yeah, sit down, sit down, yeah, yeah, sweetie! [*He reaches around and feels her breasts.*] Wow, what firm titties—like turnips!

EURIPIDES: Piper, play faster. [*To Elaphion*] Still afraid of the cop?

POLICEMAN: What a fine butt! [*Looks down at his trousers.*] You'll be sorry if you don't stay inside my pants! [*opening his trousers to reveal a huge phallus*] There!      1245
That's better for my prick!

EURIPIDES [*to Elaphion*]: Well done. Grab your dress, it's time for us to be going.

POLICEMAN: Won't she give me a kiss first?

EURIPIDES: Sure. Kiss him. [*She does so.*]                                                                                  1250

POLICEMAN: Woo woo woo! Boyoboy! What a sweet tongue, like Attic honey! Why don't you sleep with me?

EURIPIDES: Goodbye, officer. That's impossible.

POLICEMAN: No, wait, my dear old lady, please do me this favor.

EURIPIDES: Got a drachma, then?[173]                                                                             1255

POLICEMAN: Sure I do.

EURIPIDES: Well, let's have it!

POLICEMAN: But I've got nothing on me! Wait, take my shaft-case. [*He hands his quiver to Euripides.*] And give it back after! [*To Elaphion*] You come with me! [*To Euripides*] And you watch the old man, grandma! What's your name?      1260

EURIPIDES: Artemisia.[174]

POLICEMAN [*as he exits with Elaphion*]: Remember that name: Artamuxia.

EURIPIDES: Trickster Hermes, just keep on giving me this good luck! [*To Teredon*] You can run along now, kid; and take this stuff with you. [*He hands him the harp, the women's clothing and the quiver.*] And I'll release this one. [*He begins to*      1265
*free the Kinsman.*] As soon as you get loose you'd better get out of here fast and head back home to your wife and kids.

KINSMAN: I'll do that, as soon as I'm loose.

EURIPIDES: There you are! It's up to you to escape before the policeman comes back and arrests you.                                                                                   1270

KINSMAN [*Putting on his dress*]: That's just what I'm going to do!

[*Euripides and the Kinsman exit on the run.*]

POLICEMAN [*returning with Elaphion, and wearing a limp phallus*]: Old lady, your girl is nice and easygoing, no trouble at all! [*Looking around*] Where's the old lady? Oh no, now I'm in for it! Where'd the old man get to? Old lady! Lady! I don't like this at all, old lady! Artamuxia! The old bag's tricked me! [*To Elaphion*]   1275 You, run after her as quick as you can! [*Elaphion runs off, the Policeman picks up his bow and realizes his quiver is gone.*] Justly is it called a case for shafts: I traded mine for a fuck and got shafted! Oh my, what am I gonna do? Where'd that old lady get to? Artamuxia!

CHORUS-LEADER: Are you asking for the lady with the harp?   1280

POLICEMAN: Yeah, yeah! Seen her?

CHORUS-LEADER: She went that way [*pointing left*], and there was an old man with her.

POLICEMAN: Was the old man wearing a yellow dress?

CHORUS-LEADER: That's right. You might still catch them if you go that way   1285 [*pointing right*].

POLICEMAN: The dirty old bag! Which way should I go again? [*He runs off to the right.*]

CHORUS-LEADER: Right! Straight up that hill! Where are you going? No, run the other way! No, you're going the wrong way!   1290

POLICEMAN [*winded*]: Damn! I've gotta run! Artamuxia! [*Exit.*]

CHORUS-LEADER: Run off now quick as you can—straight to hell!

CHORUS:
   Well, we've had our share of fun.
   Now it's time for every woman
   to go on home.   1295
   May the Twain Gods of Thesmophoria
   well reward each and every one of you
   for your performance!

# ASSEMBLYWOMEN

# INTRODUCTION

## 1. The Historical Context

On the basis of internal evidence (no external evidence survives), *Assembly-women* was very likely produced at the Dionysia of 391,[1] twenty years after *Lysistrata* and *Women at the Thesmophoria*. During that interval the Athenians had experienced momentous upheaval and change. They had lost the Peloponnesian War, and with it their navy, their empire and much of their national pride, in 404; two oligarchic regimes had replaced the democracy, first in the summer of 411 and then immediately following the war (the regime of the thirty "tyrants" that was overthrown in a bitter counterrevolution led by democratic exiles);[2] and after they had restored the democracy the Athenians had made changes in their constitution in the hope of eliminating the most irresponsible features of full popular sovereignty, on which many blamed the loss of the war. One of the reforms relevant to *Assemblywomen* was the intro-duction of pay for attendance at assembly meetings, on the model of the payment for jury service earlier introduced by Perikles.[3] The goal was to insure a larger and more representative turnout, with more opportunity for ordinary citizens to voice their concerns.[4] These goals seem to have been achieved, since the payment quickly grew from one obol to three, and in *Assemblywomen* there is both anxiety about not getting to the assembly on time (only the first 6000 attendees were paid) and much discussion about the concerns of ordinary citizens. The reformed democracy turned out to be both stable and effective, remaining unchallenged until Athens fell under Macedonian rule in 322.

Athens also recovered a measure of her former international power. By 395 the Athenians had rebuilt their navy (though with Persian support) and their city walls, and were once again a major force in the Greek world (though Sparta

was now dominant). Indeed Athens became embroiled in the so-called
Corinthian War (395–386), which involved not only the major Greek powers but
Persia as well, and which ended with a treaty that left Sparta, now allied with
Persia and Syracuse, even more firmly in command of the Greek world.[5] At the
time of the production of *Assemblywomen*, the Athenians, on the advice of
Thrasyboulos (lines 332–333), had rejected a Spartan peace proposal on the
grounds that its terms would threaten the democratic constitution, and,
according to the play's heroine, had thus lost (as was later proved true) an
opportunity for "salvation" (185–187).

The political crisis and constitutional reforms, in combination with a revital-
ized assembly, had stimulated the Athenians to discuss and debate their
democratic system afresh, and had also stimulated theoretical speculation
about various ideal systems of government. *Assemblywomen* is a reflection
of such speculation in comic terms. One of its major themes—the fitness of
women to rule—had old roots in myths[6] and comic fantasies,[7] where the
normal order of society is traditionally inverted. But in *Assemblywomen* this
theme is developed in light of actual contemporary discussions, both popular
and philosophical, about the wisdom of women's traditional exclusion from
participation in male (executive) culture, and about the virtues and potential
civic value of women. The Athenians never put into practice, and Aristophanes
never even entertained, the idea of "emancipating" women by giving them
a share in the rights possessed by men. But Plato in *Republic* went so far as to
envision both male and female rulers in his ideal state.[8]

The other main theme of *Assemblywomen*—the elimination of the private
household in favor of the communization of property and sexual partners—
similarly takes up an idea familiar to the Athenians through contact with other
cultures,[9] but explores its particular implications for contemporary Athens on
much the same lines as Plato in *Republic* (especially books 3 and 5) a few years
later:[10] Plato's regime for elite Guardians is essentially the same as Praxagora's,
save for its abolition of the traditional distinction between men's and women's
work, and its system of eugenic breeding. A generation earlier, Perikles' socially
prominent mistress, Aspasia of Miletos, provided an actual test case, and the
sharp division of Athenian responses to her are instructive. On the positive
side, here was a woman who had been able to hold her own among the largely
male intelligentsia of her day. Her rhetorical skills and political shrewdness
(conventionally male attributes) were recalled and discussed by Plato in
*Menexenos*, by the orator Aischines in *Aspasia* and by others;[11] she thus
equipped proponents of civic roles for women with a powerful argument
against conventional views about the natural limitations of the female. On the
negative side, Aspasia's influence on Perikles and his inner circle so alarmed
conventional people that she became a not insignificant political liability; at

the onsets of both the Samian War and the Peloponnesian War it was openly rumored that Perikles' bellicose policies were the result of his passion for, or the evil influence of, Aspasia.[12]

Discussion about potential civic roles for women was no doubt stimulated also by the response of ordinary Athenian women to their experiences during the long decades of the war and its aftermath. Many women had seen their households disrupted or destroyed by the loss of fathers, brothers, husbands or sons; many maidens had been doomed to spinsterhood;[13] many had been forced to take on jobs that in ordinary times would have been beneath the dignity of respectable women;[14] and some (like the heroine of Assemblywomen) had gone into exile with their democratic menfolk in 404/3. Although we have no actual woman's testimony, the complaints about public policy and its disruption of the women's domestic world that Aristophanes gives to his female characters in Lysistrata and Assemblywomen ring true to life. But it is significant that, whereas in Lysistrata the husbands are portrayed as ignoring their wives' complaints and as ultimately being vanquished by coercion rather than argument, in Assemblywomen the heroine and the men engage in actual debate, with victory going to the heroine.[15] Furthermore, the women in Assembly-women, by contrast with Lysistrata and Women at the Thesmophoria, are not portrayed as opposing the male world by operating as a female "bloc" with a religious base or association with particular goddesses, but rather as addressing issues of universal concern to Athens from the center of Athenian political life.

## 2. The Women Take Power

In the prologue we learn that the women of Athens, alarmed by the men's inability to govern the polis competently, have devised a scheme: they will disguise themselves as men, pack the Assembly and vote to transfer political power from the men to themselves. The prologue is largely devoted to a rehearsal of this scheme: the women try out their disguises and practice speech-making. Their impersonation of male assemblymen must be flawless, since men will be attending the assembly too and cannot be allowed to discover the women's scheme.[16] As in Lysistrata one woman, Praxagora (roughly, "Woman Effective in Public"), organizes and leads the other women:[17] she alone has the discipline, rhetorical skills and imagination necessary to carry out the scheme, while the other women are hampered in their attempts to impersonate men by their usual comic shortcomings: slow minds, preoccupation with sex, wine and household chores, ignorance of politics and government, lack of vision.

In contrast with *Lysistrata*, however, the scheme in *Assemblywomen* has been devised not by the heroine alone but by all the women together, and it is only in the course of the rehearsal that Praxagora, who gives the best sample speech, emerges as the obvious candidate to address the Assembly and propose the transfer of power. And unlike Lysistrata's plot, which is temporary and limited to ending the war, Praxagora's scheme aims to give women full power permanently (though the assembly-packing turns out to be a once-only event). That her proposal is to be enacted by a legal vote in the Assembly[18] makes it seem more legitimate than the women's decree in *Women at the Thesmophoria* or Lysistrata's coercive tactics of occupation and strike. The humor of the prologue centers on satire of assembly-speeches and novel political "cure-alls," with cross-dressing adding to the hilarity: male actors portray women who disguise themselves as men and rehearse male roles, much as in the prologue of *Women at the Thesmophoria*, where men dress as women and rehearse female roles.[19]

After it becomes apparent that the other women are too womanly to be effective assembly speakers, Praxagora delivers a speech herself to illustrate how it should be done. She begins with a swift review of the polis' political problems: the Athenians choose the wrong men as leaders and have no consistent policy because everyone votes only for leaders and policies that will bring him some personal financial gain; Agyrrhios, for example, who proposed pay merely for attending assembly meetings, is now a popular leader, though before he was considered a scoundrel, while Thrasyboulos selfishly scuttled a peace treaty because it might deprive him of a lucrative command. The result has been failure to secure peace and general prosperity for Athens. This part of Praxagora's speech could have been made by a male speaker and is mostly earnest; in earlier plays Aristophanes had in fact voiced the same sort of complaints, which no doubt echoed those of many spectators. But Praxagora's particular emphasis on the tendency of selfish individualism to undermine civic cooperation and the rule of law takes up an important theme of contemporary philosophical debate and is thematically central to the plan which Praxagora is about to reveal.

In the second part of her speech Praxagora proposes a surprising remedy for all of Athens' ills: to turn over governance of the polis to the women. This she justifies on the grounds that women (1) manage each household more competently than the men manage the polis; (2) are conservative, having maintained their traditional customs and eschewed risky novelties; (3) will, as mothers, be better than men at supplying the soldiers; (4) will be more inventive at raising money; and (5) will be harder to deceive. If the household is a more stable and successful entity than the polis, the reason must be women's superiority as governors. Although Praxagora reserves a description of the particular policies that she plans to enact once the woman have been voted into power, it is already clear that her plan envisages only the transfer of *executive* power and not an exchange of gender characteristics. Her emphasis on women's expertise in the areas of sex, wine, household finance and trickery, and her specification that men will continue to be soldiers, show that women will continue to be women and men men. In other words, governance of the polis will simply be removed from the men's list of duties and added to the women's, being feminized in the process. In structural terms, Aristophanes has taken the old idea that polis management should be *like* household management, as in *Lysistrata*,[20] to its logical conclusion: the polis is actually to *become* a household, with women as its natural governors.

While the meeting of the assembly takes place offstage, we meet two characteristic men. Praxagora's husband, Blepyros, an older man, has come outside looking for a place to defecate and wearing his wife's clothes—naturally enough, we realize, since Praxagora has taken his own clothes to wear to the Assembly.[21] Presently he has a brief conversation with a neighbor, who tells him that his own wife seems to have disappeared with his clothes too. Meanwhile, Blepyros tries unsuccessfully to relieve himself, for he is constipated. This is evidently a new contribution to the genre of bowel-humor, since it is not attested in any earlier comedy, but it may also have symbolic significance: Blepyros' prayer to the goddess of childbirth to help him "deliver" his burden invites us to compare him (unfavorably) to a pregnant woman.[22] The sight of an old man dressed in women's clothes, vainly trying to defecate (give birth) and being surprised by a suspicious neighbor is both intrinsically funny and a significant twist on the traditional cross-dressing scenario, since it effectively symbolizes the play's central action:[23] the husband is confined to the house, wears a housewife's clothing, must make excuses for being outside and struggles with a degrading chore, while the wife is at the assembly taking his power just as she had taken his clothing.

After a citizen named Chremes passes by and describes the assembly meeting, Praxagora and the women return and hastily doff their disguises so that the men will not discover their trick. Almost at once Praxagora is confronted by Blepyros, who suspects she has been visiting a lover. But Praxagora deals with her obtuse husband easily, countering each accusation with a plausible lie, and then affects surprise when Blepyros tells her about the assembly's decision to turn over power to the women. Praxagora applauds the Assembly's decision, predicts great advantages for the polis, and almost at once delivers a detailed exposition of her policies.[24] At the end, she reveals that the women have elected her to be Commander and goes off to put these policies into effect, with Blepyros apparently still none the wiser.

This scene demonstrates the originality of Praxagora's characterization, for she combines qualities that in Lysistrata were divided between Lysistrata the leader and Myrrhine the wife who can outwit her husband.[25] As for Blepyros, he makes even Lysistrata's Kinesias look good, and that suits the different perspectives of the two plays. In Lysistrata the heroine forces the men to mend their ways and do a better job in the future, so that they cannot be portrayed as hopeless. The men of Assemblywomen, on the other hand, are to be permanently relieved of their duties, and so their characterization as old, tired, sterile, disorganized and easily led, while their wives are young, vital and effective, serves to make Praxagora's reform seem eminently justified.

Although later we are given to understand that Praxagora's policies, and her leadership, have been successful, we will not actually see her again. Aristophanes has concluded the first action of the play (the women attend the assembly and transfer power to themselves) and now moves directly to the second (the effect of Praxagora's new policies on the lives of typical Athenian men and women). Since Praxagora's presence is not needed for the second action, which indeed has little directly to do with the first,[26] Aristophanes simply abandons her (in contrast with Lysistrata, whose enterprise requires that she carry it through to its conclusion at the end of the play). Readers of tragedy will be reminded of the early demise of Sophokles' Ajax. By our standards of organic unity this procedure seems unsatisfactory, but in Aristophanes' time a complex plot did not require that even principal characters participate in episodes with which they were unconnected.

### 3. The Women's New Regime

Praxagora announces her plan to Blepyros, Chremes, the Chorus and the spectators: it amounts to a permanent economic, social, and sexual revolution. Private property is abolished: every citizen is to surrender his possessions to the common store, from which the women will provision all citizens equally, turning what had previously been government buildings into communal dining halls. Household and family are abolished too: dividing walls are to be removed, and any man may copulate with, and have children by, any woman, equality of opportunity being guaranteed by a regulation requiring the young and the beautiful of both sexes to copulate with the old and the ugly first. As for slaves and other non-citizens, they will do the farming and (presumably) all other manual labor, and are debarred from sexual competition with citizens. In the new order, social inequalities based on wealth, age, and beauty are thus eliminated, and with them the principal motives for civic selfishness. The main economic problem of society, together with the principal motives for civic selfishness, are thus neatly solved for men, women and children alike.

In classical Athens women were not legally competent either to acquire or to dispose of property, so that their proposal to do away with private property is both a logical consequence of the abolition of male rule and in their own interest, since they will now be in charge of the common store and free to help themselves to the wine and food that their husbands could previously deny them; with marriage eliminated, they will also enjoy the same access to sexual gratification as men, and the children will now regard all men as their fathers.[27] No free person of either sex will enjoy any sort of privilege.

It is now clear that the women will not "rule" as the men have ruled but (true to their earlier claim to be traditionalists!) will continue doing what they have always done: managing, feeding and clothing the members of their household. The difference is that now the polis has become one great household, with all the women doing communally what each woman had done in her own household before. The removal of men from rule has eliminated the need for private households each headed by one man (i.e. the household as a mechanism for maintaining and transmitting inherited wealth within a male family line), just as it has eliminated the need for a polis ruled by the aggregate of male heads of households (i.e. the polis as a mechanism for protecting the integrity of each private household). As in Lysistrata, women are portrayed as satisfied with their traditional domestic roles, complaining only that they are disrupted in their routine by the domestic suspicions and public actions of their husbands.

It must be stressed that by relieving men of their civic responsibilities the women have not simply added to their list of burdens; they realize important gains too. Now that they have freed themselves from confinement within their husbands' households they can freely associate with one another, enjoy the sexual freedom hitherto reserved for men without needing to be deceptive about it,[28] and rest assured that their households will no longer be damaged or destroyed by the men's foolish policies.

As for the men, the new regime is a typical comic utopia come true: they will have nothing to do under the new regime but put on their new clothes, eat, drink and copulate; in effect, carefree boyhood, with women doing all the chores, is to be their lifelong situation.[29] Some modern Westerners may well regard such a life as pointless and degraded,[30] but it will have appealed strongly to many ancient men: in Hesiod's Works and Days the "Golden Age" is characterized as a time when men "lived like gods, with carefree heart, free and apart from trouble and pain" (112–13), and the "Silver Age" as a time when "a boy was raised by his dear mother for a hundred years, a large infant playing in his house" (130–31); similar is the biblical Garden of Eden, where Adam ("man") enjoys a carefree life under the benign care of his "helpmate" Eve ("woman").[31] I imagine that not a few modern men, to judge from *their* fantasies, would welcome such a life, too.

In this conception of female "rule" Aristophanes differs in a very important way from Plato and the other philosophers: whereas they envisioned qualified women and men as *sharing* in governance of the ideal polis, Aristophanes maintains the traditional assignment of gender functions by eliminating the polis as such, and with it the need for men to participate in governance at all. Although the women in Aristophanes' comedies may give men good advice or interfere in their misgovernance of the polis, nowhere do we find him contemplating a situation in which women and men would share any duties civic or domestic. In tragedy, too, the usurpation of male duties by a female is always portrayed as unnatural, and vice versa (e.g. Aischylos' Klytaimestra and Aigisthos).

A pair of episodes illustrates the two main elements of the plan—community of property and equality of sexual opportunity—and the main problem that threatens their implementation: the desire of some people to take unfair advantage of the new system by holding onto the privileges that they had enjoyed under the old.[32] The first is a conversation between a likeable and lawabiding Citizen, who is preparing to turn in his property, and a cynical, scoffing Dissident, who habitually puts his own interests above the law and now hesitates to turn in his own property. At the end of the scene the Dissident goes off to claim his place at the communal dinner but still hopes to find a way to keep his property; we never learn whether or not his cheating succeeds. But Praxagora has already explained that under the new regime the desire to own property makes no sense, since everyone will be amply supplied from the common store, so that the Dissident comes off looking both selfish and stupid.

The second episode illustrates the new regime of equality of sexual opportunity, in which the old and the ugly must be served before the young and the beautiful. In this longer, livelier and more elaborate scene, a beautiful young girl and a handsome young man, Epigenes, attempt to evade the new law by copulating. Their desire is frustrated by the intervention of three hags, each one older and uglier than the last, who stake their claims to Epigenes. In the end Epigenes is dragged off by the last two hags together, since in their case it proves impossible to resolve the question of priority.

Those who think that Aristophanes was being ironic when he portrayed Praxagora's plan as successful argue that we are meant to sympathize with Epigenes on the grounds simply that the old women are disgusting. But it is precisely this kind of selfish and discriminatory attitude that Praxagora's scheme seeks to frustrate, and in fact several considerations suggest that the

Athenians are unlikely to have felt any sympathy for Epigenes: (1) like the Dissident in the previous scene, Epigenes is an arrogant scoff-law who is trying to cheat: he has eaten the free dinner but now refuses to do his duty on behalf of the old women. (2) He is attempting to sleep with an unmarried citizen girl when her parents are away—serious misbehavior in the eyes of respectable Athenians and one that in real life could result in the death penalty.[33] (3) In Aristophanes' comedies young men are without exception portrayed unsympathetically. (4) The old women, risible though they are (this is satire, after all), seem not to have husbands, and so are probably to be thought of as widows or spinsters—perhaps as a result of the loss of men in the Peloponnesian War;[34] if so, their real-life counterparts will have been accorded a certain sympathy and respect. Like the Citizen in the previous scene, they are determined to obey the new laws, and like the Citizen, who sees that the common store will provide him better than his private store, they stand to gain something that they did not have before. But no one is to be ultimately deprived, unlike the situation in real life, where poor and unattractive people *never* get a chance for sex with the most attractive mates. As we will see in the following scene, unattractive older men like Blepyros are now getting first crack at the young, beautiful girls while boys like Epigenes are servicing old hags—a reversal of real-life norms that is an element of the play's "utopian" fantasy designed to appeal to ordinary men.[35]

On the face of it, Praxagora's plans are a great success, as the final scene demonstrates.[36] Praxagora has sent a jolly, tipsy Maid to fetch Blepyros to dinner. Blepyros, who enters with his arms around two young girls (he is among the old and ugly!) and ready to eat, thus enjoys the typical rewards of the sympathetic comic man: wine, food and sex. We feel that he deserves these because he has dutifully obeyed Praxagora and (unlike the Dissident and Epigenes) behaved unselfishly (he is the last to eat). No doubt he wears his own (men's) clothes once again, and he seems to have reversed the sexual impotency hinted at earlier, in line with the common comic motif of male (but never female) rejuvenation. It is clearly implied that every man who cooperates with the new regime will fare as well as Blepyros. All that remains is for the Maid to invite Blepyros and the women of the chorus (representing all the women) to dance off to dinner, which she describes in opulent terms in a lively song.

To what degree Aristophanes was "serious" about Praxagora's communist polity has prompted much debate,[37] perhaps because Plato made a similar proposal himself in all apparent seriousness and because communism in various forms has actually been tried on a large scale in our own century. I for one see no irony in Aristophanes' manner of proposing the idea or in his portrayal of its ultimate success; in this respect *Assemblywomen* follows much the same pattern as his earlier "great idea" plays. By the same token, the communism proposed in *Assemblywomen* is no less fantastic and idealistic either: society would indeed be a better place for most of us if it were not economically and socially unequal, and (as earlier plays imagine) there were no war, dishonest politicians and obnoxious fellow citizens. But when we try to imagine how such a state of affairs might actually be realized, we become painfully or comically aware of the gap between wish and reality. Aristophanes' fantastic satire elides that gap, and to that extent *Assemblywomen* is serious on the level of wish-fulfillment.

*Assemblywomen* follows the pattern of Aristophanes' fifth-century comedies in its plot but shows significant changes in formal structure, particularly in its handling of the chorus. Though the chorus plays a prominent role at the beginning and end of the play, its silent and gradual entry, subsequent absences, and minimal involvement in the central scenes are paralleled only in tragedy; there is no parabasis and only a truncated agon; and the choral songs separating episodes are absent from the script, the lacuna sometimes indicated by the note *chorou* ("place for a chorus"), as would become the norm by Menander's time.

## CHARACTERS

PRAXAGORA, an *Athenian wife*
FIRST WOMAN, *a friend of Praxagora*
SECOND WOMAN, *Praxagora's neighbor*
BLEPYROS, *Praxagora's elderly husband*
NEIGHBOR, *Second Woman's husband*
CHREMES, *an elderly acquaintance of Blepyros*
SELFISH MAN
HERALDESS, *a woman appointed by Praxagora*
THREE OLD WOMEN
GIRL
EPIGENES, *a young man in love with Girl*
MAID *of Praxagora*
CHORUS *of Athenian wives*

Mute Characters
SICON and PARMENON, *slaves of Neighbor*
YOUNG WOMEN, *accompanying Blepyros*

## PROLOGUE

SCENE: *A street in Athens, just before daybreak. A young figure wearing a woman's white, beardless mask*[38] *enters from one of three doors in the scene-building carrying a lighted lamp, wearing men's clothing and carrying a walking-stick,*[39] *and addresses the lamp in a woman's voice.*

PRAXAGORA:[40]

> O radiant disk of my ceramic lamp,
> fairest invention of skilled artisans,
> I shall reveal your pedigree and fortunes fair.
> For, whirled on the wheel by the potter's impetus,
> you hold the Sun's radiant honors in your nozzles.                    5

Now send forth the fiery signal as arranged. [*She swings the lamp to and fro.*] You alone we've made privy to our plot, and rightly, since you also stand by us in our bedrooms as we execute Aphrodite's maneuvers, and when our bodies are flexed, no one banishes from the room your supervisory eye. You alone shine your light into the hushed-up recesses between our     10 thighs, when you singe away the hair that sprouts there;[41] and you stand by us when we stealthily open the pantry, stocked with bread and the liquor of Bakchos. And you never babble to the neighbors about the things you've abetted. So you'll be in on our present plans too, the plans my friends and I agreed on at the Skira.[42] But the women who are supposed to     15 meet here haven't shown up, though it's almost light, and the Assembly is about to begin! We "wenchmen" must grab our seats, as Phyromachus once put it, if you still remember[43]—and settle ourselves without attracting notice. [*She paces around.*] What can be keeping them? Don't they have the false beards they were told to get? Was it hard for them to steal     20 their husbands' clothes without getting caught? [*Figures wearing women's underclothing and carrying lamps, men's clothing and false beards enter the orchestra through a parodos, followed by several other figures, similarly dressed.*] But I see a lamp over there, coming this way. I'll duck out of the way in case it happens to be a man.     25

[*She retreats to a doorway; one of the entering women goes onstage, while others gather in the orchestra.*]

CHORUS-LEADER [*to her companions*]: Time to move! Just now, as we were on our way here, the Herald crowed a second time!

PRAXAGORA [*in a loud whisper, which spins the new arrivals around*]: And I was up the whole night waiting for you! Well, I'm going to get this neighbor of mine out of the house—by scratching softly at her door, since her husband mustn't     30 notice. [*She scratches on the door.*]

FIRST WOMAN [*emerging from the door, dressed in men's clothing*]: I was just getting dressed when I heard you give the secret knock: see, I wasn't asleep! You know, my dear, the husband I live with is from Salamis:[44] all night long he was sailing me all over the bed, so I just now got the chance to grab his suit.     35

[*First Woman takes from her house-door three chairs and a lectern, which she and Praxagora set up on stage; meanwhile several other women enter the orchestra.*]

PRAXAGORA: Hey, I see Kleinarete and Sostrate coming, and there's Philainete.[45]

CHORUS-LEADER [*to the new arrivals*]: Get a move on! Glyke has promised on oath that the last woman here will be fined ten quarts of wine and a bag of chickpeas!     40

PRAXAGORA: Look, there's Smikythion's wife Melistiche trying to run in her old man's boots! And I think she's the only one who had no trouble getting away from her husband![46]

FIRST WOMAN: And there's the barkeep's wife Geusistrate[47]—see her, with the torch in her hand?     45

PRAXAGORA: And there's Philodoretos' wife, and Chairetades', and a lot more women besides: anyone who's anybody in town!

SECOND WOMAN [*to Praxagora*]: I had an awful time, my dear, making my escape and getting over here quietly. My husband stuffed himself with anchovies at dinner last night and was up all night coughing!     50

PRAXAGORA: Well, now that you're all here, please sit down. [*The women except Praxagora sit in the chairs.*] I want to ask you if you've done everything we agreed on at the Skira.

FIRST WOMAN: I have! First, I've let my armpits grow bushier than underbrush, just as we agreed; then, whenever my husband goes off to the agora, I oil myself and spend the whole day in the sun trying to get a tan.     55

SECOND WOMAN: Me too! I threw my razor out of the house so I'd get all hairy and not look female at all!

PRAXAGORA: Have you all got your beards—the ones you were told to bring with you when next we met?     60

[*The women onstage produce false beards.*]

FIRST WOMAN: Sure, by Hekate![48] I've got this nice one here!

SECOND WOMAN: And mine's far nicer than Epikrates'!

PRAXAGORA [*to the Chorus*]: And how about the rest of you?

FIRST WOMAN: They've got them; look, they're nodding yes.

PRAXAGORA: All right, I see you've taken care of the preliminaries: and you've     65
got your men's boots and walking-sticks and suits, just as we stipulated.

FIRST WOMAN: [*producing a huge shillelagh*]: Look, I've brought Lamios'
shillelagh; I took it while he was asleep!

SECOND WOMAN: Must be the shillelagh he uses to fart!

PRAXAGORA: By Zeus the Savior, if he wore Argos' goat-leather jacket he'd be     70
perfectly suited to provide fodder for the public—executioner![49] But let's get
on with the next items of business, while the stars are still in the sky. The
Assembly we're prepared to attend begins at dawn.

FIRST WOMAN: By Zeus, we've got to leave time to get seats right under the
Chairman's dais.     75

SECOND WOMAN: [*taking a knitting-basket out of her bundle*]: I brought this along,
just for something to do while the men are filing into Assembly.

PRAXAGORA: While the men are filing in, stupid?

SECOND WOMAN: Sure, by Artemis![50] I can hear just as well when I'm
knitting. My kids have nothing to wear![51]     80

PRAXAGORA: Listen to you! Knitting? You mustn't risk showing any part of
your body to the men. Wouldn't we be in fine shape, if the assemblymen are
all there and then some woman has to climb over them, hitching up her
clothes, and flashes her, her—Phormisios?[52] If we're the first to get to our
seats, no one will notice that we're keeping our clothes wrapped tight. And     85
when we unfurl the beards that we're going to stick on our chins, who
would suspect that we're not men? Take Agyrrhios: now that he's wearing
Pronomos' beard he passes for a man; and yet this very man used to be a
woman! And now, you see, he's the most powerful figure in the polis.[53] And
it's because of him, I swear by this dawning day, that we must dare such a     90
daring deed, hopeful of somehow being able to take over the government
and do something good for the polis! As it is, our polis is oarless and
becalmed.

FIRST WOMAN: But how can a congregation of women, with women's minds,
expect to address the people?     95

PRAXAGORA: Much better than anybody, that's how! They say that the young
men who've been reamed the most are also the most effective orators! And as
luck would have it, that's exactly what nature suits us for!

FIRST WOMAN: I'm not so sure: inexperience is a dangerous thing.

PRAXAGORA: Well, isn't that why we've gathered here, to practice what we're    100
going to say there? Come on, attach your beard; [to the other women] and that
goes for everyone else who's been practicing how to gab.

FIRST WOMAN: Is there anyone here, friend, who doesn't know how to gab?

PRAXAGORA: All right then, you put on your beard and become a man; I'll set
out these garlands and put on my beard too, just in case I decide to make a    105
comment.

[The women attach their beards.]

SECOND WOMAN: Face this way, darling Praxagora. My dear, what a
ridiculous sight this is!

PRAXAGORA: Ridiculous?

SECOND WOMAN: Looks like somebody bearded a grilled squid!    110

PRAXAGORA: [moving behind the lectern and speaking in the voice of a Herald]: Purifier,
please make your rounds with the sacrificial cat.[54] Assemblymen, come
forward into the sanctified area. Ariphrades, stop chattering![55] You there,
come forward and take a seat! Who wishes to address the Assembly?

SECOND WOMAN: I do!    115

PRAXAGORA [indicating the pile of garlands]: Then put on the garland and may
your speech be propitious.

SECOND WOMAN [putting on the garland]: Ready.

PRAXAGORA: You may speak.

SECOND WOMAN: Don't I get a drink first?    120

PRAXAGORA: Drink?

SECOND WOMAN: Well, sir, what did I put on a garland for, then?[56]

PRAXAGORA: Get off of there! You would have done the same thing to us in the
real Assembly!

SECOND WOMAN [flaring]: What? Don't they drink in the real Assembly?    125

PRAXAGORA: Listen to you—"don't they drink"!

SECOND WOMAN: Sure, by Artemis, and they drink it straight! Their decrees,
when you think about the reasoning behind them, are like the ravings of
drunkards! By god, and they pour libations too: why else would they make

those long prayers, if they didn't have wine? And they yell at each other like   130
drunks, and the police drag away the guy who's had too much.

PRAXAGORA: Well, you may get back to your seat and sit down! You're
worthless!

FIRST WOMAN [returning to her seat]: By Zeus, I would have been better off
without this beard—I'm absolutely parched with thirst!   135

PRAXAGORA [to the seated women]: Is there another candidate orator among us?

FIRST WOMAN [rising]: Me!

PRAXAGORA [motioning her forward and extending another garland]: Put this on then.
We can't stop now, after all our planning. Now, carry on like a man and speak
cogently; lean hard on your stick like this [she adopts an oratorical posture].   140

FIRST WOMAN: I would have preferred to yield the floor to one of the usual
speakers, sitting quietly and listening to a very good speech. But as far as my
own vote goes, I say in barrooms we outlaw the use of kegs to hold water! It
is a bad policy, by the Twain Goddesses.[57]

PRAXAGORA: By the Twain Goddesses, you bungler? Where is your mind?   145

FIRST WOMAN: What's the matter? I didn't ask for a drink!

PRAXAGORA: God no, but you did swear by the Twain when you're supposed to
be a man! [Dejectedly] And the rest was so good, too.

FIRST WOMAN: Oh! [Resuming a manly voice] By Apollo . . .

PRAXAGORA: No, stop. [She plucks the garland from Second Woman's head.] I won't   150
take another step on the road to being an assemblywoman until everything's
exactly right.

FIRST WOMAN: [snatching back the garland]: Give me the garland. I want to try
my speech again; I think I've got it down nicely now. [She assumes the rhetorical
posture.] In my view, ladies of the Assembly . . .   155

PRAXAGORA: Again, you loser? You're calling men ladies!

FIRST WOMAN: [pointing to the audience]: It's that Epigonos over there:[58] I caught
sight of him and thought I was addressing women!

PRAXAGORA [pointing her away from the lectern]: Shoo. You go back to your seat
over there too. [To the seated women] To judge from what I've seen of your   160
abilities it seems best that I put on this garland and make the speech myself.[59]
[Taking the lectern] I beseech the gods to grant success to today's deliberations.

My own stake in this country is equal to your own, and I am annoyed and depressed at all the polis' conduct of affairs. For I see her constantly employing scoundrels as her leaders. If one of them turns virtuous for one day, he makes up for it by being wicked for ten. You turn to another one, and he causes even worse trouble. I realize how difficult it is to talk sense to men as cantankerous as you, who fear those who want to befriend you and consistently court those who do not. There was a time when we convened no assemblies at all, but at least we knew Agyrrhios for a scoundrel. Nowadays we do convene them, and the people who attend and draw pay for it praise him to the skies, while those who cannot attend say that the people who attend for the money deserve the death penalty.[60]

FIRST WOMAN: Well said, by Aphrodite![61]

PRAXAGORA: Pitiful! You swore by Aphrodite! Wouldn't it be charming if you spoke that way in the Assembly?

FIRST WOMAN: But I wouldn't have!

PRAXAGORA: Well, don't get into the habit now. [*Resuming her speech*] And about this alliance: when we were examining the issue, the people insisted that the polis would perish if we did not ratify it. But when it finally *was* ratified, the people were unhappy, and the alliance's staunchest supporter had to leave town in a hurry.[62] When it's a question of launching a fleet, the poor are all for it,[63] while the rich and the farmers are against it. First you are angry with the Korinthians, and they with you; then they're nice people, so you have to be nice as well. The Argives are morons, but Hieronymos is a sage. And occasionally we get a fleeting glimpse of salvation, but Thrasyboulos gets angry that you're not begging him to lead you.[64]

FIRST WOMAN: This man's intelligent!

PRAXAGORA: That's the way to applaud! [*Resuming her speech*] And you, the sovereign people, are responsible for this mess! For while you're drawing your civic pay from public funds, each of you is figuring how you can personally profit. Meanwhile the state staggers around like Aisimos. But listen to my advice and you shall escape from your muddle. I propose that we turn over governance of the polis to the women, since they are so competent as stewards and treasurers in our households.

ALL THE WOMEN: Hear hear! Well said! Pray continue, sir!

PRAXAGORA: And their character is superior to ours, as I will demonstrate. First of all, they dye their wool in hot water according to their ancient custom, each and every one of them. You'll never see them trying anything

new. Contrast the Athenian polis: never content to do well with a tried and        200
true method, they are always fiddling around with some pointless novelty.
Meanwhile the women settle down to their cooking, as they always have.
They carry burdens on their heads, as they always have. They celebrate the
Thesmophoria, as they always have. They bake cookies, as they always have.
They drive their husbands nuts, as they always have. They hide their lovers in        205
the house, as they always have. They buy themselves little extras, as they
always have. They like their wine neat, as they always have. They like to get
fucked, as they always have. And so, gentlemen, let us hand over governance
of the polis to the women, and let's not beat around the bush about it or ask
what they plan to accomplish. Let's simply let them govern. You need        210
consider only two points: first, as mothers they'll want to protect the soldiers;
and second, who could be quicker at sending rations to soldiers than the
mothers who bore them? No one is more inventive at getting funds than a
woman. Nor would a woman ruler ever get cheated, since women
themselves are past masters at cheating. I'll pass over the other arguments.        215
Adopt my resolution and you'll lead happy lives.[65]

SECOND WOMAN: Well said, dearest Praxagora! What skill! What skill! Where
did you learn such fine talk, my dear?

PRAXAGORA: I lived with my husband on the Pnyx,[66] with the refugees,[67] and
learned by listening to the orators.        220

FIRST WOMAN: Then it's no wonder, madam, that you were so impressive and
sage. What's more, your fellow women hereby elect you general if you
succeed in this plan of yours. But what if Kephalos[68] challenges you
abusively? How do you plan to handle him in the Assembly?

PRAXAGORA: I'll say he's crazy.        225

FIRST WOMAN: But everyone knows that!

PRAXAGORA: Well, I'll say he's a dangerous psychopath.

FIRST WOMAN: Everyone knows that too!

PRAXAGORA: Then I'll say that a man who does such a bad job making pottery
is sure to do a terrific job running the polis.        230

FIRST WOMAN: But what if Neokleides the squinter abuses you?

PRAXAGORA: I'll tell him to go squint up a dog's butt.

FIRST WOMAN: And what if they try to screw you?[69]

PRAXAGORA: I'll screw them right back: I know a good many tricks myself.

FIRST WOMAN: There's another danger we haven't discussed: if the police          235
jump you, what will you do then?

PRAXAGORA [*assuming a wrestler's stance*]: I'll be ready for them like this—they'll
never get on top of me!

FIRST WOMAN: And if they do hoist you, the rest of us will—ask them to put
you down!          240

SECOND WOMAN: I think this is a fine plan we've thought up. But one thing
we haven't given much thought to is how we'll remind ourselves to put up
our *hands* when voting; we're used to putting up our *legs*.[70]

PRAXAGORA: That's a tough one. [*Demonstrating*] Just remember that you vote
by undraping your right arm and raising that hand. Go ahead, now, hitch          245
up your tunics. [*The women do so. To the chorus*] Now hurry up and put on your
boots, just the way your husbands *used* to when they went off to the Assembly
or on some errand. Then when you're all dressed up, fasten your beards. And
when you've attached them exactly right, put on the men's coats that you
stole and drape them correctly. Now lean on those walking-sticks as you          250
walk, and sing like old men, country-style.

CHORUS [*fully disguised*]: Great instructions!

PRAXAGORA: Let's go forward just so, because I expect some women from the
country are on their way directly to the Pnyx. Well, hurry then, since the drill
on the Pnyx is: in by dawn or go back home with nary a clothespin.[71]          255

[*Praxagora, the First and Second Woman depart; the women in the orchestra, now disguised as
men, form up a chorus.*]


## PARODOS

CHORUS-LEADER: Gentlemen, it's time for us to march—and "gentlemen" is
the word we must remember to use, and never let it slip from our minds. We
run no small risk if we're caught dressed up for so dark a deed of daring.

CHORUS (*strophe*):
      So it's off to the Assembly, gentlemen!
      The magistrate has sounded his warning:          260
      if anyone fails to come bright and early,
      covered with dust, happy
      with a breakfast of garlic soup

with a spicy look in his eye,
he'll not get his three-obol pay.                                    265
Hey Charitimides,
Smikythos and Drakes,[72]
get a move on! Watch your step,
don't strike a false note
in the role you've got to play.                                      270
When we've got our tickets
let's be sure to sit down together
and raise our hands in favor
of whatever our ladies propose.
What am I saying? *Gentlemen*                                        275
is the word I ought to have used!

[*Half of the chorus exits.*]

(*antistrophe*)
Let's make sure to jostle
the assemblymen from town,
who never used to attend:
when the pay was only one obol,                                      280
they sat around gossiping
in the garland-shops,
but now they fight for seats.
Never in the good old days,
with noble Myronides in command,                                     285
would anyone have dared
to husband the polis' affairs
for a fistful of money.
No, everyone would come to assembly
with a little bag lunch:                                             290
something to drink, dry bread,
a couple of onions and three olives.
Now what they want is three obols
for doing a public service,
like common laborers.                                                295

[*The rest of the chorus exits.*]


## EPISODE


[*Through the door by which Praxagora had entered now enters an old man, dressed in women's shoes and a skimpy yellow shift.[73]*]

BLEPYROS [74] [*to himself*]: What's going on? Where has my wife got to? It's getting near dawn and she's nowhere to be seen. I've been lying awake for ages, needing to shit, trying to find my boots and coat in the dark.[75] I've groped everywhere but couldn't find them, and all the while the dung man kept pounding at my back door, so finally I grabbed my wife's slip here and     300 put on her Persian slippers.[76] [*Looking around and advancing into the orchestra*] Now where, where could a man find an out-of-the-way place to take a shit? Well, *anywhere* is fine at night. At this hour no one's going to see me shitting. God, what a fool I was—getting married at my age! I deserve a good flogging! You can be sure she didn't go out on any decent errand. Anyway, I've got to do     305 my business. [*He squats down and begins to grunt loudly; another old man, holding a lamp, appears at the Second Woman's window.*]

NEIGHBOR: Who's that? Surely not my neighbor Blepyros? Yes, by Zeus, the very same! Say, what's this yellow all over you? Kinesias hit you with his droppings?[77]     310

BLEPYROS: Say what? No, I had to come out here and I put on my wife's little yellow shift.

NEIGHBOR: Where's your coat?

BLEPYROS: Can't say. I looked for it all over the bedroom and couldn't find it.

NEIGHBOR: Well, why didn't you get your wife to tell you where it is?     315

BLEPYROS: By Zeus I couldn't: she doesn't happen to be in; she slipped out of the house on me. And I'm worried she's up to no good.

NEIGHBOR: Poseidon! Exactly the same thing just happened to me: the woman of my house has gone off with my clothes! That wouldn't be so annoying, but she's taken my boots too! I couldn't lay my hands on them anywhere.     320

BLEPYROS: Dionysos! I couldn't find my Spartan boots either! But as luck would have it I had to shit, so I threw on these pumps and dashed out. Didn't want to shit on the comforter; just had it cleaned.

NEIGHBOR: What can she be doing? Did one of her lady friends invite her out for breakfast?     325

BLEPYROS: That's probably it. She's not a tramp—as far as I know.

NEIGHBOR: You must be pooping a ship's cable! Me, I've got to be getting along to the Assembly, that is, if I can get hold of my coat—it's the only one I've got!

BLEPYROS: Me too, as soon as I finish my business. At the moment some kind of     330 choke-pear has got my food blockaded.

NEIGHBOR [*disappearing from the window*]: Like the blockade Thrasyboulos proposed against the Spartans?

BLEPYROS [*laughing*]: Dionysos, yes! It's got me pretty uptight anyway. [*To himself*] What am I going to do? This present predicament isn't my only        335
anxiety: what's going to happen when I *eat* something? Where will the poop go? As it is, he's got me bolted up tight, this fellow from Cul-de-Sac. [*Surveying the audience*] Is there a doctor in the house, with the right treatment? Any of you asshole-experts knowledgeable about my condition? I know: Amynon! But maybe he'll refuse. Somebody call Antisthenes right away! As far as        340
grunts and groans go, he's the man to figure out the meaning of an asshole that needs to shit.[78] O Mistress Hileithya,[79] don't let me down when I'm bursting and bolted! I don't like the role of comic potty!

[*Enter Chremes.*]

CHREMES [*catching sight of Blepyros*]: Hey there, what are you doing? Not taking a shit, are you?        345

BLEPYROS [*hurriedly straightening up*]: Who, me? No indeed, not any longer anyway, by god. I'm on my feet again!

CHREMES: Is that your wife's slip you're wearing?

BLEPYROS: Yes, it was dark in the house when I grabbed it, by mistake. But tell me, where have you been?        350

CHREMES: At assembly.

BLEPYROS: You mean it's adjourned already?

CHREMES: By god it has, and before daylight too! And the ruddle-rope got a big laugh too, by Zeus Most Dear, when they swung it around![80]

BLEPYROS: You got your three obols anyway?        355

CHREMES: I wish I had! But this time I was too late. God, I'm ashamed to admit <that I left empty-handed.

BLEPYROS: So you got nothing?>

CHREMES: Nope, absolutely nothing but my shopping bag.

BLEPYROS: But what made you late?        360

CHREMES: A huge crowd of people showed up en masse at the Pnyx, an all-time record! In fact we thought they all looked like shoemakers.[81] Really, the assembly was awfully pale-faced to behold. So I didn't get my pay, and a bunch of others didn't either.

BLEPYROS: So, I wouldn't get paid if I went there now?                                      365

CHREMES: Hah! Not even if you'd gotten there before the cock finished crowing!

BLEPYROS [*tragically*]: Ah, what a blow! Antilochos, raise not the dirge for those three obols but rather for me who yet live: for all I had is gone.[82] But what business could have fetched such a mob together so early?                                      370

CHREMES: It could only be that the chairmen decided to schedule deliberation about the salvation of the polis. And right away Neokleides the squinter[83] groped his way to the podium to speak first, but the people started to yell as loud as you please, "Isn't it awful that this guy dares to address us, on the subject of our salvation no less, when he can't even save his own eyelids?"                                      375
And he squints around and yells back, "Well, how can I help it?"

BLEPYROS: If I'd been there I would have said, "Grind up garlic and figs and add Spartan spurge, and rub the mixture on your eyelids at bedtime."

CHREMES: After him, that success-story Euaion[84] stepped forward—wearing only a shirt, most people thought, though he insisted he was wearing a coat.                                      380
His speech appealed mainly to the masses: "You see that I'm in need of salvation myself—about four bits would do it—but nevertheless I shall tell you how to save the polis and her people. If the clothiers were to donate coats at the winter solstice to those who need them, none of us would ever again catch pneumonia. And you should allow anyone without a bed or a blanket                                      385
to sleep in the tanneries[85] after they've 'washed up';[86] if a tanner won't open his doors in wintertime, fine him three comforters!"

BLEPYROS: By Dionysos, what a noble thought! He would have won unanimous approval if he'd added that grain-dealers should give the needy three quarts for their dinner or face punishment. They could have collected                                      390
that benefit from Nausikydes![87]

CHREMES: Well, after that a pale, good-looking young man[88] sprang to his feet to address the people—looked very much like Nikias.[89] He made a case for handing the polis over to the women! And they all cheered and yelled their approval, this mass of cobblers, while the people from the country made                                      395
deep rumbles.

BLEPYROS: They had sense, by god!

CHREMES: But they were the minority, and the speaker drowned them out. In his view, women could do no wrong, and you no right.

BLEPYROS: What were his arguments?                                      400

CHREMES: First, he called you a criminal.

BLEPYROS: And what did he call you?

CHREMES: I'll get to that. Then he called you a crook.

BLEPYROS: Only me?

CHREMES: That's right, and an informer too. 405

BLEPYROS: Only me?

CHREMES: That's right, you and [indicating the spectators] this crowd here as well!

BLEPYROS: Well, that's a different story—who'd deny that?

CHREMES: He went on to say that a woman is a creature bursting with brains
and productive of profit, and furthermore that women never divulge the 410
secrets of the Thesmophoria,[90] by contrast with you and me, who leak what
we say in Council all the time.

BLEPYROS: By Hermes, that last point's fair enough.

CHREMES: Then he said that women lend each other dresses, jewelry, money,
drinking cups, privately and without witnesses,[91] and always return 415
everything with nothing held back; while most of us men, he said, cheat.

BLEPYROS: By Poseidon, we cheat even when there are witnesses!

CHREMES: He included other items in his long eulogy of the women: that they
don't inform on people, don't sue them, don't try to overthrow the
democracy, but instead do it lots of good. 420

BLEPYROS: And what was voted?

CHREMES: To turn the polis over to them. That seemed to be the only thing that
hasn't been tried.

BLEPYROS: And this passed?

CHREMES: That's what I'm telling you. 425

BLEPYROS: They've been put in charge of everything that used to be the
business of the citizens?

CHREMES: That's the way it is.

BLEPYROS: So I won't be going to court anymore, but my wife will?

CHREMES: And you won't be taking care of your dependants anymore—your 430
wife will.

BLEPYROS: And I won't have to groan myself awake at dawn anymore?

CHREMES: God no, all that's the women's concern now; you can stop groaning and stay at home farting all day long!

BLEPYROS: But there lies the danger for men our age:[92] once they've taken the reins of power they'll force us against our will to— 435

CHREMES: To what?

BLEPYROS: To screw them!

CHREMES: And what if we can't?

BLEPYROS: They won't make us breakfast! 440

CHREMES: By Zeus you'd better this then [miming cunnilingus]: then you could eat breakfast and screw at the same time.

BLEPYROS: But it's absolutely terrible when you're forced!

CHREMES: But if this is the policy of the polis, every true man's got to do his part! 445

BLEPYROS: Well, there is that traditional saying: however brainless and foolish our policies may be, all our affairs will turn out for the best.

CHREMES: And I hope they do turn out for the best, Lady Pallas[93] and all you Gods! Well, I've got to go. Be well, friend. [He walks offstage.]

BLEPYROS: You too, Chremes! [He goes inside his house.] 450

## CHORAL INTERLUDE

[The Chorus begins to return in small groups to the orchestra, still costumed as men.]

CHORUS-LEADER [still offstage, shepherding the women]: Forward march! Is any man following us? Turn around, take a look, guard yourselves carefully—lots of no-good men about—one of them might be at our rear, inspecting our deportment!

CHORUS (strophe):
Right! As you march along 455
see that you stomp your feet
as loud as you can.
Getting caught red-handed in this business

would disgrace us in our husbands' eyes.
And so stay closely wrapped,                                    460
look this way and that,
left and right,
to avoid catastrophe for our operation.

CHORUS-LEADER: Come, let's make the dust fly: we're near the place where
we first set off for the Assembly. We can see the house now where our      465
commander lives, who thought up the plan that the citizens have now
enacted.

CHORUS (antistrophe):
So we've no further need to hang around
with these beards stuck on our chins;
someone might see us in the daylight                            470
and maybe turn us in!
So come this way, into the shade
by the house-wall, keeping an eye peeled,
and change yourselves back to the way you were.

CHORUS-LEADER: And don't dally, for I see this commander of ours coming    475
this way from the Assembly. Everyone, get a move on, get rid of those
hateful hairbags on your cheeks; we've grudgingly worn them for a long
time now.

## EPISODE

[Praxagora enters and moves to the doorway of her house, removing her beard.]

PRAXAGORA [to the Chorus]: We're in luck, ladies: the business has turned out as
we planned. But now you must get rid of those suits and kick off those shoes   480
as quick as you can, before anyone sees them. You, undo the knotted reins
Lakonian. Lose the walking-sticks. [To the Chorus-Leader] And you, get these
women into some kind of order! I'd like to sneak back into the house before
my husband sees me, and put his suit back where I got it, and all this other
stuff I borrowed.                                              485

CHORUS-LEADER [after the chorus have removed all their male costuming]:
Everything's off, just as you ordered. We're ready for further instructions and
will obediently do whatever you think is most helpful to you. For I know that
I've never encountered a woman more impressive than you are.

PRAXAGORA: Then stick around: I'll use all of you as counsellors in running
the office I've been elected to. Yes, at the Assembly, amid hubbub and danger,    490
you were all very manly!

[Just as Praxagora starts to open her door, Blepyros emerges, still dressed in her clothes.]

BLEPYROS: It's you! Where have you been, Praxagora?

PRAXAGORA: Is that any of your business, sir?

BLEPYROS: Any of my business? What innocence!

PRAXAGORA: Now don't start saying I've been at some lover's house.    495

BLEPYROS: Maybe more than one!

PRAXAGORA: OK then, there's a way for you to test it.

BLEPYROS: How?

PRAXAGORA: See if you can smell perfume on me.

BLEPYROS: What? Can't a woman get fucked without perfume?    500

PRAXAGORA: Not I—more's the pity.

BLEPYROS: Then why did you leave the house so early, without telling me, and
taking my coat with you?

PRAXAGORA: A woman I know, a dear friend, was in labor and asked me to
attend her.    505

BLEPYROS: And so you couldn't let me know you were leaving?

PRAXAGORA: And not give a thought to a woman brought to bed, husband, in
her condition?

BLEPYROS: You could at least have told me. There's something fishy here!

PRAXAGORA: Not at all, by the Twain. I dropped everything and went as I was.    510
The maid who came for me asked me to come right away.

BLEPYROS: Then shouldn't you have taken your own dress with you. Instead,
you swiped my coat and threw your slip over me, leaving me there like a
corpse at the undertaker's—you all but laid me out with a wreath and urn!

PRAXAGORA: It was cold outside, and I'm thin and delicate, so I put this on    515
to keep warm. But before I left I made sure you were snugly covered,
husband.

BLEPYROS: And why did my Spartan boots go with you, and my walking-stick?

**PRAXAGORA**: I didn't want your coat to get stolen, so I put these on to sound like you, stomping my feet and poking at stones with the stick. 520

**BLEPYROS**: You realize you've cost us eight quarts of wheat—what I'd have gotten by attending Assembly?

**PRAXAGORA**: Don't worry about it: she had a baby boy![94]

**BLEPYROS**: Who, the Assembly?

**PRAXAGORA**: No no, the woman I attended! So, an Assembly was held? 525

**BLEPYROS**: God yes. Don't you remember me telling you about it yesterday?

**PRAXAGORA**: Yes, now I remember.

**BLEPYROS**: So you don't even know what's been decided?

**PRAXAGORA**: No idea.

**BLEPYROS**: Well, sit down and chew cuttlefish! They say you women are in charge of the polis. 530

**PRAXAGORA**: To do what? Our knitting?

**BLEPYROS**: No, by Zeus: to govern!

**PRAXAGORA**: Govern whom?

**BLEPYROS**: All the city's affairs. 535

**PRAXAGORA**: Then, by Aphrodite, the polis has a rosy future in store.

**BLEPYROS**: How do you figure?

**PRAXAGORA**: For lots of reasons. From now on aggressive people won't be allowed to treat the polis shamefully in any way: no more perjury, no more trumped-up charges— 540

**BLEPYROS**: Good heavens, don't do that! You'll take away my livelihood!

[*Neighbor has come out of his house to listen.*]

**NEIGHBOR**: Please, friend, let your wife talk.

**PRAXAGORA**:—no more mugging, no more envying the next guy, no more wearing rags, no more poor people, no more wrangling, no more dunning and repossessing. 545

**NEIGHBOR**: Poseidon, that would be great, if it's true.

**PRAXAGORA**: Let me explain it; you'll have to agree that I'm right, and even my mister here will have nothing to say against me.

## DEBATE

CHORUS:[95]

>Now you must summon up a shrewd intelligence
>and a mind sage in the task of defending your comrades!          550
>For it's to the prosperity of all alike
>that your creative ingenuity
>will gladden the lives of the citizens
>with countless benefits—
>now is the time to show what that ingenuity can do!              555
>You know how much our polis needs some sage plan;
>describe it in full, making sure only
>that it's never been said or done before:
>[indicating the spectators] for they hate to watch
>the same old stuff again and again!                              560

CHORUS-LEADER: No more delay! Here and now you must put your idea in play: what the audience most appreciates is instant gratification!

PRAXAGORA: Well, then, I'm sure my proposals are worthwhile, but I'm awfully worried about the spectators: are they ready to quarry a new vein and not stick with what's hoary and conventional?          565

NEIGHBOR: Don't worry about quarrying what's new: for us, indifference to precedent takes precedence over any other principle of government![96]

PRAXAGORA: Then let no one object or interrupt until you've heard the speaker out and understand the plan. Very well: I propose that everyone should own everything in common and draw an equal living. No more rich          570 man here, poor man there; no more division between the man with a big farm and the man without land enough to be buried in; between the man with many slaves and the man without even an attendant; no, I will establish one and the same standard of life for everyone.

BLEPYROS: How will it be the same for everyone?          575

PRAXAGORA [crossly]: If we were eating dung you'd grab the first bite!

BLEPYROS: We'll be sharing the dung too?

PRAXAGORA: God no! I mean you jumped in with the point I was about to make! As I was about to say, my first act will be to communize everyone's land, money and other property. We women will manage this central pool          580 with thrift and good judgment, and we'll take good care of you.[97]

NEIGHBOR: And what about the man who owns no land but has gold and silver stashed away?

PRAXAGORA: He'll contribute it to the central pool.

BLEPYROS: And if he refuses, he'll perjure himself: after all, that's how he got        585
the money in the first place!

PRAXAGORA: But look, it won't be of any use to him anyway.

BLEPYROS. What do you mean?

PRAXAGORA: No one will be forced to do anything out of poverty: everyone
will have all the necessities: bread, salt fish, barley-cakes, cloaks, wine,        590
garlands, chickpeas. So where's his profit in not contributing? If you can
find it, do tell me.

BLEPYROS: Isn't it true that the people who have all this now are the biggest
thieves?

NEIGHBOR: Before now, my friend, yes, when we lived under the previous        595
system. But now that everyone will be living from a common fund, where's
the profit in holding out?

BLEPYROS: What if someone fancies a girl[98] and wants the pleasure of a poke?
He'll take her price from this common fund, and when he's slept with her
he'll have all that's commonly wanted.        600

PRAXAGORA: No, he'll be able to sleep with her free of charge. I'm making
these girls common property for the men to sleep with and make babies with
as they please.

BLEPYROS: Then won't everyone be looking for the prettiest girl and trying to
bang her?        605

PRAXAGORA: The second-rate and the bob-nosed will sit right beside the
classy ones, and if a man wants the latter he'll have to ball the ugly ones
first.[99]

BLEPYROS: But what about us older men? If we go with the ugly ones first,
our cocks won't have anything left when we get to where the classy ones are!        610

PRAXAGORA: They won't complain, don't worry about it. Never fear, they
won't complain.

BLEPYROS: What do you mean? Complain about what?

PRAXAGORA: About not getting to sleep with you! Anyway, you've got that
problem as it is.        615

BLEPYROS: Your side of the equation makes a certain sense; you've planned it that no woman's hole will go unplugged. But what do you mean to do for the men? The women will shun the ugly ones and make for the handsome ones!

PRAXAGORA: Well, the ugly men will have to tail the handsome men as they leave their dinner-parties, and keep an eye on the public places, for it won't be lawful for the tall and handsome to sleep with any women who haven't first accommodated the uglies and the runts.    620

BLEPYROS: So I suppose Lysikrates[100] will now be sticking up his nose with the best of them!    625

PRAXAGORA: By Apollo, he will. And what's more, the idea favors ordinary people. It'll be a great joke on the big shots with their signet rings when a guy wearing sneakers speaks up and says, "Step aside and wait till I'm finished; then I'll give you sloppy seconds!"

BLEPYROS: But under your regime, how in the world will any man be able to recognize his own children?[101]    630

PRAXAGORA: Why should he? Everyone in the younger generation will consider all older men to be their fathers.

BLEPYROS: I suppose that from now on sons will start methodically strangling each and every older man, since they strangle their acknowledged fathers as it is. What will they do to a *stranger*? Not only strangle him but shit on his corpse too!    635

PRAXAGORA: But the bystanders won't allow that! Nobody used to interfere with sons who beat up their fathers, but now if someone hears a man being beaten he'll be afraid that the victim is his *own* father and he'll fight the attackers.    640

BLEPYROS: That's all well and good, but if Epikouros or Leukolophos start hanging around and calling me "daddy" it's going to be awful.

NEIGHBOR: Well, I can think of even more awful things.

BLEPYROS: Such as?    645

NEIGHBOR: If Aristyllos[102] claims you're his father and kisses you!

BLEPYROS: If he does he'll sorely regret it!

NEIGHBOR: And you'd smell of *eau d'ordure*!

PRAXAGORA: But he was born before our decree, so there's no need to worry that he'll be kissing you.    650

BLEPYROS: He'd have been sorry if he had! But who will there be to farm the land?

PRAXAGORA: The slaves. Your only concern will be to get all slicked up when the shadow-clock says it's time for dinner.

BLEPYROS: And overcoats: who will supply them? It's a reasonable question.     655

PRAXAGORA: The current stock will do for now; later we'll weave you new ones.[103]

BLEPYROS: One more question: what happens if someone loses a lawsuit? How will he pay his expenses? It wouldn't be fair to take these from the common pool.     660

PRAXAGORA: There won't be any lawsuits in the first place.

BLEPYROS: That statement will be your undoing!

NEIGHBOR: I think so too.

PRAXAGORA: But why should there be any lawsuits, poor dear?

BLEPYROS: For lots of reasons, by Apollo. To give just one example: when a     665
debtor refuses to repay.

PRAXAGORA: But where did the creditor get the money to lend? If all funds are common, he's got to be a thief!

NEIGHBOR: By Demeter, she's right!

BLEPYROS: But let her answer me this: a dinner party ends in assault; how are     670
the fighters going to pay their fines? I think I've got you in a corner now!

PRAXAGORA: They'll pay out of their own food-allowance. A decrease there will hit them right in the belly, so they'll think twice before they get rowdy again.

BLEPYROS: No more thieves, then?

PRAXAGORA: Of course not: why would anyone steal what he's got a share in?     675

BLEPYROS: No more muggers at night?

NEIGHBOR: Not if you sleep at home!

PRAXAGORA: Not even when you go out, as was previously the case. All will be content with their condition. If someone demands your cloak, let him have it. Why put up a fight? Go to the common store and get yourself a better one.     680

BLEPYROS: Won't people still gamble at dice?

PRAXAGORA: To win what?

BLEPYROS: And what standard of living will you establish?

PRAXAGORA: The same for all. I propose to remodel the city, knocking down all partitions and remodeling it into one big household, where everyone can come and go as they please. 685

BLEPYROS: And where will you serve dinner?

PRAXAGORA: I'll turn all the courthouses and porticoes into dining-rooms.

BLEPYROS: What will you do with the speakers' platforms?

PRAXAGORA: I'll use them to store mixing-bowls and water-jugs, and the children can use them to recite epics about brave men in battle—or about anyone who was cowardly, so he'll be ashamed to share the meal. 690

BLEPYROS: By Apollo, what a charming idea! And what will you do with the ballot boxes?

PRAXAGORA: I'll have them set up in the marketplace by Harmodios' statue and use them for allotment: everyone will draw his lot and go off happily to whatever place at table the lot assigns. Thus the Herald will instruct everyone with the letter R to proceed to dinner at the Royal Stoa; the Thetas will go to the appropriate place; the G's to the Grain Market. 695

BLEPYROS: G as in guzzle? 700

PRAXAGORA: No, as in gourmandize.

BLEPYROS: But the guy who draws a blank—will everyone push him away from the table?

PRAXAGORA: That won't happen with us, for we'll provide everything for everyone unstintingly. Every single man will go away drunk, with his garland still on and a torch in his hand, and as they go through the streets after dinner the ladies will accost them: "Come to my place! There's a fine young girl in here!" "And over here," another one will cry from a second-story window, "is a very fine and exquisitely pale girl! You may sleep with her after you've slept with me first!" And the inferior men will chase after the handsome young lads, saying "Hey you, where do you think you're running off to? You're not going to get anything anyway: the law says the ladies've got to fuck the pug-nosed and the ugly men first. Meanwhile you can grab the petals of your double-hung fig-branch and jerk off in the doorway!" So tell me, does my plan meet with your approval? 705 710 715

BLEPYROS AND NEIGHBOR: Absolutely![104]

PRAXAGORA: Then I'll be going off to the marketplace to receive the goods as they come in; I'll pick up a girl with a loud voice to be my crier; these are my duties as the woman elected to rule. I must also organize the communal dinners, and I'd like you to have your first banquet this very day.          720

BLEPYROS: The banquets are to start right away?

PRAXAGORA: That's what I'm telling you. Then I want to put a stop to all prostitution.

BLEPYROS: Why?

NEIGHBOR [indicating Praxagora and the Chorus]: That's obvious: so that these          725
women can have the best young men all to themselves!

PRAXAGORA: Correct. What's more, slave-girls will no longer be allowed to wear make-up and steal away the fond hearts of the free boys.[105] They'll be allowed to sleep only with slaves and may trim their pussies only in the style of a woollen barn-jacket![106]          730

BLEPYROS: Say, I'd like to tag along, right at your side, and share the spotlight, with people saying, "Look, that's none other than the Lady Commander's husband!"

[Praxagora and Blepyros depart for the marketplace.][107]

NEIGHBOR: As for me, if I'm to be taking my possessions to the marketplace, I'd better collect them all and take inventory of what I've got. [He goes into one          735
of the houses.]


## EPISODE[108]

[The Chorus sing a brief song, not preserved, after which the Neighbor comes out of his house, followed by two slaves who bring out household utensils and, on the Neighbor's instructions, line them up on the street outside the doorway.]

NEIGHBOR [addressing the utensils as if they were women forming up a festive procession]: You there, my pretty Miss Sifter, first of my possessions, come outside here prettily: you'll be the Basket-Bearer,[109] being well powdered—after emptying so many sacks of my flour! And who will be the Chair-Bearer? Miss Pot, come outside here. By Zeus, you're black! You must have boiled the concoction Lysikrates uses to dye his hair! This way, stand next to her; you're the          740
Maid-In-Waiting. Water-Bearer, bring this water-jug over here. And you come over here as Lyre-Player—since you've so often woken me up too early,

in the middle of the night, to go off to Assembly, with your morning tune.[110]
Whoever's got the Bowl come forward; bring the honeycombs, and put the
branches down beside them; bring out the Tripod and the Oil Flask. You may     745
now produce the little things: they'll be the rest of the parade.

[*As Neighbor forms up his line of goods, a citizen walks by and regards him scornfully.*]

SELFISH MAN: Imagine me turning in my stuff! I'd be a sorry excuse for a man,
and virtually brainless. Never, by Poseidon! First of all I'll have to test and
study the situation very carefully. On the strength of mere words I'm hardly
about to throw away the fruits of my sweat and thriftiness in this sort of     750
mindless way, not until I've made thorough inquiries about the entire affair.
[*Walking up to Neighbor.*] You there! What's the meaning of these utensils here?
Are you moving? Are you pawning them?

NEIGHBOR: Neither.

SELFISH MAN: Then why are they lined up like this? It's not a procession you     755
people are arranging for Hieron the auctioneer, is it?

NEIGHBOR: God no! We're getting them ready to go to the marketplace for
surrender to the polis: it's the law of the land.

SELFISH MAN: You mean to turn them in?

NEIGHBOR: Of course.     760

SELFISH MAN: Then, Zeus save us, you're a fool!

NEIGHBOR: How so?

SELFISH MAN: It's easy to see.

NEIGHBOR: Really? Am I not supposed to obey the law?

SELFISH MAN: The law? You're pitiful!     765

NEIGHBOR: The law that's been duly enacted!

SELFISH MAN: Duly enacted! How stupid can you get?

NEIGHBOR: Stupid?

SELFISH MAN: Well, aren't you? And not just stupid, but the most simple-
minded man in the world?     770

NEIGHBOR: Because I do what I'm told?

SELFISH MAN: So you think the man of sense ought to do what he's told?

NEIGHBOR: Above everything else.

SELFISH MAN: No, that's what the imbecile does!

NEIGHBOR: So you don't intend to turn in your goods?    775

SELFISH MAN: I intend to be cautious; first I want to see what everyone else does.

NEIGHBOR: Why, they're getting ready to turn in their goods, of course!

SELFISH MAN: Well, I'll believe it when I see it.

NEIGHBOR: That's what they're saying around town, anyway.    780

SELFISH MAN: Say it? Sure they will.

NEIGHBOR: They're promising to carry in their stuff personally.

SELFISH MAN: Promise? Sure they will.

NEIGHBOR: You'll be the death of me with your total skepticism!

SELFISH MAN: Be skeptical? Sure they will.    785

NEIGHBOR: Zeus destroy you!

SELFISH MAN: Destroy? Sure they will: the plan, that is! Look, do you really think that anyone with a brain is going to turn in their stuff? That's not in our national character!

NEIGHBOR: You mean, we should only take?    790

SELFISH MAN: Zeus, yes! The gods are the same way. Just look at their statues and you'll see that: whenever we pray to them to give us something, they stand there with their hands out, palm up, not to give us something but to get something from us!

NEIGHBOR: Listen, you nut, let me get on with my business here. These things    795
need to be packed. Where's the twine? [He and the slaves begin to wrap up the utensils.]

SELFISH MAN: You're really going to do it?

NEIGHBOR: Zeus yes. Look, I'm wrapping up these tripods here.

SELFISH MAN: What foolishness, not to wait and see what others are going to do, and then and only then—    800

NEIGHBOR: Do what?

SELFISH MAN:—wait a little longer, then put it off.

NEIGHBOR: The object being what?

SELFISH MAN: There might be an earthquake, or some ill-omened lightning, or a black cat darting across the street. That would put a stop to their depositions, you mental case!    805

NEIGHBOR: Well, wouldn't I be delighted if I waited and then found there was no more room to deposit this stuff!

SELFISH MAN: No more room! Don't worry, they'll take your deposit even if you wait a couple of days.    810

NEIGHBOR: What do you mean?

SELFISH MAN [indicating the spectators]: I know these people: they're quick to vote on something, then they turn around and refuse to abide by it.

NEIGHBOR: They'll bring in their stuff, my friend.

SELFISH MAN: And what if they don't?    815

NEIGHBOR: Don't worry, they will.

SELFISH MAN: I repeat, what if they don't?

NEIGHBOR: We'll fight them!

SELFISH MAN: And what if they outnumber you?

NEIGHBOR: I'll leave my stuff and go home.    820

SELFISH MAN: And if they sell your stuff?

NEIGHBOR: Blast you to bits!

SELFISH MAN: And if I'm blasted to bits?

NEIGHBOR: You'll be doing a great service.

SELFISH MAN: Do you really want to surrender your stuff?    825

NEIGHBOR: I do. [Indicating the spectators] And I see my own neighbors doing the same.

SELFISH MAN: Antisthenes would contribute his stuff—sure! It would suit him much better to take a month-long shit first!

NEIGHBOR: Damn!    830

SELFISH MAN: And Kallimachos the chorus-master: would he contribute anything?

NEIGHBOR: More than Kallias.

SELFISH MAN [to the spectators]: This guy's gonna lose everything he has!

NEIGHBOR: That's putting it pretty drastically.      835

SELFISH MAN: Not at all. As if I don't see decrees like this all the time! Don't you remember the one about salt imports?

NEIGHBOR: Sure.

SELFISH MAN: And how we voted in the matter of the bronze coinage—remember that?      840

NEIGHBOR: Yes, that was certainly bad for me! After I sold my grapes I shoved off with a mouthful of those coppers, over to the market for barley, and as soon as I held out my sack the crier yelled, "Bronze coins are no longer honored; we're back to silver now."

SELFISH MAN: And didn't we all recently swear that the polis would raise      845
talents from the two and a half percent tax levied by Heurippides?[111] And how Heurippides was everyone's golden boy? But finally we looked into the matter more carefully and it turned out to be just the same old story, a quite inadequate measure; then Heurippides became everyone's tar baby.

NEIGHBOR: But all that's different, sir: *we* were in power then; now the *women*      850
are.

SELFISH MAN: And I mean to keep an eye on them, by Poseidon, so they don't piss all over me!

NEIGHBOR: I don't know what you're going on about. [*To one of his slaves*] Boy, pick up that baggage.      855

[*Enter a female Herald.*]

HERALDESS [*to the spectators*]: Now hear this, all you citizens—you heard correctly: in the new arrangement *all* citizens are included: get a move on and go straight to the Lady Commander's place, where the luck of the draw will determine where each man among you will be dining. The tables are set and heaped high with every kind of goodie, and the dining couches are draped      860
with cushions and coverlets. They're mixing the wine in bowls, and the perfume-girls are standing by. The fish fillets are on the grill; they're spitting hares; the rolls are in the oven; they're weaving garlands; the desserts are baking; the little girls are boiling pots of pea soup. Smoios is with them, wearing his riding-suit, ready to lick at the women's boxes. And old man      865
Geron's there wearing a new suit and fashionable pumps, joking with another young blade; his old boots and shabby cloak lie discarded. This is what you're invited to: come along! The slaves are waiting with your daily bread: just open your mouths! [*Exit Heraldess.*]

SELFISH MAN: Well, if that's how things are going, I'm ready to go! Why stand    870
around here when the polis is throwing us a party?

NEIGHBOR: Just where do you think you're going, when you haven't turned in
your goods?

SELFISH MAN: To dinner!

NEIGHBOR: Oh no you don't! If the women have any sense they won't feed    875
you till you're paid up!

SELFISH MAN: Don't worry, I will be.

NEIGHBOR: When?

SELFISH MAN: I won't be holding anybody up.

NEIGHBOR: Meaning what?    880

SELFISH MAN: I mean that others are bound to turn their stuff in later than I
will.

NEIGHBOR: And you mean to go to dinner anyway?

SELFISH MAN: Sure! How can I help but go? All sensible people should
cooperate with the polis in any way they can.    885

NEIGHBOR: And what if the women won't let you in?

SELFISH MAN: I'll lower my head and charge them!

NEIGHBOR: And if they beat you like a slave?

SELFISH MAN: I'll sue them!

NEIGHBOR: And if they laugh at your threats?    890

SELFISH MAN: I'll stand in the doorway—

NEIGHBOR: And do what? Tell me!

SELFISH MAN:—and snatch the food that people come to turn in!

NEIGHBOR: In that case you'd better follow me in. [To the slaves] You there,
Sikon, and Parmenon too, hoist my estate.    895

SELFISH MAN: Let me help you.

NEIGHBOR: No, no thank you! I don't want to bring my contribution to the
Lady Commander and have you pretending that part of it's yours! [The
Neighbor and his slaves depart with the goods.]

SELFISH MAN: By Zeus, I need some kind of scheme to save the property I've    900
got while at the same time sharing in the goodies these people are getting.
[*He ponders.*] I think I've got it! I've got to run off to dinner with the rest of
them, and quick! [*Runs after the Neighbor.*]

[*Here the Chorus performed, but the text is not preserved.*]


## EPISODE[112]


[*In the doorway of one of the stage houses is an old woman, and at the upper window of the
house next door is a young girl; both look anxiously up and down the street.*]

FIRST OLD WOMAN: Where in the world are the men? Dinner must be over
by now! Here I am, all plastered with makeup and wearing my party dress,    905
just standing around, whistling myself a song, with my trap all set to catch
one of the men who walk by. Ye Muses, descend to these my lips with some
spicy Ionian tune!

GIRL: This time you've got downstairs ahead of me, old hag. You thought
you'd strip the vines when I wasn't looking and entice some guy with your    910
singing! If you try it, I'll sing a song of my own. And if the audience expects
this to be boring, I trust they'll find something sweet and comic in it anyway.

FIRST OLD WOMAN [*pointing to her rump*]: Put your complaints in here, and get
lost! [*To the flute-player in the orchestra*] You, my dear little piper, take up your
pipes and blow us the kind of tune that's wanted here.    915

    Whoever wants to have a good time,
he's gotta sleep with me!
Finesse dwells not in girls
but in grown-up women!
No one's readier than I    920
to take really good care
of the boyfriend I live with
and never fly off to another man.

GIRL:

    Don't despise the girls,
for softness resides    925
in their tender thighs
and blossoms on their boobs.
But you, old bag, tweeze your hair
and paint your face:
the Grim Reaper's heartthrob!    930

FIRST OLD WOMAN:

> I hope your twat falls off
> and when you hanker for humping
> you can't find your back seat!
> And in bed when you're ready for kissing          935
> I hope you open up your arms
> and hug a snake!

GIRL:

> Ah, what will become of me?
> My boyfriend hasn't come,
> I'm alone in the house,                            940
> my mother's gone out:
> need I say any more?
> Well, granny, you better call
> Doctor Dildo
> so you can enjoy yourself!                         945
> Pretty please!

FIRST OLD WOMAN:

> Poor thing, you're already
> itching for the Ionian toy,[113]
> and it looks like you also want
> to suck like the Lesbians.[114]                    950

GIRL:

> But you'll never snatch
> my boytoys away,
> nor spoil my youth
> or take it from me!

FIRST OLD WOMAN: Well, sing any tune you like and prowl around like a cat:  955
no man's going to visit you before me!

GIRL: Not for my funeral, anyway! That's a new one, old hag!

FIRST OLD WOMAN: Oh no: who can tell an old lady anything new? It's not
my age that'll hurt you.

GIRL: What then? Your makeup and rouge?                             960

FIRST OLD WOMAN: Are you still talking?

GIRL: Are you still hanging out of the doorway?

FIRST OLD WOMAN: Me? I'm singing for my sweetheart Epigenes.

GIRL: You've got a sweetheart? You must mean Father Time!

FIRST OLD WOMAN: Even you'll have to admit it, since he'll soon be coming to     965
see me! [*Epigenes, wearing his banquet garland and holding a torch, walks tipsily up the street.*] In fact, here he comes now!

GIRL: Not for you, old pest; he's got no business there!

FIRST OLD WOMAN: Au contraire, miss twiggy!

GIRL: You'll see I'm right, you moldy old hag; I'm going inside! [*She disappears*     970
*from the window.*]

FIRST OLD WOMAN: Me too; you'll see that my confidence is much more
justified than yours! [*She ducks inside the door, but comes out again as soon as the Girl is gone.*]

EPIGENES:[115]
How I wish I could sleep with the girl     975
and not have to bang a pug-nosed crone first!
That doesn't sit well with a free man!

FIRST OLD WOMAN [*unheard by Epigenes*]:
You'll bang to your sorrow then, by Zeus;
the days of Charixene are past![116]     980
If this is still a democracy,
we've got to do it legal and proper!
But I'll go inside to see what he's going to do. [*She ducks inside again, but leaves the door slightly ajar.*]

EPIGENES: Ye gods, just let me get the pretty girl alone! It's her I got drunk to     985
visit and her I've so long been longing for!

GIRL [*appearing in her window*]: I've completely fooled the damnable old thing;
she's gone inside, thinking that I'm going to stay inside. But here's the very
boy we were talking about!
Hither now, hither now,     990
my dear one,
come to me and be
my bedmate tonight!
A powerful passion
sets me awhirl     995
for your curly hair!
What is this strange longing
that attacks me and holds me

in its grinding grip?
Release me, Eros, I beg you!                                    1000
Please make this boy
come to my very own bed!

EPIGENES:
Hither now, hither now,
my dear one,
run to the door for me                                         1005
and open it wide!
If you don't I'll fall down
and die!
I want to lie in your lap
and play see-saw with your butt!                               1010
Aphrodite, why have you driven
me mad for this girl?
Release me, Eros, I beg you!
Please make this girl
come to my very own bed!                                       1015
And yet nothing I've said
comes near to matching my need!
I beg you, dearest,
open the door for me,
throw your arms around me;                                     1020
I'm hurting for you!
Oh my gold-bauble delight,
flower of Aphrodite,
honeybee of the Muses,
child of the Graces,                                           1025
personification of utter
voluptuousness,
open the door for me,
throw your arms around me;
I'm hurting for you!                                           1030

[He knocks at the Girl's door, but before she can come down to him the First Old Woman bursts from her doorway and accosts him.]

FIRST OLD WOMAN: Hey you, what's this knocking? Looking for me, are you?

EPIGENES [recoiling]: Surely you jest!

FIRST OLD WOMAN: Yes you are; you were banging on my door!

EPIGENES: I'll be damned if I was!

FIRST OLD WOMAN: Well, what *is* your business, then, with the torch and all?     1035

EPIGENES: I'm looking for a fellow from Wankton.

FIRST OLD WOMAN: Which one?

EPIGENES: Not Mr. Humpus, whom *you're* perhaps expecting.

FIRST OLD WOMAN [*seizing him by the arm*]: By Aphrodite, whether you like it
or not—     1040

EPIGENES [*shaking her off*]: Wait, I'm not in your jurisdiction; the statute of
limitations is sixty years! You're tabled. I'm involved only in cases under
twenty!

FIRST OLD WOMAN: That might have been true under the old system, my
sweet; but according to current law you've got to deal with *me* first.     1045

EPIGENES: When gambling it's legal to pass the deal.

FIRST OLD WOMAN: You didn't obey that law when you had your dinner.

EPIGENES: I don't know what you're talking about. I've got to bang on this
door.

FIRST OLD WOMAN [*pointing to her crotch*]: Not until you bang this one first!     1050

EPIGENES: No thanks, I don't need a bucket just now.

FIRST OLD WOMAN: I know you like me; you were just surprised to see me
here. Come on, give us a kiss.

EPIGENES [*retreating*]: No! I'm, ah, terrified of your lover!

FIRST OLD WOMAN: Who's that?     1055

EPIGENES: The best-selling painter.

FIRST OLD WOMAN: Who are you talking about?

EPIGENES: The one who decorates funeral urns. Better get out of here before
he spots you in the doorway!

FIRST OLD WOMAN: I know what you want, I know!     1060

EPIGENES: And I know what *you* want, by Zeus!

FIRST OLD WOMAN: By Aphrodite, who gave me the luck of the draw, I'm not
giving you up!

EPIGENES: You're a crazy old lady!

FIRST OLD WOMAN [*waggling her fingers at him*]: Nonsense! I'm personally     1065
going to escort you to my bed!

EPIGENES: Why do we need tongs for our buckets, when we could run a crone
like this down the well and use her to haul them up?

FIRST OLD WOMAN: Very funny, my boy! But you just get over here to my
place!     1070

EPIGENES: No! I don't have to obey you unless you've paid the polis the 2% tax
on me.

FIRST OLD WOMAN: By Aphrodite, you do too! I just *love* sleeping with boys
your age!

EPIGENES: And I just *hate* sleeping with women your age! I'll never consent.     1075

FIRST OLD WOMAN [*producing a piece of paper*]: This will make you, by Zeus!

EPIGENES: What is it?

FIRST OLD WOMAN: The regulation that says you've got to come to me.

EPIGENES: Tell me what in the world it says.

FIRST OLD WOMAN: All right, I shall. [*Reading*] The women have decreed: "if a     1080
young man desires a young woman he may not hump her until he first bangs
an old woman. Should he in his desire for the young woman refuse to do this
preliminary banging, the older women shall be entitled with impunity to
drag off the young man by his pecker."

EPIGENES: Dear me, this very day I'm to be Prokrustes![117]     1085

FIRST OLD WOMAN: Our laws must be obeyed!

EPIGENES: What if one of my fellow demesmen or friends comes and goes bail
for me?

FIRST OLD WOMAN: No man is any longer permitted to transact business over
the one-bushel limit![118]     1090

EPIGENES: Can't I swear off my duty?

FIRST OLD WOMAN: You can't squirm out of this duty!

EPIGENES: I'll get myself exempted as a merchant.

FIRST OLD WOMAN: You'll be sorry if you do!

EPIGENES: So what am I to do?                                                    1095

FIRST OLD WOMAN: Follow me into my house.

EPIGENES: Is it a necessity?

FIRST OLD WOMAN: Diomedes' necessity![119]

EPIGENES:[120] In that case, begin by strewing the bier with marjoram and four
broken vine-branches as kindling, and deck it with ribbons, and put the urn     1100
beside it, and set the water-jug outside the door.

FIRST OLD WOMAN: Surely you're going to buy me a wedding garland too.

EPIGENES: Yes, by Zeus, provided I can find a waxen one somewhere,[121]
because I think you're going to disintegrate pretty quick in there!

[As the First Old Woman draws Epigenes into her house, the Girl emerges from her doorway.]

GIRL: Where are you dragging him off to?                                          1105

FIRST OLD WOMAN: I'm bringing my own man home!

GIRL: That's not very prudent. He's the wrong age to be sleeping with you—
you're more his mother than his wife! If you old women start enforcing a
law like this, you'll fill the whole country up with Oedipuses![122] [She steps
between Epigenes and the First Old Woman.]                                        1110

FIRST OLD WOMAN: You dirty slut, you've thought up this objection out of
pure envy. But I'll make you pay for it. [She goes into her house.]

EPIGENES [embracing the Girl]: By Zeus the Savior, sweetest, you've done me a
favor by getting that crone off my back! When the lights are out I'll slip you a
big, juicy token of my gratitude! [The Girl leads him toward her door.]          1115

[Enter a Second Old Woman, older and uglier than the First.]

SECOND OLD WOMAN [to the Girl]: Hey you! Where are you taking him, in
violation of the law? It's clearly stated that he's got to sleep with me first.

EPIGENES: Good grief! Where did you pop out of, you apparition of
damnation! This one's even more revolting than the last one!

SECOND OLD WOMAN: Get over here!                                                  1120

EPIGENES [to the Girl, who runs in terror back to her own house]: Don't let her drag me
away, I beg you!

SECOND OLD WOMAN: Not I but the law drags you away!

EPIGENES: No, some kind of Empousa[123] covered with one big blood-blister!

SECOND OLD WOMAN [*pushing him along the stage*]: Come along, you sissy. This    1125
way. Make it snappy and no back talk!

EPIGENES: Wait! May I go to the bathroom first? It would help me get hold of
myself. If you don't let me, I'll do something right here and you'll soon see
me go brown with fear!

SECOND OLD WOMAN: Buck up and get moving. You can shit when we get in    1130
the house.

EPIGENES: I'm afraid alright: afraid that I'll shit more than I want! But I'll be
glad to deposit two valuable sureties with you (*indicating his testicles*).

SECOND OLD WOMAN [*giving him a shove*]: Don't bother.

[*Enter a Third Old Woman, older and uglier than the Second.*]

THIRD OLD WOMAN [*to Epigenes, whose back is turned*]: Hey you! Where are you    1135
going with her?

EPIGENES: I'm not going anywhere; I'm being kidnapped! But whoever you
are, bless you if you don't just stand by while I'm being tormented! [*He turns
and takes a good look at the Third Old Woman.*] Herakles! Pan! Korybantes!
Dioskouroi! That one's much more revolting than this one! Please, someone    1140
tell me what in the world it is! A monkey plastered with makeup? A crone
arisen from the underworld?

THIRD OLD WOMAN [*taking hold of Epigenes' arm*]: Cut the jokes and follow me.

SECOND OLD WOMAN [*holding onto Epigenes; other arm*]: Oh no you don't. This
way!    1145

THIRD OLD WOMAN: I'm never letting you go!

SECOND OLD WOMAN: Me neither!

EPIGENES: You're going to rip me in half, you hellbound creatures!

SECOND OLD WOMAN: The law says you've got to follow me!

THIRD OLD WOMAN: No it doesn't, not if an even uglier old woman appears.    1150

EPIGENES: If I'm to be miserably destroyed by you two, tell me how I'm
supposed to get to that pretty girl?

THIRD OLD WOMAN: That's your problem. [*She makes a sexual gesture.*] Just now
you've got to do this.

EPIGENES: So which of you do I have to poke first in order to get away?     1155

THIRD OLD WOMAN: Isn't it plain? Come this way!

EPIGENES: Then make this other one let go of me!

SECOND OLD WOMAN: No! He's coming this way with me!

EPIGENES: If she'll let go!

THIRD OLD WOMAN: By Zeus, I will not!     1160

SECOND OLD WOMAN: Nor will I!

EPIGENES: You two are rough enough to be ferryboat captains!

SECOND OLD WOMAN: How's that?

EPIGENES: You'd fight over your passengers hard enough to wear them out!

THIRD OLD WOMAN: Shut up and get moving. This way!     1165

SECOND OLD WOMAN: No, this way!

EPIGENES: This is obviously Kannonos' Law put into practice: I've got to appear in custody before the people and fuck my accusers![124] But how can I manage to man both boats with a single oar?

SECOND OLD WOMAN: Just fine—after you've wolfed down a potful of love-     1170 bulbs!

[Both old women try to pull Epigenes through the same doorway.]

EPIGENES: Ah what a sorry end! I'm poised on the very threshold, and getting shoved!

THIRD OLD WOMAN: That's not going to save you, because I'm going to follow you right in.     1175

EPIGENES: Gods, no! Better to grapple with one evil than two!

THIRD OLD WOMAN: By Hekate, you've got no choice in the matter.

EPIGENES [to the spectators]: Ah, thrice ill-fated me, that must fuck a decrepit woman all night and all day, and after I've got free of her, to start in again on an old toad with a funeral urn already standing by her chops! Am I not then     1180 ill-fated? Nay, a man heavily doomed, by Zeus the Savior, and unlucky, that shall be closeted with such wild beasts as these! But if the very worst really does befall me as I sail into port atop these two floozies, bury me right where I penetrated the channel. [Indicating the Third Old Woman] As for her, while she's

still alive, cover her with pitch all over and put her feet in molten lead up to    1185
her ankles, then stick her over my grave instead of an urn!

[*The two Old Women drag Epigenes into the house and slam the door behind them.*]


## EPISODE

[*A tipsy Maid enters and walks up to Praxagora's house.*]

MAID: Blessed is our citizenry, favored is our land, and most blessed is our
    mistress herself, as are you women who stand at our door, and all the
    neighbors and fellow demesmen, and me too, the maid, with my head
    perfumed with fine perfumes, Zeus be praised! But those nice little bottles of    1190
    Thasian wine have a much greater impact than all these fragrances: it stays in
    your head a long time, while those others lose their bouquet and completely
    evaporate. So it's far the best, yes, by far, the gods be praised! Pour me a cup
    neat! It makes women merry all night when we pick out the one with the
    best bouquet![125] [*To the Chorus*] Women, tell me where master is, I mean my    1195
    mistress' husband.

CHORUS-LEADER: If you wait right there you're bound to run into him. That's
    right, here he is on his way to dinner.

[*Blepyros enters with his arms around two young girls and walks by the house.*]

MAID: Oh master! You happy and three-times lucky man!

BLEPYROS: Who, me?    1200

MAID: Sure you, by Zeus, and like nobody else in the world! Who could be
    luckier? Out of more than thirty thousand citizens you're the only one who
    hasn't had dinner!

CHORUS-LEADER: Yes, he's a lucky fellow, you're quite right.

MAID: Hey, where can you be off to now?    1205

BLEPYROS: Why, I'm off to dinner.

MAID: By Aphrodite, you're absolutely the last one. Still, your wife told
    me to gather you up and escort you and these girls you've got with you.
    There's some Chian wine left over and some other good stuff. So don't be
    late. And any of you spectators who favor us, and any of you judges who's    1210
    not looking elsewhere for a winner, come along with us! We'll supply
    everything.

**BLEPYROS**: Why don't you address all of them, like a lady, leaving no one out? Be liberal, invite the old man, the boy, the little child: there's dinner specially made for all of them—if they hurry home! Me, I'm shoving off to my dinner 1215 now; [indicating one of the girls] and fortunately I've got this little torch here to light my way!

**CHORUS-LEADER**: Then why waste time here? Come on, take these girls and get going! And while you're going offstage, I'll sing a little tune anticipating our dinner! [Blepyros, the Maid and the girls descend from the stage into the orchestra.] 1220 But first I want to make a small suggestion to the judges: if you're sage judges, declare me the winner by virtue of my sagacity; if you're after humor, declare me the winner by virtue of my jokes. Thus it's virtually all of you that I'm asking to vote for me. And don't hold it against me that the luck of the draw has put me onstage first. So, bearing all this in mind, don't break your 1225 oath, but always judge the choruses fairly. Don't act like dishonest whores, who only remember their latest customers!

**CHORUS**:
> Hey, hey, it's time, dear ladies,
> to shake a leg and hop off to dinner,
> if we mean to do it at all. 1230
> So everyone move your feet
> to a Cretan tune!

**BLEPYROS**: That's what I'm doing!

**CHORUS**:
> And these women here,
> with their wonderfully lithe bodies, 1235
> encourage them to move their gams
> rapidly to the rhythm of the dance!
> For soon there'll be served
> limpets and saltfish and sharksteak and dogfish
> and mullets and oddfish with savory pickle-sauce 1240
> and thrushes with blackbirds and various pigeons
> and roosters and pan-roasted wagtails and larks
> and nice chunks of hare marinated in mulled wine
> and all of it drizzled with honey and silphium
> and vinegar, oil and spices galore![126] 1245
> Now that you've heard what awaits you,
> grab your dish double-quick,
> get a move on to dinner—

and don't forget some porridge:
you might need it!                                               1250

BLEPYROS: I'm sure that they're stuffing it in.

CHORUS [*exiting behind Blepyros, the Maid and the girls, all dancing gaily*]:
Lift your legs aloft, hey hey,
We're off to dinner, hoy hoy,
and victory, hurray!                                             1255
Hurray hurrah!

# Appendix

## *Selected Fragments of Lost Plays*

Here is a selection of fragments bearing on women from Aristophanes' (Ar.'s) lost plays, using the Greek text and numbering of R. Kassel and C. Austin, eds., *Poetae Comici Graeci* III.2 (Berlin/New York 1984); when something is known about the date, plot or characters of a play I have given a brief synopsis.

Aside from a few scraps of papyrus, most of the fragments of Ar. and other comic poets come from ancient works of scholarship whose authors quote from plays now lost to us. Sometimes the authors tell us something about the plot or characters of the play they are quoting, or drop other hints about how to interpret the quotations, but for the most part the context of a fragment must be inferred from the fragment itself or from other fragments cited from the same play; when that can be done at all, the inferences are usually tentative to some degree. Still, it is worthwhile to be aware, as much as possible, of Ar.'s dramatic range beyond the eleven extant plays, and to that extent the fragments assist us in forming a more comprehensive picture of his artistry.

## AIOLOSIKON I/II

The title suggests that Sikon played the role of the mythical Aiolos in parody of Euripides' play of that name, which portrayed as incestuous the marriage of Aiolos' six sons to his six daughters (cf. Homer *Od.* 10.8–9). The chorus contained women (fr. 9) but there may have been a semichorus of men (Aiolos' sons and daughters?), as in *Lysistrata*. Herakles seems to have been a character.

Two versions of *Aiolosikon* were known in antiquity. The date of the first production is unknown; the date of the second, the last play of Ar. ever produced, was after *Kokalos* (Dionysia of 387).

1

Back from the bakery of Thearion I come,
where lie the abodes of ovens[1]

2

But hurry up: no more delay, so I can shop
for everything you'll want, woman.

6

One bed and one bath will be enough for all the women[2]

8

And we see everything,
as in a new lantern,
shining through the cloak[3]

9

Not without reason, women,
are the men always belaboring us
with every sort of abuse:
for when we do dire deeds
they always catch us out.


## AMPHIARAOS

A man and his wife visit the oracular and healing shrine of the Theban hero
Amphiaraos, probably in Oropos (on the Attic-Boiotian frontier, and at this time
subject to Athens), and there undergo incubation and a strenuous cure for some
(sexual?) ailment. *Amphiaraos* was produced at the Lenaia of 414.

17

(A)    Woman, what was it made that noise?
(B)                                            The hen
       knocked over the wine-cup.
(A)    She'll be sorry for that!

18

By Zeus, fetch us out of the bedroom
a cushion and a pillow, the linen ones.

21

Scholion Ar. *Plutus* 701: Iaso, named for her healing function, served Asklepios,
but Ar. called her also the daughter of Amphiaraos in those lines:

But, my daughter Iaso, I spoke propitiously[4]

25

I'm bringing him this meat from someone's wife

## OLD AGE

The chorus seems to have been composed of old men who are rejuvenated and then behave like licentious youths. The only indication of the production year might be the mention of *kleroteria* (allotment-machines), if these were introduced in connection with the new system of seat-allocation in the Council chamber that was introduced in 410/09.

131

you[5] should've been cast into Halmyrides[6]
and not have caused trouble for this daughter of yours

136

she, having uncovered a bowl of gruel

137

she, having taken a position on the walk by the tenement

140

a girl raised on gray-skinned sprats[7]

144

Scholion Nikandros *Theriaca* 295 ("short cruise"): Ar. *Old Age* has a woman drawn by a span of asses and brings on a lover of hers, whom she excites by saying:

(A)   Are you truly cruising away?
(B)                                             To the bridegroom
       I'm to marry today.

146

the old man's [like] a girl trading thrusts with some boy's balls[8]

147

bend in the rhythm of a wagtail-strut[9]

148

Old man, do you fancy the call girls who are ripe,
or the fresh ones who are firm as salted olives?

## DAIDALOS

Zeus makes use of the arts of Daidalos in an erotic adventure (with Leda?). The date of production is unknown.

191

all wives without exception are alike
in having an adulterer ready as a side-dish

193

Athenaios 9.374C: The ancients used "cock" also for "hen": Ar. *Daidalos:*

she's laid a huge egg, like a cock

194

it happens that many cocks by necessity
often lay wind-eggs[10]

## DIONYSOS SHIPWRECKED

iii. Life of Aristophanes (Testimony 1.59): Ar. wrote 44 plays, four of which are said to be spurious . . . *Poetry, Shipwrecked, Islands* and *Niobos*, written, some say, by Archippos.

277

why, wicked man, are you banging me like
a buggy cot?[11]

## PEACE II

Ar. wrote two plays entitled *Peace*. Only one—the extant play that won the second prize at the Dionysia of 421—was preserved in the library at Alexandria. In the lost play the goddess Agriculture was a character with a speaking part (fr. 305): evidently Ar. had decided not to repeat his earlier portrayal of the goddess Peace as a mute statue, an idea ridiculed by rival comic poets (Eupolis, fr. 62 and Platon, fr. 86).

305

(A)    Of Peace, so dear to all mankind,
        a faithful nurse, housekeeper, helper, steward,
        daughter and sister: all these she had in me.
(B)    So what is your name?
(A)                                            Mine? Agriculture.

## WOMEN AT THE THESMOPHORIA II

Whereas the extant *Women at the Thesmophoria* (Dionysia 411) is set on the second day of Thesmophoria, a day of fasting, this play is set on the festive third day; Demetrios of Troizen called it *Women Who Have Celebrated the Thesmophoria* (test. ii). A date after 411 is suggested by an allusion to Euripides' *Antiope*, and a date before 405 by ridicule of Agathon (who emigrated to Macedonia in that year). Evidently this play was not a reworking of the earlier play but either a sequel to the earlier play (whose ending leaves open that possibility) or an entirely new one.

### 331

Scholion Ar. *Women at the Thesmophoria* 298 (Kalligeneia): a deity associated with Demeter, whom he makes prologue-speaker in the second *Women at the Thesmophoria*. Photios 127.8 Kalligeneia: Apollodoros makes her the earth (244 F 141 Jacoby), others the daughter of Zeus and Demeter, Ar. the comic poet Demeter's nurse.

### 332

(A)    razor, mirror, scissors, wax, soap,
        wig, dress-trimmings, headbands, barrettes,
        rouge—sheer devastation![12]—white face-powder,
        perfume, pumice-stone, brassiere, hairnet,
        veil, orchil paint, necklaces, mascara,
        soft gown, hellebore, hairnet,
        slip, shawl, negligé, bordered robe, long gown,
        the stocks, death-pit![13] striped jacket, curling-iron.
        I haven't come to the best of this stuff.
(B)                              What's next?
(A)    Earrings, set gems, hoops, choker, cluster-pin,
        bracelet, brooches, wrist-band, necklaces, anklets,
        signets, chains, rings, plasters,
        bubble-hats, brassieres, dildoes, carnelians,
        leis, hoops, and lots of other things that
        you[14] couldn't name if you tried.

### 333

(A)    Has anyone bought seafood, a cuttlefish
        or jumbo prawns or octopus?
        Or is a dogfish being roasted or a mullet or squids?

(B)    No indeed, by Zeus.
(A)                                        No ray?
(B)                                                        I must say no.
(A)    No haggis, then, or beestings or boar-liver
       or honeycombs or pork belly,
       no eel or crayfish? Great had been
       your[15] aid to tired women if there were.

### 334
I won't permit the drinking of Pramnian wine
nor Chian, nor Thasian, nor Peparethian,
nor any other that will rouse the boffing-ram.

### 335
                              With great benefits for the city
they say the Amphictyonic delegates have returned,
from Pylaea, and the Sacred Remembrancer

### 336
Most holy Zeus, how the blasted leather purse,
as soon as I opened it, blew at me a stench
of perfume and hazelwort

### 337
So much superfluous stuff they[16] had,
so many attachments they decked themselves with

### 338
she undid the flap of her girlish shirt
and the bands that held her little titties

### 341
and, in the manner of Agathon, a shaven antithesis[17]

### 344
I want to mount the woman[18]

### 348
nor summon the curly-tressed Muses
nor yell for the Olympian Graces to the dance,
for our producer says they're already present

### 352
Athenaios 14.619A: another kind of song is sung by women winnowing, as Ar.
in *Women at the Thesmophoria*.

355

Anonymous commentator on Aristotle's *Nikomachean Ethics*, *CAG* 20.200.10 Heylb: *Baukides*, a kind of Ionic shoe worn by Ionian women, which Ar. also mentions in *Women at the Thesmophoria*.

356

Antiatticist 88.28: "Converse with": Ar. in *Women at the Thesmophoria*. Pollux 2.125. Hypereides (fr. 171 Bl.-J.) uses "converse with" of sexual intercourse, and Ar. as well.

358

Hesychios λ 224: "Play the Lakonian": use boys. Ar. in the second *Women at the Thesmophoria*.

## KOKALOS

The story of Kokalos, King of Kamikos in Sicily, was treated in Sophokles' play *Kamikoi*. Daidalos, escaping from Crete, took refuge with Kokalos, who refused to surrender him to Minos and his army. Kokalos' daughters, charmed by Daidalos' art, contrived to kill Minos in his bath. The *Life* says that "Ar. gave the first example of the style of New Comedy in *Kokalos*, which both Menander and Philemon took as their starting point as dramatists" (4–6) and that the plot contained "rape, recognition and all the other elements that Menander imitated" (50–51).

The play was produced by Ar.'s son Araros at the Dionysia of 387 and won first prize.

364

and others, some rather old bags,
got a bottle of vintage red Thasian,
and with oversized ladles poured it
pell-mell right into their skins,
overcome with lust for the dark
unmixed wine

370

Stephen of Byzantium 374.5. To play the Korinthian is to consort with prostitutes, from the prostitutes of Korinth, or to be a procurer: Ar. in *Kokalos*.

## LEMNIAN WOMEN

Aischylos, Sophokles and Euripides each treated the story of Hypsipyle, who saved her father, King Thoas, and fell in love with Jason, when the other women of Lemnos killed their husbands. If fr. 373 ridicules the etymology of Thoas' name given in E.'s *Iphigeneia among the Taurians* (line 32), a date after 410 is probable.

### 373

here reigned the sire of Hypsipyle as king:
Thoas, the slowest runner of all mankind[19]

### 374

they did away with the men who had got them children

### 375

every colonnade[20] swarms with alien men

### 376

why, just now I left her soaping herself
in the bath

### 378

while her bloom is at its very peak

### 382

*Etymologicum Genuinum* AB, Hesychios δ 2230: *Doriallos* or *dorillos* in Ar. is used of the female genitals, to insult the tragedian Dorillos.[21]

the women fence off their pussy shelleys

### 383

Pollux 9.126 on the game "five-stones" (resembling jacks) played mostly by women:

<playing> five-stones with bits of a broken pot

### 384

Photios 251.7: Ar. in *Lemnian Women*, perhaps meaning Bendis, for she was Thracian:

the Great Goddess[22]

### 386

Harpokration 58.4: To serve as a bear: ... of maidens consecrated before marriage to Munichian or Brauronian Artemis ... because such maidens are called "bears," as in Euripides' *Hypsipyle* (fr. 767 N.), Ar.'s *Lemnian Women* and *Lysistrata* (645).

## POESY[23]

466
<through>all of Greece
seeking the woman[24] we've come to this place;
they say she's here with you: her[
                    ]and you will be pleasing th[
                    ]of some, you're well aware[
                            ]hot coal[
                            ]by Zeus, that[
                    ]       ?       [
                            ]deeds and the[
                            ]say to you all[
                            ]she for whose sake [we've come
                            ]said she was wronged[
                            ]then I[
                            ]the woman wronged[
                            ]we think it's in your [interest


## WOMEN CLAIMING TENT-SITES

Spectators at festivals who lacked local accommodation might erect temporary shelters. In this play women compete with men over such shelters at a festival which the fragments suggest is theatrical; this may perhaps count as evidence that women did attend performances of drama. The speaker of fr. 488 is said by its testimonium to represent Ar. himself; if so, this is the only such self-reference in Ar. outside a parabasis other than in *Acharnians* 377–82, 497–503, where the character Dicaeopolis speaks for Ar.; it is possible that in this play Ar., like Cratinus in *Flagon*, was a character. There is no firm evidence for dating the play.

487
the carrying-flask—
three-quart capacity, ceramic, fine quality—
that I'd gotten for company while I watched the show

489
yet listen, woman, with anger put aside,
without heartburn, and be yourself the judge

490
just as in *Kallipides*[25]
I'm sitting in the garbage on the ground

494
they call the strumpet the Leopardess

496
but you've got to draw your buttocks in

497
s/he's as punctured as a sieve

503
Hesychios t 1451: "third-row choruswoman" in Ar.'s *Women Claiming Tent-Sites*. Pollux 4.106: (choristers) standing on the right, standing on the left, standing in the second row, standing in the third row, and Ar. calls a woman "third-row choruswoman."

## TRIPHALES

The title means "Three-Phallused." The fragments suggest a date after 411.
iv. Lucian *Fugitives* 32: (A) There's a book, sir, called *Trikranos (Three-Headed)*. (B) That's nothing; there's also one called *Triphales (Three-Phallused)*.

560
I/they asked the women for a little money

561
now she had three tube-holders instead of one

562
Scholion Plato *Phaidon* 72C: In Ar.'s *Triphales* . . . the woman giving birth to Triphales says

take hold of me; the time is near

## PHOENICIAN WOMEN

Apparently a send-up of Euripides' play of the same title, which was produced after *Andromeda* (412) and before *Orestes* (408).

573

and lamp that by night
restrainest the flame
on my lampstand

## FRAGMENTS OF UNSPECIFIED PLAYS

592[26]
(12–31)

(A)    insulted[27] (fem. pl.).
(B)                        No, by Zeus; I [have an idea.
        If we've got sense we'll look for [a way to stop]
        these men from any longer [
(A)    What's to be done?
(B)                        Look, [answer me this:]
        what's the thing they say the Milesian women
        use to play with themselves, the leather thing?
(A)    Nonsense and inanity [full of] outrageousness,
        and shameful too, and [very] laughable.
        Whenever they use one of them it's just like using one
        of those so-called wind-eggs: nary a chick inside.
        That's the way it is with this too: [whenever hubby's away,]
        that's what it's for, and it's a lot of botheration.
(B)    But still they say the thing is very like
        a genuine pecker.
(A)                        Sure it is, my dear,
        as the moon is to the sun: same general hue
        when you look at it, but no heat at all.
(B)    And isn't that fitting?
(A)                        [
(B)    Well, what if we share the matter in hand
        with the slaves? Secretly [
(A)    I wouldn't [                          ] ahead of her
        (32–39)
                        ]                    [
                ]rather tragic[
                ]outside[
bring out what Agathon calls "light-bringing pines"
    ]
    ]

]god
]in songs

## 596

Euripides *Life* 6: He mocked women through his poems for the following reason. He had a home-bred slave-boy named Kephisophon, with whom he caught his own wife misbehaving. At first he tried to make her mend her ways, but when he failed to persuade her he gave up the woman to him, since Kephisophon was willing to take her. As Ar. also says,

> finest and swarthiest of men, Kephisophon,
> you lived for the most part with Euripides
> and helped him compose his arias, they say

## 599

> and other girls sprout beans upon their chests,
> and are just about ready to fly off toward the men

## 604

Aristophanes *Life* 55: He passed away leaving three children . . . but some say two, Philippos and Araros, whom he himself mentions:

> my wife
> I'm ashamed to face, and the two infant children
>     perhaps speaking of them

## 608

Eustathios *Odyssey* 1467.36: Hekate's images are bitches, for these are sacrificed to her, they say, and she is also portrayed as having a bitch's face; Ar.:

> a prickly-tempered bitch,
> the image of light-bearing Hekate I'll become[28]

## 616

> for a young wife an old husband is a disgrace

## 623

> you'll pit a sour-sweet pomegranate then[29]

## 662

> but truly he will betroth to you
> the beautiful girl

## 664

> my brassiere unfastened,
> out fell my nuts

676

I'll be beaten till the lint flies off my sweater[30]

715

you who on fragrant
coverlets spend the night
humping the mistress

721

Hesychios ι 835 (Hippokleides): Ar. impishly refers to the female genitals by this name.

## OF DUBIOUS ATTRIBUTION

926

I'm afraid that Ariphrades will grate our business for us[31]

928

the voyage to Korinth is not for every man[32]

961

I've got four women sitting idle

# Notes

## Introduction

1. Attika was divided into 139 demes, semi-autonomous communities each belonging to one of ten tribes and serving as the political district of its citizens.

2. For full details and ancient testimonia about these festivals see Pickard-Cambridge 1988, Csapo/Slater 1995, P. Wilson 2007.

3. On this material, which has roots in fertility cults (particularly those of Dionysos and Demeter), see Henderson 1991; on its abusive and satirical functions see Edwards 1991; on Aristophanes' language generally, see Willi 2003.

4. For a political history of this period see Ostwald 1986; for theatrical festivals as a venue for experimental politics see Longo 1990; and for a detailed analysis of comedy as a privileged extension of political debate see Henderson 1990, 2007.

5. Women occupied some of these religious positions: see *Lysistrata*, Introduction 2, Connelly 2007.

6. For a full account of the history and operation of the choregic system see Wilson 2000.

7. On carnival and Old Comedy see Edwards 1993, Platter 2007; on comedy and ritual laughter see Halliwell 2008:206–14.

8. For the composition of the audience at the Dionysia see III, below, and Henderson 1991b, 1998–2007 I:19–22, Sommerstein 1998b; for theatrical rituals, see Chaniotis 2007.

9. On the phallephoria and associated rituals see Cole 1993.

10. For a survey and interpretation of these features see Henderson 1991.

11. See Halliwell 2002, 2008:242–63. Attic visual art of the late archaic period is also rich in erotic themes: for a survey see Kilmer 1993.

12. The anti-democratic pamphleteer known as the "Old Oligarch" (Pseudo-Xenophon, *Constitution of the Athenians*), writing c. 425 BCE, claims that while the comic poets criticised prominent individuals, they did not criticize the demos (2.18).

13. For discussion see Wallace 1994a and 1994b, Henderson 1998.

14. Contrast the criticisms of the demos and of democracy that are found in such non-public writings as Thucydides' *History* and the works of Plato.

15. During the Peloponnesian War the number of comedies may have been reduced to three, though this is uncertain.

16. For review and discussion of the evidence for women's attendance see Henderson 1991a; for a much more cautious response, inclining toward women's nonattendance, see Goldhill 1994, though his attempt to discredit the Platonic testimony is unconvincing (the principal texts are *Gorgias* 502b–d and *Laws* 658a–d) and his emphasis on the theater as civic (and therefore male) space neglects its festive/religious dimension.

17. See MacDowell 1995:257–58. For a critique of the attempt by Taafe 1993 to find comic rupture of this illusion see Gilbert 1995.

18. Thus the employment of approaches from film criticism, with its emphasis on close-ups and directorial shaping of the viewer's gaze, to analyze Aristophanic comedy is inappropriate.

19. See Schaps 1977, Sommerstein 1980. For the important dichotomy between public and private in Athenian life see IV, below.

20. See Thucydides 2.45.2 (Perikles' plea for public decorum to the war-bereaved women), with Kallet-Marx 1993.

21. Taking the advice of a woman could indeed be cited in court to prove an opponent's incompetence: Demosthenes 46.16, Isokrates 2.20.

22. In general see Stone 1981.

23. The phallos, in addition to being a traditional element of comic and satyric costumes, was a traditional symbol of fertility and masculine power, and it was especially associated with the worship of Dionysos; on the *phallephoria* see II, above.

24. There was no ancient counterpart of the "choral speaking" often heard in modern performances of Greek drama.

25. For a selection of epitaphs see Lattimore 1942, and for cult-records see Turner 1983, Connelly 2007.

26. The archaic period, by contrast, did produce female poets, notably Sappho of Lesbos, who flourished around the turn of the sixth century BCE.

27. Schaps 1977, Sommerstein 1980; for women's conventional invisibility in the theatrical audience see III, above.

28. Euripides' alleged violation of this protocol motivates the women's conspiracy against him in *Women at the Thesmophoria*.

29. The women of tragedy often protest their lot too, but they are significantly distanced by their confinement to the heroic age and mostly to places other than Athens.

30. For more detailed overviews of the material background see Blok and Mason 1987; Cohen 1989, 1991; Dover 1974:95–102; Foxhall 1989; Gould 1980; Henderson 1988; Just 1989; McClees 1920; Schaps 1979, 1982; Turner 1983; Versnel 1987; Winkler 1990; for dramatic portrayals see Assaël 1985; Blundell 1995:130–49; Foley 1981b, 1982; Gardner 1989; Henderson 1987b, 1991a; Muecke 1982; Said 1979; Shaw 1975; Sommerstein 1980; Taafe 1993; Zeitlin 1985.

31. Athenian cults, festivals and religious societies at both the local and national levels offered many opportunities for citizen women to serve the community outside the household. As priestesses women could even have a public identity and some public

influence, since they were public officials subject to official scrutiny and review; see further Lysistrata, Introduction 2, Blundell 1995:160–69, O'Higgins 2003, Connelly 2007.

32. For the ways in which women's corporate public esteem was managed according to proper gender-norms see Kallet-Marx 1993.

33. A wife who came with a large dowry (which remained with her during her lifetime and would be passed on to her male children after her death) could have considerable influence over her husband.

34. See Henderson 1987a:121–26.

35. For the prominence of women at the local (deme) level see Whitehead 1986:77–81; for the heroines worshipped in local communities see Larson 1995.

36. See n. 31, above.

37. Hitherto non-mythic women had appeared in comedy only sporadically and as minor characters, representing disreputable types like prostitutes, market-women and the female relatives of "demagogues." See Henderson 2000.

38. See further the Introduction to Women at the Thesmophoria; the character Agathon (a follower of Euripides) would not be so concerned to turn himself into a woman if the verisimilitude of his female characters were not actually characteristic. For the question of verisimilitude as it involves male actors portraying women, see III, above.

39. For drama's often critical stance toward civic ideology see Goldhill 1990.

40. Cohen 1991:166.

41. See above, Introduction III.

42. For the age-distinction see Henderson 1987a.

43. Euripides' Alkestis (produced in 438) is the only extant tragedy that portrays a loving relationship between a husband and a wife.

44. The emphasis on this motif in comedy suggests that in real life women may not have been fed as much as men (they did not typically take meals with the men, but with the children and slaves) and that their access to wine was strictly regulated—presumably to deter its potential interference with their household work and their sexual propriety. In classical Athens, drinking occurred in occasional religious festivities but as an everyday activity was confined to bars (public) and symposia (all-male), so that respectable women would normally have no licit opportunities to drink.

45. Unless the wine-drinking in Women at the Thesmophoria counts as misbehavior. For courtesans and comic wives see Stroup 2004, Faraone 2006.

46. See Blundell 1995:143–44.

47. See Lysistrata, Introduction 2.

48. This view has been most systematically advanced by Zeitlin, cf. esp. Zeitlin 1985.

49. This may indeed have been a consideration in Aristophanes' choice of women to argue against continuing the war in 411; see Lysistrata, Introduction 1.

50. See Halperin 1990:145–47.

51. For the distinctively sex-based language of comic women see Willi 2003:157–97, Sommerstein 2009b.

## 1 Lysistrata

1. The principal historical source for the Peloponnesian War is Thucydides' *History*; book 8 records the events of 411.

2. Thucydides 8.53.

3. See further Introduction II.

4. It would not be surprising if, in the course of the long war and in the aftermath of such a great loss of men as in 413, normal male supervision of women was relaxed, allowing women greater scope for independent action and expression than was usual in normal times.

5. On these see further Introduction IV. For Lysistrata, like Athena, as champion of all Athenians, and a leader who is shown to bring them peace on the most favorable terms, see Sommerstein 2009c.

6. For the dramatic typology of a household's women taking public action to save it from the men see Bowie 1993:199–200, Foley 1981b, Shaw 1975; for historical examples see Schaps 1982.

7. For the characterization of older women in comedy generally see Henderson 1987a.

8. Ordinary Athenians (like their counterparts in modern democracies) envied but also admired the rich and privileged, and tended to identify with people (including politicians) higher in the social hierarchy than lower.

9. But not (like Artemis) chastity, despite Loraux 1993:147–83: Athena was the patron of both girls and married women, and her Akropolis cult was the polis' symbolic household.

10. For more details see Henderson 1987a:xxxviii–xl; Vaio 1973; for the special social, economic and legal benefits that priestesses enjoyed see Connelly 2007, Gould 1980, Turner 1983:383 ff.; and for the importance of religion in connecting women with the polis see Introduction IV. Modern readers should bear in mind that in classical Greece priestesses were not, like nuns for instance, expected to devote their whole lives to religion; except when performing their offices for a particular divinity (usually only on certain days of the year), they lived the same sort of lives as other women.

11. She is apparently appealed to by name in the cause of peace in Aristophanes' *Peace* (991–92).

12. The name Lysistrata was in fact borne by more than one Polias priestess in later times, and perhaps in earlier times too, since Lysimache is the first identifiable incumbent.

13. Some scholars have suggested that the other wives in the play also represent priestly personnel, since they seem to be familiar with one another and with the Akropolis; in particular, the Athenian wife Myrrhine is given the same (admittedly common) name as a woman known to have served in the latter fifth century as the priestess of Athena Nike ("Victory"), whose bastion was at the entrance to the Akropolis (see MacDowell 1995:241–42, and *Lysistrata* n. 79). But even if this is so, none of the other women in the play is so strongly characterized in terms of cult as Lysistrata is in terms of the Akropolis cult of Athena.

14. See *Lysistrata*, n. 116. It may well be that Euripides borrowed elements of *Lysistrata* in composing *Bakchai*.

15. For a survey see Burkert 1983:168–79 (including the Skira festival, p. 170).

16. See Bowie 1993:184–85.

17. See Martin 1987, Bowie 1993:186–94.

18. Dillon 1987 points out that the threat to fertility represented by the Spartan occupation of the Attic countryside (see section 1, above) is an element underlying the idea of the women's conjugal strike (a threat to human fertility that is equally "abnormal").

19. See n. 6, above.

20. The central text for this role of Athena is Aeschylus' *Eumenides*.

21. The wine-god Dionysos (here referred to by his epithet Bakchos) was worshipped by private groups of men, women or (if disreputable women were involved) both together; respectable women, whose access to wine was ordinarily restricted (Minieri 1982), were in comedy typically portrayed as bibulous and thus as being fond of "Bacchic" religion.

22. Pan was especially associated with "wild" music and dancing, activities that for women could be enjoyed only in the context of religious festivals; he also had erotic associations, embodying the power of animal procreation.

23. The Genetyllides were goddesses of procreation who also had erotic associations.

24. These *tympana* were used (mainly by women) in ecstatic worship of Dionysos and such Asiatic deities as Sabazios (below, n. 92) and the Great Mother.

25. Comic poets often refer to women's religious activities as being mere excuses for drinking, dancing and illicit sex. In *Lysistrata* the young wives conform to this stereotype, but from the start the heroine herself is exempted.

26. The name means "Fair Victory."

27. The name means "Disbander of Armies."

28. Kalonike seems to be older than Lysistrata, but not very much older, since she aligns herself with the other housewives; she plays the role of bawdy sidekick in the Prologue.

29. Meaning "difficult" but also implying that wives who go out are likely to cause mischief. Note that the wives' freedom to leave their houses is assumed, but at the same time they must be sure that their husbands would have no reason to deny permission.

30. Young women are conventionally portrayed as incapable of controlling their sexual appetites, whereas men were supposed to be capable of disciplining their own. In *Lysistrata* these gender-roles will be comically reversed, the wives resisting sexual temptation and the husbands succumbing.

31. The Peloponnesians (headed by Sparta) and the Boiotians (headed by Thebes) were Athens' chief enemies in the war.

32. Eels from Lake Kopais in Boiotia were a great delicacy, now contraband.

33. An expensive import from a place (probably in Asia Minor) no longer identifiable.

34. Kalonike represents the stereotypical wife of a prosperous husband: a frivolous and spoiled spendthrift.

35. The chief deities of the Eleusinian Mysteries, Demeter and Kore (Persephone), whose worship was intimately associated with human and agricultural fertility and thus with women.

36. Two regions of Attika that evoke the names of Athens' two fastest ships, the Paralos and the Salaminia.

37. An allusion to the "equestrian" mode of sexual intercourse (woman on top), apparently a risqué posture, since it was a favor for which a prostitute might charge extra.

38. The name (meaning "Myrtle") was a very common one in life and in comedy, but it is particularly appropriate for the character in *Lysistrata* because it was a slang term for the vulva ("Pussy" would be a rough modern equivalent), was associated with Aphrodite and myrtle was used in bridal garlands.

39. The *zone* was a waistband worn just above the hips.

40. Lampito was an actual royal name in Sparta, though no contemporary of that name is known.

41. In the following introduction of the foreigners the women show physical interest in one another, which may have erotic overtones (for female homoeroticism see Dover 1978:171–84); at the same time we must remember that the scene was played by men for a notional audience of men.

42. Spartan girls, unlike their Athenian counterparts, took outdoor physical training, so that Spartan women were stereotypically portrayed as "masculine": see Cartledge 1981a.

43. In *Lysistrata* the Spartans speak a caricatured version of their local dialect of Greek (Lakonian).

44. The Dioskouroi, Kastor and Pollux, brothers of Helen and special patrons of the Spartans.

45. For women, partial or total public depilation (by plucking or singeing) was considered to be a necessary element of good grooming; for the Greek male's preference for the sexually immature look in females see Kilmer 1982.

46. Humorously substituting the name of an Athenian commander for the name of a city that the Athenians were besieging; comedy routinely assumes that all military commanders are cowardly, incompetent or corrupt.

47. Though adultery was in reality a very serious offense at Athens, comic wives are typically portrayed as ready to take lovers.

48. The Ionian city of Miletos, Athens' former ally, was famous for its leather dildoes, either as a major exporter or because Milesian women were thought to be sexually insatiable. Six inches (literally "eight fingers") was a comparatively short size for a dildo.

49. Lysistrata, whose speech has been rather demure up to this point, uses the Greek "four-letter word" for the penis, *peos*, which would have been shocking on the lips of a respectable woman and which here emphasizes the shocking nature of Lysistrata's proposal.

50. Here and elsewhere in comedy, characters often speak in "paratragedy": either quoting from, or mimicking the general style of tragedy.

51. Comparing the women to the mythical Tyro, who was seduced by the god Poseidon disguised as her lover (the river-god Enipeus) and who exposed the twin boys born of that union in a tub or trough by the riverbank; the myth had been twice dramatized by Sophokles. Lysistrata's point is that young women cannot rise above sex and procreation.

52. Comically adapting the typical male compliment, "real man."

53. After the fall of Troy Menelaos (the King of Sparta) intended to kill his unfaithful wife Helen, but at the sight of her beauty dropped his sword; apparently Euripides in his play *Andromache* had added the detail about Helen's breasts.

54. In Attic slang "skinning" meant "causing an erection" and "skinned dog" meant "dildo." Pherekrates was a contemporary comic poet, but the context of the phrase quoted is unknown.

55. The Greek word *bia*, here translated as "force," is commonly used to denote rape. While at least some Athenian men may not have equated forced sex with a spouse with rape if they considered sexual compliance to be a wifely duty that they could choose to command, nevertheless men who beat their wives were considered brutes (see below, nn. 110–11), consensual marital sex was the normative ideal (see nn. 56 and 193), and later in the play Kinesias, though desperate, never thinks of forcing his wife Myrrhine to sleep with him.

56. Meaning sexual unresponsiveness: see preceding note.

57. Playing on the contrast (and conflict) between the authoritarian Spartan monarchy and the Athenian direct democracy ("mob rule," according to its critics).

58. The temple of the citadel-goddess, Athena, on the Akropolis, was Athens' main treasury; for the importance of Athena to the play's symbolism, see Introduction 2.

59. That is, the women who are too old to participate in the sex-strike; they are the counterparts of the older men of the "home guard" who are too old to serve on military expeditions.

60. What follows is a parody of an old-fashioned oath-ceremony, in which a black sacrificial animal was slaughtered and its testicles severed; participants stood on the severed parts while taking the solemn oath. The principal humor lies in the spectacle of women performing such a ceremony, which was ordinarily the prerogative of men.

61. The Athenians used slave-archers, mostly from western Asia, as policemen and security guards for officials (like the Magistrate later in the play); the slave-girl here, apparently dressed like such a policeman (hence her possession of a shield), increases our impression of Lysistrata's ability to challenge males on their own ground (cf. Stone 1984:306). We are not to ask where Lysistrata came by a Skythian warrior-girl.

62. Lysistrata seems more warlike than her comrades. The reference is to Aischylos' *Seven Against Thebes* 42–48, where the Seven vow to take Thebes or die trying.

63. A "white horse" made a rare and costly sacrifice normally associated with myths (e.g. the oath of Helen's suitors, taken over a severed white horse) and with the fabulous East; its appropriateness here is as a slang term for the erect penis or as an allusion to the Amazons (a mythical, eastern race of women who rejected and battled with men: see below, n. 151).

64. The Greeks typically mixed their wine with water; a liking for neat wine—which more quickly intoxicates and was therefore considered excessive—was a comic stereotype about women. Wine from Thasos was exceptionally fine. The vessels used in this scene are the kylix, the standard drinking bowl, and a *stamnion*, a large jar more appropriate for festive cult than private drinking. The women violate the protocol of an oath-ceremony, in which nothing was eaten or drunk.

65. Alluding to the practice at male drinking-parties (*symposia*, from which respectable women were barred) of determining the drinking-order by drawing lots.

66. That is, on all fours, to be penetrated (vaginally or anally) from behind. The handles of household utensils were often made in the form of crouching animals.

67. For the importance of the women's solidarity see Konstan 1993.

68. The Greek word *ololyge* designated (1) women's ritual shouts at the completion of a sacrifice (here, the old women's pretext for being on the Akropolis) and (2) any victory-cry.

69. The favor of the goddess of sexual enjoyment is of course crucial for the conspiracy's success.

70. Chorus members in comedy (but not in tragedy) are often given personal names; the men's names here seem to be generic for old men.

71. The ancient olive-wood image of Athena Polias was both a venerable symbol of Athens and an important guarantor of the goddess's goodwill toward the polis.

72. Since the Akropolis was in actuality open to the public at large, both men and women, and since virtually every Athenian participated in some way in its many sacred activities, the men's proprietary and exclusive attitude toward it is unwarranted; for mythical and cultic exemplars of the men's assault and the women's resistance see Faraone 1997.

73. The men imagine (wrongly) that the ringleader of the conspiracy must be Lykon's wife, a citizen woman who had a reputation for promiscuity in Athens at the time.

74. A Spartan king (c. 520–490) who in 508 had occupied the Akropolis for two days on the invitation of Athenian oligarchs and was allowed to leave under truce, paving the way for the restoration of the democratic leader Kleisthenes.

75. The men speak of Athens and of the Akropolis in a proprietary way, since they boast of having personally taken part in glorious actions of the past that would make them about 120 years old!

76. Euripides' reputation as a misogynist—based on his unprecedentedly vivid portrayals of female deviousness (e.g. Phaidra) and even criminality (e.g. Medeia)—underlies the plot of Aristophanes' play *Women at the Thesmophoria*.

77. The stone monument that commemorated the great Athenian victory over the Persians in 490.

78. For the myth of the Lemnian women and its significance for the plot of Lysistrata see Introduction 2.

79. That is, Athena Nike, whose temple stands on your right as you face the Propylaia (the main entrance to the Akropolis).

80. The women's names, like the men's, are apparently generic for old women, but Nikodike ("Victory for Right") probably has additional significance in immediately following the men's appeal to Lady Victory, and Kritylla (also the name of a character in *Women at the Thesmophoria*) may allude to an actual person (see *Women at the Thesmophoria*, n. 70).

81. Drawing water from a well was a typical morning chore for women.

82. Branding was meted out to slaves who had run away or committed some other serious offense. The women emphasize the toughness of the competition at the well (to match the men's martial exploits).

83. Around 175 pounds (an exaggeration).

84. An ancient epithet of Athena thought to recall her birth near a mythical river or lake and thus suited to the women's task of dousing the men's fire.

85. A Chian sculptor vilified by the sixth-century iambic poet Hipponax.

86. For Euripides' reputation for misogyny see *Women at the Thesmophoria*, Introduction.

87. That is, not a slave or foreigner but a citizen entitled to the Athenian right of free speech.

88. Jury service, for which a small stipend was paid by the polis, was popular with impecunious old men and with others unfit for more remunerative occupations.

89. Acheloos, a river in north-west Greece, was metonymic for "water," especially in ritual contexts—suggesting that the women are countering an impious action by the men.

90. For these slave archers see n. 61, above.

91. Exemplifying the typical male assumptions about women's business (and echoing Lysistrata's first words), though this time these assumptions are wrong.

92. A Phrygian (and therefore barbarian) god similar to Dionysos, whose worship had recently become popular at Athens, especially among women and slaves; but the women in the play associate themselves only with the major polis gods.

93. Adonis (in myth, the mortal youth whom Aphrodite loved) was another eastern (Semitic) import who was not officially recognized by the city. His cult was celebrated by women in the heat of midsummer on rooftops: the women planted quickly flowering and quickly withering gardens and lamented the death of the young god.

94. That is, in the summer of 415; for the disastrous Sicilian expedition, see Introduction.

95. A very bad omen, considering that the Athenians were moving to send the flower of their youth to Sicily, and one that proved only too accurate.

96. Still a prominent politician at the time of the play.

97. Note that the Magistrate's anecdote actually demonstrates the recklessness of Demostratos and the male assemblymen rather than any ill-effects resulting from the women's festival.

98. An overnight voyage. In addition, "sailing" and "Salamis" can connote sexual intercourse.

99. Like women, slaves were stereotypically bibulous.

100. Artemis, sister of Apollo, was a fearsome maiden huntress associated with wild places and untamed beasts.

101. One of the daughters of the mythical King Kekrops; along with her sister Aglauros she was worshipped as a heroine on the Akropolis, and their myth may well be commemorated in the ritual of the Arrhephoria (see n. 139, below).

102. A title of Hekate, a popular women's goddess associated with the moon and with the birth and rearing of children; her epithet here puns on "eye" or "eye-salve."

103. An impossibility in actual life, but we are reminded of Athena, who was imagined as bearing arms in her capacity as polis-guardian.

104. Market-women were (conventionally) older women of the lower citizen or slave classes and (proverbially) bold, tough and abusive, so that they make perfect "combat troops" for Lysistrata.

105. Emphasizing the sanctity of the Akropolis by invoking the name of a mythical king of Athens.

106. In the typical comic agon (contest) both contestants state and argue a case as if in a lawcourt; in this one, the Magistrate is given no argument in favor of continuing the war but merely challenges Lysistrata's arguments against it.

107. See Introduction 1.

108. For women and domestic management, see Introduction IV.

109. A common male oath.

110. It was illegal (because undemocratic) to strike any male citizen, and in terms of democratic ideology physical violence against women was disapproved behavior as well, being attributed in all our sources only to drunks and scoundrels. Violence against wives is stressed in this play as one element of its portrayal of males as intemperate and ill-behaved (though the husbands who appear later on are not at all violent).

111. The following account of dispute between husbands and wives about the war is modelled on the famous conversation between Hektor and Andromache in the sixth book of Homer's *Iliad*. There Andromache gives Hektor sound tactical advice (to defend Troy from the walls) that he refuses to follow, preferring the more masculine path of honor (to confront Achilleus in single combat), with results disastrous for himself, his city and his wife and small son. But even in refusing his wife's advice Hektor, in contrast with Lysistrata's husband, nevertheless treats her with tact, sympathy and compassion—traditional marks of the civilized man: see also *Iliad* 19.287 ff., 24.762 ff., *Odyssey* 20.105 ff. By echoing this scene Aristophanes not only evokes the ideal (heroic) models of husband and wife, but also singles out the one episode in the heroic tradition when a leader would have done well to heed a woman's advice.

112. Quoting Hektor's words (previous note); proper gender-roles were conventionally epitomized by the antithesis weaving/fighting.

113. Respectable women normally veiled their faces when they went outside the house.

114. The ancient equivalent of gum-chewing, and associated with menial tasks.

115. The feminization and (thus) disempowerment of the Magistrate by dressing him as a housewife scenically underlines the play's wholesale gender-reversals, and it recalls such mythical prototypes as Pentheus in Euripides' *Bakchai*; see Zeitlin 1985, Levine 1987.

116. The list combines conventionally male and female attributes.

117. Not necessarily indicating that Lysistrata is old, for she is here addressed in her role as leader of the occupying (older) women.

118. In Greek *Lysimachai*, possibly alluding to Lysimache, the current priestess of Athena Polias; see *Lysistrata*, Introduction.

119. Eastern divinities associated with ecstatic dancing, and a popular way to refer to lunatics.

120. During the war many wealthy young men had taken to wearing their hair long and affecting other "Spartan" mannerisms, to the disgust of older, more conventional Athenians.

121. Thracian mercenaries struck Athenians as wild and uncivilized. Tereus was the mythical Thracian king who raped and mutilated Philomela, the sister of his wife Prokne, daughter of the Athenian King Pandion; when Prokne found out, she killed

their son Itys and served him to Tereus for dinner. In the end, Tereus was transformed into a hoopoe, Prokne into a nightingale and Philomela into a swallow. The myth was dramatized by Sophokles.

122. Lysistrata's polis-as-ball-of-wool metaphor appeals to the item of domestic management most characteristic of wives, and is thus a central illustration of Lysistrata's main argument, that female skills are a better model for running the polis than the male predilection for aggression.

123. Here Aristophanes signals a departure from the comic plot: his heroine is about to give advice about how the men ought to govern the actual polis; that is why her following metaphor does not include women in its list of useful citizens to be included in a newly constituted polis: see MacDowell 1995:238–39.

124. Referring both to open political cliques and to antidemocratic conspiracies, cf. Thukydides 8.54.

125. She was about to add, "never to see them again," an indication of the intended seriousness of Lysistrata's words; the men in the audience are being asked to see the situation through women's eyes.

126. That is, wives and widows.

127. In the Greek world, every woman was expected to marry and bear children, and it was considered her right to have a husband. Those women who for some reason did not marry faced social isolation, were both an embarrassment and an unwelcome expense to their families, and represented for the community a horrible and ill-omened wastage that called the basic social order into question. The recent destruction of the Sicilian expedition had in fact significantly reduced the number of young citizen men and created real fear that many young women might go without husbands. The future dearth of citizen males was of course an additional consideration if the marriage-rate dropped.

128. That is, omens foretelling marriage.

129. The Magistrate might have continued "has a perfect right to take the most attractive woman he chooses as a wife" (crudely disregarding the right of every woman to have a husband: see n. 127, above).

130. Lysistrata and her comrades playfully enact one of the traditional duties of older women, managing funerals.

131. Charon ferries dead souls across the river Styx into the underworld.

132. That is, dressed first as a housewife and then as a corpse.

133. This last Athenian tyrant was expelled in 510, but a public curse against anyone aiming to be or to abet a tyrant was still solemnly pronounced on important civic occasions. Since Hippias' name is based on *hippos*, "horse," there is an allusion here to the "equestrian" position in sexual intercourse (woman on top).

134. A beardless man teased for effeminacy and for taking the woman's role in sexual intercourse in eight of Aristophanes' eleven extant plays; in *Women at the Thesmophoria* he is the intermediary between the women and the polis. Here he would be a suitable intermediary between the women and the Spartans, since the latter were thought by the Athenians to be especially fond of performing anal intercourse: see Dover 1978:185–96.

135. Pay for jury service, introduced by Perikles, enabled the poorer classes of citizens to serve and was especially attractive to older men with nothing better to do with their time. Many conservative Athenians regarded this pay as a needless expense and even as a danger to democracy, since it tended to introduce a class imbalance between litigants (mostly wealthy) and jurors that demagogues might exploit for their own political purposes.

136. Quoting from a patriotic drinking-song about the tyrant-slayers (see next note); the phrase could also have a slang double meaning referring to male sexual penetration of women.

137. In the marketplace stood bronze statues of Harmodios and Aristogeiton, the young men who killed Hipparchos, the brother of the tyrant Hippias, in 514; they and their descendants were subsequently revered as "tyrant-slayers" and freedom-fighters. (Thucydides' account [6.53–59], that the two were merely lovers avenging a personal insult, is unlikely to have been common knowledge at the time of the play.) Here the Old Men pose incongruously as the young and handsome Harmodios.

138. Aristophanes further develops the contrast between the well-born and well-trained old women and the poor, ignorant old men. The résumé of religious distinctions offered by the old women here is the most prestigious that any Athenian woman could boast. For the importance of service in the public cults for women's status in the polis see Introduction IV and Gould 1980:50–51, Connelly 2007.

139. The Arrhephoroi were two girls who spent a year living on the Akropolis in ritual service to the cult of Athena Polias and under her priestess's supervision. Among their other duties, they began the weaving of Athena's Panathenaic robe and marched in the procession at the Panathenaia, a great festival honoring Athena and held every four years. The girls had to be at least seven and no more than eleven years old and came only from the noblest Athenian families; their selection was made by the people's assembly and the King Archon, the polis' chief religious magistrate. The Arrhephoroi ritually represented all Athenian girls' preparation for their married lives as domestic managers, and their service helped assure the goddess's favor toward the polis itself. In general see Burkert 1983:150–54, Simon 1983:38–46, 66–69, Sourvinou-Inwood 1988:58–59, 73–74.

140. Well-born girls who served a goddess—probably Demeter at Eleusis—by grinding ritual cakes; see Sourvinou-Inwood 1988:142–46.

141. That is, Artemis (see n. 100, above), the patron deity of the Brauronia.

142. The Brauronia, an elaborate ritual sequence celebrated every four years, was open to select girls five to ten years old (criteria for eligibility are unknown). Its climax was the Arkteia (Ritual of the Bears), in which the girls donned various costumes representing their passage from girlhood to adulthood (eligibility for marriage); at one point they removed a saffron-dyed robe and performed naked. See in general Burkert 1985:263, Simon 1983:83–88, Sourvinou-Inwood 1988. Here the old women, who shed their jackets, thus reenact their youthful Arkteia, producing a humorous incongruity to match the old men's imitation of the young tyrannicides.

143. Maiden basket-bearers were a feature of many processions, and figs symbolized fertility; see Simon 1983:77–78. The climactic placement of basket-bearing here perhaps suggests the most prestigious of all processions, in the Panathenaia.

144. The word hubris ranges in significance from "outrageous conduct" to "assault" to "behaving as if more than human."

145. Leaving them "naked," that is, wearing only their theatrical skin (leotard and phallos).

146. A military nickname of unknown but evidently patriotic significance (opposition to the tyrants); perhaps it refers to the dusty feet of peasant soldiers.

147. In the hills of northern Attika where rebels battled the tyrant Hippias after his brother's assassination (see n. 137, above).

148. The following items of martial activity have double meanings suggesting fear that the women will take command in sexual relations—an idea dramatized in *Assemblywomen*.

149. A queen of Halikarnassos who commanded naval actions against the Greeks during the Persian invasion of 480.

150. Yet another allusion to the equestrian (woman-on-top) mode of sexual intercourse.

151. According to legend the Amazons, a mythical race of women who shunned men, once invaded Attika and occupied the Akropolis in order to rescue an Amazon princess who had been captured by Herakles and given to the Attic king Theseus as a prize; but they were routed by the Athenians in battle. See in general DuBois 1982, Tyrrell 1984, Bowie 1993:184–85.

152. They will be "naked" like the old men—something that in actual life no respectable woman would ever do except as a performer in the Ritual of the Bears (see n. 142). But now the need to match the men's aggression overrides concern for their own dignity.

153. Alluding to an Aesopic fable, the beetle avenges a wrong done it by an eagle by breaking the eagle's eggs; these had been placed in Zeus' lap for safekeeping, but when the beetle dropped its dung-ball into Zeus' lap, he unthinkingly jumped up and spilled the eggs. Here the eggs seem to indicate the men's testicles.

154. See n. 102.

155. See n. 32. The women liken the Greek world at war to a neighborhood disrupted by a troublemaker.

156. The elevated style incongruously parodies tragedy, in which the stage building typically represents a troubled palace.

157. The (obscene) word she uses, being grammatically in the active voice, would typically be used by horny men.

158. For Pan see n. 22, above. This grotto, on the northern slope of the Akropolis, was where Apollo raped Kreousa; later in the play it serves as a trysting-place for Kinesias and Myrrhine.

159. Sparrows were emblematic of sexual appetite and eaten as aphrodisiacs, and "sparrow" was a slang term for both "penis" and "vagina"; thus the sparrow was sacred to Aphrodite.

160. Evidently a "ladies' man." For a wife to visit her lover's house is a sign of sexual desperation because it was normal for an adulterer to visit the wife at her own house.

161. Birth and death were forbidden in sanctuaries like the Akropolis.

162. That is, the helmet from the great bronze statue of Athena Promachos on the Akropolis.

163. Like omens and even dreams, oracles were frequently used in political persuasion and deliberation, but Aristophanes, like many educated people, considered those who believed in them to be gullible; here the gullible wives are being treated to the sort of "demagogic" tactics that were familiar to their husbands in Assembly.

164. An allusion to the myth of Tereus (see above, n. 121).

165. The mythical Melanion is best known for using the trick of the golden apples to win a footrace against the huntress-maiden Atalante and thus her hand in marriage; here the old men seem to be thinking of an earlier phase of the myth, in which Melanion was celibate and Atalante was his divine companion (compare Hippolytos and Artemis in Euripides' play Hippolytos).

166. Two Athenian generals, now dead, who were remembered for their toughness and bravery. Hairy hindquarters were a sign of strength and courage in men.

167. A legendary misanthrope who (despite the old women's claim in this song) reportedly hated both men and women. He was a main character in several Greek comedies and in Shakespeare's Timon of Athens. For his portrayal here see Hawkins 2001.

168. Just as body hair was a sign of virility, so its absence was a sign of femininity; see above, n. 45.

169. The ensuing scene, which illustrates the sex-strike in action, reverses the Greek norm of seduction, in which the male takes the lead. But it also takes off on such well-known precedents of female seducers as Hera in book 14 of Homer's Iliad; for an analysis see Taafe 1993:67–69.

170. Kinesias was an actual (though uncommon) name that was borne by a contemporary poet whom Aristophanes had caricatured in Birds three years earlier; if Aristophanes is caricaturing him here, then it is possible that Myrrhine represents his actual wife, perhaps the priestess of Athena Nike (see Lysistrata, Introduction, n. 13). But the name alone suits the role of the representative husband in this play, since it reminds us of the verb kinein "screw (a woman)"; the deme-name Paionidai similarly reminds us of paiein, "bang"—we might translate "Roger Balling from Bangor." Myrrhine's name ("myrtle" = "pussy," see above, n. 38) is similarly significant.

171. The typical toast for an absent loved one, except that here Myrrhine is represented as toasting with food rather than with drink, which would be inappropriate for a respectable wife.

172. Although Kinesias is bribing a "sentry" here, the audience will think of the usual association of men and purses: negotiation with prostitutes; see Keuls 1985:153–203.

173. A line of text has been lost here, but its gist must be as indicated by the supplement offered here.

174. That is, "had sex with me," which Kinesias tries to portray as a sacred duty.

175. See above, n. 158.

176. No one who had had sex was allowed to enter a sanctuary until (s)he had bathed; for this and other taboos involving sex see Parker 1983:74–103.

177. It was in this spring, in a cave below the north-west side of the Akropolis, that Zeus' wife Hera was said to have recovered her virginity; in Aristophanes' time the image of Aphrodite Peitho ("The Persuader") was ritually bathed there.

178. Women, being legally incompetent to swear an oath, were popularly regarded as being too untrustworthy to live up to one.

179. The he-man hero Herakles was portrayed in myths as having a huge appetite for food and sex; various kinds of trouble about meals is a typical feature of his comic persona.

180. Apparently an inferior brand.

181. This duet parodies scenes in tragedy where a stricken hero is consoled by the chorus (-leader).

182. The nickname of the pimp or brothel-keeper Philostratos.

183. Early morning is often mentioned as a conventional time for conjugal sex.

184. A demon or divinity associated with ithyphallic dances.

185. The joke is obscure. Since Pellene was a safe Spartan ally, a "need" for it is hard to explain: perhaps the ample cloaks for which Pellene was noted would better conceal the Spartans' condition than the short cloaks they are wearing, or perhaps it puns on some word for, or metaphorically meaning vagina or anus, for example, *pella* "milk-pail." Alternatively, we might accept Taillardat's emendation to "Pallene," an Athenian colony coveted by Sparta as well as a personal name that could have been borne by (though it is not attested for) a courtesan.

186. Pan (above, n. 22) was frequently portrayed as ithyphallic and thus able to inflict ithyphallism.

187. The deme Trikorythos abutted a large marsh on the Bay of Marathon.

188. Choral songs in the latter parts of an Old Comedy often ridiculed or abused specific members of the audience; here, by contrast, Aristophanes wants to underline the theme of general reconciliation, so that the chorus merely teases the spectators by making comically insincere promises; this routine is continued in another pair of songs after the following Episode.

189. The only passage in surviving Greek comedy that explicitly recognizes the presence of women in the audience (see further Introduction); note that the women are thought of as having a need for money of their own.

190. A substantial amount of money.

191. Troops from this ally were stationed in Athens and were (to judge from this passage) attractive to Athenian women.

192. The Greek puns on *asketikon* ("pertaining to athletic training") and *askitikon* ("suffering from abdominal swelling").

193. See above, n. 134. This was not, of course, the only available outlet for an Athenian husband denied access to his wife: though masturbation was considered slavish, and no free man would admit to resorting to it, slaves and prostitutes were freely available. But it is unlikely that most Athenians could afford, or would normally resort to, prostitutes or slave-rape, so that consensual marital sex was (as the play assumes) the real-world norm.

194. In 415, just before the departure of the Sicilian expedition, the faces and phalli of the pillar-images of Hermes, which stood in the streets throughout Athens, had been mutilated. Since not all of the perpetrators had been identified, Aristophanes suggests that some were among the spectators.

195. The men's references to Lysistrata by name in these final scenes are the only exceptions in extant comedy and oratory to the rule of Athenian etiquette that a free man does not publicly refer by name to a respectable woman not holding public office: see

Sommerstein 1980. This exception may have to do with the heroine's assimilation to the Polias priestess Lysimache (see Introduction 2), but in any case it is significant that Lysistrata is not so named until her victory (and thus her extraordinary status) is assured.

196. Either the Spartan (who can know nothing of Lysistrata) does not care whether the mediator is male or female, or Aristophanes is poking fun at an effeminate Lysistratos.

197. Humorous oxymoron (because "manly" was an inappropriate epithet for a woman), but also calling attention to the fact that Lysistrata has done, in the fantasy of the play, what no man has been able to do in reality.

198. That is, a man (or boy) wearing a girlish mask and a leotard to which false breasts and genitalia were attached; similar "naked girls" appear in most of Aristophanes' plays. Aristophanes typically portrays peace concretely and in terms of sensory enjoyments (food, drink, sex and festivals).

199. Intelligence and knowledge of the world were attributes not conventionally associated with women (cf. Dover 1974:99); that Lysistrata has paid attention to her father plausibly explains her possession of these masculine attributes and is yet another detail linking her with Athena, who had a father (Zeus) but no mother; see Introduction 2.

200. Some scholars think that the following appeals cannot have been intended seriously: the context is ludicrous and salacious, and the appeals themselves are both historically dubious and impracticable (see MacDowell 1995:244–46). Yet the context can be explained as Aristophanes' way of defusing a potentially outrageous moment (sympathetic portrayal of Spartans), and the appeals as more in tune with popular sentiment and wish-fulfillment than with a realistic analysis of the combatants' diplomatic options. But evidently some of the same arguments were made in actual debate at the time.

201. Lysistrata recalls the great earthquake that devastated Sparta in 464; it was followed by the revolt of Sparta's helots (serfs) and other subject communities, who waged a guerrilla war from bases on Mt. Ithome; Athens was among the cities that agreed to send military assistance. Lysistrata omits to mention the sequel: the Athenian commander Kimon, who advocated a friendly policy toward Sparta, was ignominiously dismissed by the Spartans—an act that led to Kimon's exile and strengthened anti-Spartan sentiment at Athens.

202. Referring to the expulsion of the Athenian tyrant Hippias in 510, when the assistance supplied by the Spartan king Kleomenes was decisive. Again Lysistrata omits the sequel: the return of Kleomenes to Athens three years later, this time to undermine its fledgling democracy.

203. Of this negotiation-scene Taafe 1993:71 writes, "Creatures who play to the male gaze have caused that gaze to refocus upon masculine desire. In addition, woman has been put back into one of her rightful places, as a silent token of exchange between men."

204. The places mentioned during these comic negotiations might have been relevant were actual negotiations held, but for Aristophanes' purposes their main attraction was that they all had sexual double meanings that could be illustrated by reference to Reconciliation's "naked" body.

205. Pylos ("gate"). Throughout this scene Aristophanes exploits the stereotype of Spartan predilection for anal intercourse (both homo- and heterosexual); since the Athenians prefer the vagina, the "settlement" turns out to be satisfactory to both sides.

206. Echinous ("sea-urchin place" = female pubis), Malian Inlet (*malon*, "apple", was slang for breasts or, as here, buttocks), Legs ( = "connecting walls") of Megara.

207. See above, n. 176.

208. Possibly Lysistrata's last words in the play: but see n. 215.

209. A continuation of the chorus's previous song (see above, n. 188).

210. See above, n. 143.

211. The Telamon Song (Telamon was the father of the epic hero Ajax) was warlike, while the Kleitagora Song (named after and/or composed by a woman, perhaps a courtesan) began (we have only the opening words) by referring to peace and prosperity.

212. The Athenian naval battle against the Persians in 480.

213. In the valiant Spartan stand at the pass of Thermopylai, where all 300 Spartans were killed; this land action occurred at the same time as the sea action off Artemision.

214. Artemis under this special title (Agrotera) was worshipped at both Sparta (where she was invoked before battle) and Athens (where a yearly sacrifice commemorated a vow made to her before the battle of Marathon).

215. Since Lysistrata's conspiracy was successfully concluded in the earlier negotiation-scene and normality has been restored, we might expect that the control of affairs would revert to the (newly reformed) men, with the final business of celebration and the return of the wives to their husbands being orchestrated by one of the Athenian delegates: for a woman, even a heroine so closely assimilated to Athena, to assume the authoritative role that the speaker takes in the final scene would have been unthinkable in actual life and perhaps dilute the impact of her achievement; Praxagora's absence in the finale of *Assemblywomen* would be a parallel. For detailed arguments for this assignment see Henderson 1987a: 214–15 (who imagines a mute Lysistrata present during the final scene) and Mastromarco and Totaro 2006:428–29 n. 236. On the other hand, the manuscripts, evidently on ancient authority, assign the role to Lysistrata, and the speaker's references to each group of Spartans and Athenians as "you" (lines 1274–75) suggest that the speaker belongs to neither group. I am now persuaded by the arguments in Sommerstein 2009c:244–46, 252–53 that Lysistrata should be allowed to finish what she started. Like Lysistrata's presiding function, the following dance by couples is exceptional in Greek drama, and was probably rare in Greek life as well.

216. Goddesses who personify the beauty and joy of the dancers themselves.

217. Apollo.

218. Dionysos was the patron of the dramatic festivals and emblematic of peace; Nysa was the legendary place of his rearing.

219. Hera.

220. Aphrodite.

221. Apollo.

222. The Spartan equivalent of Athena Polias at Athens.

223. The divine horsemen Kastor and Polydeukes (Lat. Pollux).

224. That is, Helen, who was worshipped at Sparta not as the adulterous wife familiar to us from epic poetry but as the ideal Spartan maiden and bride.

## 2 Women at the Thesmophoria

1. The idea that an author's characters reflect the character of the author himself was widespread in antiquity and exploited by Aristophanes in other plays, especially *Acharnians* and *Frogs*; no doubt there were actors and writers in Athens, as there are today, who prepared for a role by imitating real-life examples. For the character of performers' *mimesis* in our play generally see Lada-Richards 1997/98:70–79.

2. For these see Introduction IV.

3. For this see *Lysistrata*, Introduction 1. Reckford 1987:299–300 suggests, however, that despite its apolitical focus, the play, with its irrepressible Kinsman, "suggests that Athenians can play many parts, can survive humiliation and defeat, can find a way out of seemingly hopeless difficulties."

4. Of course the two stereotypes—virtuous wives as loyal defenders of their households and horny wives as deceivers of their husbands—can coexist in the same culture, as they do today.

5. See Introduction IV.

6. On the Aristophanic conception of gender and genre see Muecke 1982, Zeitlin 1981 and 1985 and Bowie 1993:217–27; on the themes and structure of the play as a whole see Hansen 1976, Taafe 1993:74–102.

7. Fuller descriptions and analyses of the Thesmophoria can be found in Brumfield 1981, Burkert 1985:242–46, Detienne and Vernant 1989, MacDowell 1995:259–62, Parke 1977:82–88, Parker 1983:81–83, Simon 1983:17–22, Zeitlin 1982, Zanetou 2002. The festival, which had its origins in neolithic times, when grain-growing and hog-raising were still done by women, is named for one of its central acts, the "carrying of *thesmoi*" (literally "things laid down"); in terms of the ritual the word *thesmoi*, which in classical times had come to mean "laws" or "ordinances," retained its earlier meaning, "fertilizer."

8. For women and sacrifice generally see Detienne 1989, who, however, is wrong in positing a connection between restrictions on women's sacrificial roles and their political disabilities: Osborne 1993.

9. *Inscriptiones Graecae*, ed. J. Kirchner (Berlin 1913–40) ii.2 1006.50–51.

10. F. Sokolowski, *Lois sacrées de l' Asie Mineure* (Paris 1955), #61.5.

11. The principal text is the Homeric *Hymn to Demeter*, for which see Foley 1994.

12. Parker 1983:83; for similar ritual analogues to the action of *Lysistrata* see *Lysistrata*, Introduction 2.

13. Aristophanes' second *Women at the Thesmophoria* (produced a few years later: see Appendix) was set on the final day, when feasting and good spirits prevailed.

14. For examples see Bowie 1993:212–14.

15. See *Lysistrata*, Introduction 2.

16. Aristophanes' *Acharnians* (produced in 425) parodies and criticizes Euripides' portrayal of heroes reduced to beggary, but contains no mention of his female characters.

17. For detailed discussions see the essays in Powell 1990; all of Euripides' fragmentary plays are available in translation in Collard and Cropp 2008–9; for *Stheneboia* see Collard et al. 1995:79–97.

18. See Introduction IV; Sommerstein 1980.

19. It is worth noting (1) that the impact of fictional characters on the behavior and self-image of actual people—a question which Plato was later to take up systematically (especially in *Republic*)—is still a live issue today with regard to such media as novels, films, television and pornography, and (2) that the response of men and women to the same fictions is often different.

20. See Henderson 1991b; Introduction III.

21. For the polarity of the dramatic genres see Taplin 1986; for comic elements in Euripides see Seidensticker 1982; for Aristophanes' play with theatrical expectations see Bobrick 1997.

22. It is significant that the Kinsman and the Policeman are the only characters in the play who display the comic phallos.

23. Bowie 1993:223.

24. Aether was a substance thought to lie between the air earthly beings breathe and the dome of the sky. Although Aether could be considered divine, it was not worshipped as a god: here Euripides speaks as an adept in the scientific or intellectualist theories currently in vogue among sophistic thinkers.

25. Agathon, who had won the first prize in his first competition five years earlier, was the most innovative tragic poet of the younger generation, incorporating the "new music" (n. 29, below), writing choruses unconnected with the action, and even inventing fictional plots. He was also very handsome, and in Plato's dialogues *Protagoras* and *Symposium* is represented as having maintained an erotic relationship with an older man, Pausanias, long into adulthood, and as championing homosexual relationships.

26. Paleness in men, suggesting the indoor life of women, was a sign of effeminacy.

27. Since most Athenian men wore beards, to be clean-shaven could be considered effeminate.

28. Implying that Agathon, like a (male or female) prostitute, has submitted sexually to every man in Athens; the Kinsman "might not know it" because he might have seen Agathon only from behind.

29. In the following songs, and throughout the Agathon-scene, Aristophanes parodies the "new music" of the later fifth century (see West 1992:356–66), with its novel instrumentation, complex rhythmic modulations and florid poeticism.

30. The Kinsman's expressions of hostility toward Agathon and his slave characterize him as holding conventionally macho views about what is appropriate for each gender in terms of manner, appearance and behavior. For normative distinctions between the manly hoplite (active) and the effeminate *kinaidos* (passive) see Winkler 1990:46–54.

31. The Kinsman brandishes his stage-phallos. His threat of anal rape reveals his own arousal at the sight of effeminate males, which in Greek terms is a conventionally masculine reaction.

32. In this year the Thesmophoria, which normally fell in October, had in fact fallen in November, after the start of the winter season.

33. The solemn day called Nesteia ("Fast"), when, in preparation for the rites of the joyful and climactic third day, the celebrants abstained from food and reverted (as one ancient

source puts it) to "the ancient way of life." For the Thesmophoria generally, see Introduction 2.

34. That is, Demeter and Kore, the goddesses in whose honor the festival is held.

35. For the Thesmophoria women formed their own cultic organization under the leadership of their own elected leaders (*archousai*, the feminine equivalent of the polis's male *archontes*); here Aristophanes imagines the women turning their cult-gathering into a special political assembly, meeting as the men do on the Pnyx: see *Women at the Thesmophoria*, Introduction.

36. For Euripides' reputation as a misogynist see *Lysistrata*, n. 76.

37. Referring to the convoluted melodies characteristic of the "new music" (n. 29, above).

38. The following "chorus" imagines the maidens of Troy celebrating after the Greeks had lifted their siege, leaving behind the Trojan Horse. Its rhythm is largely Ionic, suggesting Asiatic luxury and effeminacy.

39. Demeter and Kore.

40. The Muses, nine maiden daughters of Zeus, embodied and were thought to inspire poetry.

41. That is, the god Apollo, who with Poseidon built the walls of Troy; the Simois was a river in the Trojan plain.

42. Artemis was Apollo's maiden sister.

43. See *Lysistrata*, n. 23.

44. The Kinsman attributes to Agathon's song (exemplifying "artsy" contemporary tragedy) the power to make men want to be sodomized, but his macho sarcasm shows that he himself is immune.

45. These lost plays by Aischylos (who is often portrayed by Aristophanes as the favorite playwright of older, more traditional Athenians) dramatized the confrontation between the hyper-masculine King Lykourgos and the sexually ambivalent god Dionysos; Euripides' extant play *Bakchai* was later to explore much the same kind of confrontation. In both cases the god humiliates and destroys his opponent: in *Bakchai* Dionysos persuades King Pentheus to dress as a woman and infiltrate the women's rites, where he is exposed and ripped to pieces. In addition, the Kinsman's allusion reminds the spectators of Agathon's resemblance to the theatrical image of Dionysos.

46. The second wife of the Attic hero, Theseus, who, when her stepson Hippolytos rejected her advances, committed suicide after writing a note that accused Hippolytos of attempted rape and so led to his death. Euripides' dramatization of this story in *Hippolytos* of 431 had alarmed the more straitlaced Athenians, since it depicted Phaidra propositioning Hippolytos. Despite a second (our extant) version of the play produced in 428, which omitted the propositioning-scene and treated Phaidra more sympathetically, she became a byword for the wanton wife; shameless enjoyment of sex is here epitomized by reference to the "equestrian position" (possibly recalling Euripides' play, lines 228–31, where Phaidra imagines herself riding with Hippolytos). For a discussion of her treatment in our play see Cowan 2008.

47. Dionysiac creatures, half man and half beast, who symbolized sexuality unrestrained by the norms of civilization.

48. All these were lyric poets of the previous century, known for their love songs.

49. A tragic poet of the Aeschylean period, noted for the sweetness of his poetry.

50. From *Alkestis* (produced in 438), where Pheres rejects his son's request to die in his place.

51. Male intrusion on the rites of Thesmophoria was a very serious crime, and legends told of the mutilation and/or murder of intruders at the hands of the women.

52. That is, Aphrodite = "sexual enjoyment"; Agathon fears that he would make a more attractive woman than the women themselves, and so provoke their hatred.

53. Euripides, the tragic director, must now "direct" a comic actor in a comic plot.

54. The Eumenides ("Kindly Ones"), who defended justice (especially when crimes against kin were at issue) and gave sanctuary; their definitive dramatization was in Aischylos' *Eumenides*.

55. For this man see *Lysistrata*, n. 134, and below, where he appears as a character.

56. The removal of body hair (by singeing or plucking) was an essential feature of female grooming; see *Lysistrata*, n. 45.

57. Perhaps with a secondary allusion to the metaphorical sense of pig = woman.

58. A woman's oath.

59. Unlike Agathon, the Kinsman feels degraded by adopting a feminine appearance, and he does not succeed in losing his true male identity, though for a while he hides it under female clothing.

60. A man's oath.

61. A "scientific" entity (n. 24, above) and so useless in an oath.

62. Paraphrasing a notorious line from Euripides' *Hippolytos* (see n. 46, above), "It was my tongue that swore, but my heart remains unsworn," spoken by Hippolytos of the oath of silence Phaidra had made him swear before he knew what her secret was. Taken out of context, the line was criticized as encouraging dishonesty.

63. For the first time in the play we see male actors playing women who are supposed to be real women.

64. The Kinsman's monologue is in effect the prologue-speech of the "play" being staged by Euripides, whose starring role the Kinsman has reluctantly agreed to play.

65. Demeter and her daughter Pherephatta, elsewhere called Persephone, or Kore ("Maiden"), were the principal deities of the Thesmophoria.

66. Literally "piglet," an animal sacred to Demeter but also Greek slang for vulva.

67. The Kinsman satirizes the sort of prayer for the success of one's children that would be characteristic of actual matrons.

68. Now the Kinsman plays the role of spectator, but as a spy at a meeting he is not entitled to attend. In this he resembles the play's male spectators.

69. Torches played a prominent part in actual rites for Demeter and Kore.

70. This invocation and the other procedures to follow parody those of male political assemblies. The disguised Kinsman has gained entrance to a "polis" of women forbidden to men, much as disguised women gain forbidden entrance to the men's assembly in *Assemblywomen*. It is possible that the old priestess Kritylla (who gives her father's name, Antitheos, and deme in 898) somehow represented an actual person active (as a priestess?) in this period: a member of the chorus of old women in *Lysistrata*

is also named Kritylla (323), and one Antitheos is listed on an inscribed table (*Inscriptiones Graecae* ii² 2343) along with fifteen other men, one of whom, Philonides, was a producer of some of Aristophanes' plays and another, Simon (from Aristophanes' own deme), is mentioned in *Knights*.

71. Kritylla invokes deities appropriate to the Thesmophoria rather than to a political assembly.

72. This last category is, of course, a comic invention.

73. Apollo.

74. Athena.

75. In a contest with Poseidon over the possession of Attika, Athena prevailed by her gift of the olive tree (Herodotos 8.55).

76. Artemis.

77. The parody begins by echoing fairly closely the curses uttered at political assemblies against enemies of the polis. But the list of female "enemies of women" comically confirms male stereotypes of the secret misbehavior of wives—or, put another way, the accuracy of Euripides' "misogynistic" portrayals (and Aristophanes' too, of course).

78. That is, the Persian Empire, the traditional barbarian enemy of the Greeks; Kritylla inserts Euripides into the familiar curse.

79. A wife who failed in her principal duty—to produce a male heir for her husband—might be tempted to try such a trick. Such babies were purchased from slave-women whose masters refused to pay for the babies' rearing.

80. Apparently the women on stage are young wives; older women looking for lovers (a comic stereotype exploited in *Assemblywomen* and *Wealth*) would be widows, who had greater control over their money and their movements; see Henderson 1987b:117–19.

81. Alluding to the stereotype that women are overfond of alcohol.

82. When applied to the current political situation (see *Lysistrata*, Introduction) these provisions have a serious ring, even though when applied to the wives' enemies (particularly their husbands) they are comic.

83. The name Sostrate is not uncommon but Archikleia (the reading in a papyrus) occurs only here and in an inscription listing donors to the sanctuary at Brauron (for which see *Lysistrata* n. 142): was she perhaps (like Kritylla: n. 70, above) an actual person? The manuscript reads Timokleia, a more common name; how they came to be variants is obscure.

84. Because this was a day of fasting and relative inactivity (see above, n. 33). In addition, Aristophanes perhaps did not want to imply that his comic assembly bore any resemblance to the actual rituals of the Thesmophoria.

85. The following debate is conducted like an assembly-meeting, no mention being made of the Thesmophoria.

86. Note that women's attendance at the dramatic festivals is taken for granted.

87. For some reason Aristophanes habitually refers to Euripides' mother as a seller of wild herbs—a disreputable social category, implying both poverty and public visibility (see Henderson 1987b:121–26)—even though in reality she was well-born (though the jibe could conceivably refer to a younger woman, a stepmother otherwise unknown).

88. As we have begun to suspect, the women are angry at Euripides not for lying about them but for revealing the truth!

89. Alluding to Euripides' play *Stheneboia*, whose adulterous heroine constantly pines for her husband's young "Korinthian guest" Bellerophon.

90. The (Euripidean) source is unknown.

91. From Euripides' play *Phoinix*.

92. This last item is the most significant one.

93. To duplicate the husband's seal on the door.

94. The tragic poet earlier referred to as "base."

95. Just as purists today might charge an artist with "commercialism" or "selling out," so Aristophanes frequently charged Euripides with lowering the tragic art to suit mass tastes.

96. Euripides' plays often reflect ideas of contemporary intellectuals (Sokrates, for example) that could strike conventional people as immoral or sacrilegious.

97. See above, n. 87.

98. The Kinsman's speech, like Dikaiopolis' in *Acharnians* (497–566), is modelled on the one made by the hero of Euripides' lost play *Telephos*, produced in 438 (for fragments of this play and discussion see Collard et al. 1995:17–52, Collard and Cropp 2008–9). Telephos was the Greek king of barbarian Mysia, whose land was mistakenly attacked by the Greeks on their way to Troy. During the attack Telephos was wounded by Achilleus, who alone could cure the wound. Telephos disguised himself as a beggar in order to enter Agamemnon's palace and plead his own (and the Trojans') case. When his disguise was exposed and he was threatened with death, he seized the baby Orestes, Agamemnon's son, and took refuge at an altar: this scene is also parodied in *Acharnians* (325–51) and later in our play.

99. As medicine for his wife's indigestion.

100. That is, the pillar and statue of Apollo Agyieus in the street before the house (and also part of the permanent decor of the theatrical stage house: thus the Kinsman might illustrate his account before our eyes); this wife's act was both shameless and sacrilegious (intercourse at any shrine was forbidden).

101. See above, n. 46.

102. See above, n. 79.

103. Greek women did not allow husbands to be in the room when a baby was born.

104. We are apparently to imagine that the old woman had been the father's nanny. For the criteria applied by Athenians to penile beauty (small and with shapely foreskin, as here) and ugliness (large and circumcized) see Dover 1978:125–32.

105. That is, the Kinsman, like a politician, only pretends to work for the public good, while secretly working against it.

106. A quote from Euripides' play *Melanippe in Chains*.

107. Comic characters often say of themselves, or accept from others, what would shame or anger a real-life counterpart; here, where the theme is gender-disguise and deception, the male actor may momentarily drop his role to make an aside.

108. Aglauros and Pandrosos, daughters of the mythical Attic king, Kekrops, had

sanctuaries on the Akropolis whose cults, celebrated by girls and women, were among the polis's most ancient and important; see Simon 1983:43–46.

109. As in a male assembly.

110. Why the maiden Melanippe is singled out as a "bad" woman is unclear: the subject of two plays by Euripides, she was seduced (or perhaps raped) by Poseidon and bore twin sons, then was accused by her father of unchastity; for fragments and discussion see Collard et al. 1995:240–80, Collard and Cropp 2008.

111. See above, n. 46.

112. Odysseus' virtuous wife in Homer's *Odyssey*. Note, however, that the two recent Euripidean plays that are parodied in the second half of our play—*Helen* and *Andromeda*—do feature virtuous heroines, a new direction Euripides apparently took after the failure of his Trojan trilogy in 415.

113. The Apatouria was a kinship festival for men and boys from which women were excluded.

114. For Kleisthenes see *Lysistrata*, n. 134. Of this scene Taafe 1993:92 remarks that Kleisthenes, as a male whose gender identity is female, "speaks for women and . . . takes their place in a different sort of theater, in the ecclesia."

115. Literally "I am your *proxenos*" (a foreign citizen recognized by a polis and empowered to represent the interests of fellow countrymen before it). This relationship explains why the women do not resent Kleisthenes' intrusion on their meeting.

116. Kleonymos was an obese politician frequently ridiculed in comedy for cowardice, because he is said to have dropped his shield in battle, probably in the general Athenian retreat at Delion in 424. It is unclear why Mika is supposed to be his wife; perhaps (as Sommerstein 1994:194 suggests) she is obese too.

117. A real deme, chosen perhaps because the first syllable suggests a word meaning "penis."

118. The Kinsman makes two safe guesses, since (according to stereotype) women will take any opportunity to drink wine, their access to it being normally restricted.

119. The *hamis* (urinal), used at male drinking parties, was a jug with a narrow opening at the top and thus unusable by women.

120. The hill on which Athenian assemblies were held; for the women's Thesmophorian assembly see *Women at the Thesmophoria*, Introduction.

121. For the parody see n. 98.

122. The feminine equivalent of the masculine name Manes, frequently given to Asiatic slaves at Athens.

123. This scene is portrayed on a mid-fourth century Apulian bell-krater in the Martin von Wagner Museum at the University of Würzburg (H5697); it is the frontispiece of Sommerstein 1994.

124. Referring to the spring festival of Anthesteria, which honored Dionysos and where, in addition to adult wine-drinking, small children were garlanded and given small jugs and toys as presents.

125. See n. 46, above.

126. Priestly personnel at a sacrifice normally received some portion of the victim.

127. Aristophanes makes Kritylla the Kinman's new guard because older women were stereotypically tougher than younger women and because she suits the later parody of Euripides' *Helen*.

128. In Euripides' lost play *Palamedes* (produced, like the extant *Trojan Women*, in 415) the hero, the inventor of writing and a Greek fighting against Troy, was framed for treason and executed; his brother Oiax got a message through to their father by writing it on oar-blades and floating them back to Greece. For details see Collard and Cropp 2008–9.

129. For this Old Comic structure (the self-revelation of the chorus and its leader, who "step aside" from the plot) see in general Dover 1972:49–53 and Hubbard 1991, who (pp. 182–99) finds in this parabasis a resumption of some of the themes and concerns addressed in *Lysistrata*.

130. As in Aristophanes' *Birds* (produced in 414), this chorus speaks on its own, rather than the poet's, behalf.

131. For the workings of this criterion of female modesty see Cohen 1991:133–70.

132. That is, at an all-night women's festival, a wedding or a betrothal.

133. Charminos was an Athenian naval commander defeated the previous year, whereas the woman's name Nausimache—a typical name, like the other women's names to follow except for Salabakcho—means "victory at sea."

134. Kleophon was a politician, Salabakcho a courtesan: as often, Aristophanes insinuates that successful politicians gained their success by submitting to sexual penetration by influential men.

135. The names mean "Excellence in Battle" and "Military Victory," here understood as feminine personifications of the Athenian triumph over the Persians at Marathon in 490. The Athenians, the premier naval power in Greece, had not won a major land battle in the past 46 years, and are chided here for not daring to dislodge the Spartan army that had invested their territory two years earlier.

136. The name means "Good Counsel."

137. With sex, presumably.

138. The idea that women manage their households more prudently than men manage the public treasury—a biting charge in a time of fiscal distress caused by failure in the war—is a central theme in *Lysistrata*.

139. A surprise for "shields." The women accuse the men not only of fiscal recklessness and dishonesty but also of cowardice in battle, referring to the current Athenian situation in the war.

140. These two festivals, like the Thesmophoria, honored Demeter and were celebrated only by women; they also seem to have been run by a women's "government." See in general Brumfield 1981:156–81, Simon 1983:19–24, Burkert 1985:230. The Chorus-Leader's complaint here implies that women's seating at their own festivals was normally determined by (the status of?) their husbands.

141. Hyperbolos was a popular politician who had been ostracized (voted into exile by the Assembly) c. 417 and was to be assassinated shortly after the production of this play. He had been the frequent object of comic ridicule and attack during his political heyday in the 420s, along with his mother, who had been caricatured in at least one play as an alien, a whore and a drunk. She would now have been in her fifties.

142. This Athenian commander, ridiculed in Aristophanes' *Acharnians* in 425, had died a hero's death in the Sicilian expedition; his mother would now be in her seventies.

143. Although women could not make a legally binding contract for more than a small amount of money, they could lend any amount of money if the loan was underwritten by a man; but any public business activity by a citizen woman, let alone money-lending, could be considered disreputable (Henderson 1987b: 121–26). In this case, Hyperbolos' mother may merely have been seeing to her son's business interests during his exile.

144. In Euripides' (extant) play, produced a year earlier, in 412, the Helen whose abduction to Troy "launched a thousand ships" turns out to have been a phantom, while the real Helen spent the war in Egypt as a prisoner in the palace of Proteus, who has decreed that she marry his son Theoklymenos. After the war, her estranged husband Menelaos goes there, discovers the truth and (with the help of an Egyptian prophetess Theonoe) escapes with Helen. This play, with its novel and romantic plot, its emphasis on exotic adventure and its happy ending, marked a new departure for Euripides after 415, perhaps (as the Kinsman seems to suggest) to change his luck in the tragic competition.

145. In the following scene, the Kinsman and Euripides speak exclusively in tragic style (except for a few comic touches), with about half the lines being quoted or adapted from *Helen* and the rest composed by Aristophanes in paratragic style. Meanwhile Kritylla, being ignorant of myth and tragic theater, cannot enter into, and thus be deceived by, the "tragic" performance being staged for her.

146. A proverbial villain.

147. An Athenian commander.

148. See n. 70, above.

149. For the original *es cheras* (into my arms) Aristophanes has substituted *escharas* ("brazier," a slang word for vulva).

150. Who were, according to the Greeks, dishonest people. Ironically, Kritylla will have reminded the audience of the old Egyptian prophetess, Theonoe, who in Euripides' play had helped Menelaos and Helen escape.

151. A length of planking on which criminals were executed by suspension, as on the cross.

152. In reality, no citizen could be summarily punished without a hearing.

153. Pauson is elsewhere mocked for being poor; for the fasting see above, n. 33.

154. For the chorus's avoidance of mockery of individual spectators, which typically occurs in the second half of a comedy, see also *Lysistrata*, n. 188.

155. Apollo.

156. This epithet usually refers to Apollo, but here seems to refer to his sister Artemis; both use the bow.

157. That is, in the dramatic competition, and also perhaps in the war.

158. Since these are gods associated with the countryside, the chorus may be acknowledging the Athenians' hope for an end to the Spartan occupation.

159. This Policeman, like those who accompany the Magistrate in *Lysistrata*, is a Skythian archer and public slave, and so speaks broken Greek.

160. In Euripides' lost play *Andromeda*, produced together with *Helen* in 412, the flying hero Perseus, equipped by Hermes with winged cap and sandals (for the costume see Stone 1981:325–27), rescues the maiden Andromeda, whose father Kepheus, the king of Ethiopia, had chained her to a rock to be eaten by a sea-monster, hoping thus to appease the angry sea-god Poseidon. As the play opens, the desolate Andromeda speaks with the echo of her own voice from the caves on the shore, then is joined by a chorus of sympathetic maidens; Aristophanes reverses these scenes in his parody. The songs closely imitate Euripides' arioso style, while both songs and dialogue are a pastiche of tragic quotations and comic bathos.

161. The maiden Andromeda had enjoyed dancing, while the Kinsman (as was stereo-typical of Athenian old men) had enjoyed jury service.

162. An Athenian elsewhere mocked for his passion for gourmet seafood.

163. The nymph Echo had foiled Hera's attempt to punish other nymphs with whom Zeus had been having affairs; in revenge Hera made her able to say only what she had just heard. In Euripides' play Echo lived in the cave where Andromeda was chained. In this parody Aristophanes spoofs Euripides' use of an invisible character.

164. See n. 24, above.

165. Before spotting Andromeda Perseus had beheaded Medousa, one of three sister Gorgons, whose gaze turned anyone who saw it to stone; he kept Medousa's head in a leather bag and used it to petrify his own enemies before finally turning it over to Athena.

166. Confusing the mythological character with an otherwise unknown public official (not the famous orator Gorgias of Leontinoi). The Policeman is no more knowledgeable or sympathetic a spectator than Kritylla was.

167. "Fig" (*sukon*) was a common Attic slang term for the female genitals, "fig-tree" (*suke*) for the male; the Policeman uses the former sarcastically.

168. This hymn to the city's most august deities—Athena, Demeter and Persephone—has, in spite of its farcical dramatic environment, an earnest and patriotic tone.

169. By contrast with the jocular references to tyranny in *Lysistrata* a few months earlier, this is a more earnest-sounding reference to the current climate of political and military instability at Athens, which a few months later did indeed succumb to a right-wing coup d'état and changes in the democratic constitution.

170. Demeter and Persephone.

171. Elaphion's name means "Fawn" and Teredon's "Woodworm." Like all "naked women" in Old Comedy (a frequent feature of final scenes), Elaphion is played by a male actor wearing a leotard to which false breasts and genitalia were attached.

172. Euripides finally transforms himself into a woman (as had Agathon), but into a comic rather than tragic one, and his winning stratagem turns out to be the staging not of a tragic, but of a typical comic, scene.

173. A very high price (see Halperin 1990:107–12): probably Euripides is counting on the slave-policeman not having so much money, so that he will offer his quiver as surety (and thus facilitate their escape).

174. See *Lysistrata*, n. 149.

## 3 Assemblywomen

1. For the date see MacDowell 1995:302–3, Sommerstein 1998a:1–7.

2. The heroine of *Assemblywomen* claims to have been with the exiles.

3. For jury-pay see *Lysistrata*, n. 135.

4. In *Acharnians* of 425 Aristophanes had complained that assemblies were poorly attended and that ordinary citizens were discouraged from speaking up.

5. On the postwar period generally see Xenophon, *Hellenica*; Sommerstein 1984, Strauss 1986.

6. See Pembroke 1967 (matriarchy), Tyrrell 1984 (Amazons).

7. Pherekrates, for example, had written a play entitled "Woman Tyrant" and Theopompos had written "Women on Campaign."

8. Note that Sokrates, too, reportedly believed in the natural equality of women (Xenophon, *Symposion* 2.9).

9. Herodotos, for example, notes the absence of monogamy in some non-Greek cultures of Africa and central Europe (4.104, 180).

10. Scholars have long debated whether Plato or Aristophanes derived from the other the idea of a communist state with women participating in rule. Since *Assemblywomen* cannot on chronological grounds have caricatured *Republic*, Plato may have been influenced by the play. Aristotle tells us that Plato's system had no antecedents (*Politics* 1266a31–36, 1274b9–10), but he would have meant only published philosophical antecedents. Since theoretical discussions along these lines were probably in general circulation, Aristophanes and Plato may each have developed their own particular responses, though it is hard to believe that Plato, who knew and often incorporated ideas from Aristophanes' plays, did not somehow respond to *Assemblywomen*. In general see Ussher 1973:xv–xx, Halliwell 1993:224–25, MacDowell 1995:314–15.

11. See Rothwell 1990:22, 35–36, 92–95, 103; for philosophical thinking about women's potential for participation in polis governance see Blundell 1995:181–87; for the Diotima of Plato's *Symposion* and the traditions surrounding Sokrates' philosophical relationships with women see Halperin 1990:113–51, 190–211.

12. See Aristophanes' *Acharnians* 524–33, *Peace* 605–9; for Thucydides' "earsplitting silence" about Aspasia see Cartledge 1993; for Aspasia generally see Henry 1995.

13. See *Lysistrata*, n. 127.

14. For prejudices about women's work in public spaces see Demosthenes 57 (*Against Euboulides*), Henderson 1987b:121–26.

15. For Praxagora's success in terms of her possession of both erotic and political persuasiveness see Rothwell 1990.

16. Two contemporary politicians, Neokleides and Euaion, are later reported as having spoken at the meeting.

17. For typical features of Aristophanes' "heroic" plots see *Lysistrata*, Introduction 2.

18. The men never do find out that the women had packed the assembly.

19. For the dramatic dynamics see Taafe 1991, and for cross-dressing generally, see Said 1987.

20. See *Lysistrata*, Introduction 2.

21. Some scholars interpret Blepyros' lack of clothing as indicating general impoverishment in Athens, but ordinary Athenians would normally possess only one suit of clothes at a time.

22. Rothwell 1990:53 thinks that the constipation symbolizes "individualistic hoarding of material possessions," but that is an issue taken up only in a later scene.

23. See Bowie 1993:258–59, MacDowell 1995:311.

24. As in Lysistrata there is no real "contest" (agon); instead, Praxagora gives a kind of news conference, expounding her policies and answering Blepyros' objections or questions.

25. See Rothwell 1990:90.

26. For the distinctness of the two actions see MacDowell 1995:320–21.

27. Since in classical Athens marriage was arranged by fathers as a mechanism for transmitting property through their male successors, wives were thought of as being part of the household's property. Thus communism of property would naturally be taken to include sexual communism (so Plato in Republic).

28. Even better, they have ordered the desexualization of slave-girls and thus eliminated sexual competition from them; they say nothing about slave-boys.

29. Presumably they will still be soldiers, but nothing is said about that in the description of the new regime.

30. So Foley 1982:18, "men are reduced to leading a drone-like life of pleasure in a world run by others."

31. Aristophanes' contribution to the paradise scenario is the introduction of sex(uality) as a good thing; in the Hesiodic and biblical accounts sexuality is either absent or evil. For the psychodynamics of paradise myths see Caldwell 1989:126–42, 156–61.

32. In Aristophanes' plays it is typical that the hero(ine)'s plan is threatened by representatives of the very ills the plan is designed to eliminate.

33. Cf. Demosthenes 23.53.

34. See Lysistrata, n. 127.

35. For a good analysis of this scene see Sommerstein 1984.320–21.

36. Critics (e.g. Said 1979:49–60) who see the two illustrative scenes as ironically demonstrating the failure of Praxagora's plan wrongly assume that the Dissident and Epigenes are intended to arouse sympathy, and they overlook the final scene.

37. See Rothwell 1990:5–10, MacDowell 1995:321–23.

38. Making it clear that the male actor is supposed to be a woman dressed as a man.

39. Men normally carried a walking-stick to the Assembly but not in their everyday business.

40. Praxagora's opening lines parody (an) unknown tragic source(s) and probably contemporary dithyramb as well. Praxagora's name (not revealed until line 115 and probably a comic invention) means roughly "Woman Effective in Public." The lamp— an interior, female "sun" with secret knowledge—symbolically foreshadows the usurpation of the male (exterior) sphere by the female (interior) sphere: see Bowie 1993:255–56, who compares Klytaimestra's manipulation of the beacons in Aischylos' Agamemnon, and Parisinou 2000 for women and lamps generally.

41. For depilation and women's grooming see Lysistrata, n. 45.

42. A festival for Demeter celebrated only by women: see *Women at the Thesmophoria*, n. 140 and, for the special appropriateness of the Skira for women's plotting, Taafe 1993:184 n. 12. As usual, Aristophanes exploits the stereotype of wives as deceptive, stealthy, thievish and unwholesomely fond of sex and wine, to which access was controlled by their husbands.

43. Evidently Phyromachus (otherwise unknown) had somehow mispronounced *hetairoi* "associates" as *hetairai* "courtesans"; and *hedras* "seats" can also mean "rear ends."

44. For a female variation on this joke see *Lysistrata*, n. 37.

45. The women's names in this scene are for the most part typical, though the first three might have suggested public prominence if they were masculine.

46. Since the identity of this Smikythion is unknown we cannot say why his wife would have no trouble slipping away from him; perhaps he was reputedly negligent or too old to demand the usual morning sex.

47. A comic version of women's names ending in '–strate': Geusi-suggests wine-drinking.

48. For this popular women's goddess see *Lysistrata*, n. 102.

49. The meaning of the jokes about Lamios are obscure. Presumably this Lamios (according to the scholia, a nickname for one Mnesitheos) was likened to the fabled ogre Lamia, who carried a stick and "farted when captured." Argos was the many-eyed giant sent by Hera to stand guard over Zeus' human favorite, Io, whom she had turned into a heifer.

50. For this goddess see *Lysistrata*, n. 100.

51. Spoken not literally (indicating poverty) but in harmless exaggeration, as often in English.

52. For some reason this man's appearance (beard) suggested female genitalia.

53. It was on Agyrrhios' recent proposal that assemblymen began to be paid for attendance (see Introduction 1); Aristophanes insinuates that he had attained political prominence by submitting to sexual penetration—a stock comic assumption about politicians.

54. Actually the Assembly was purified with a piglet; the women, normally confined to the house, naturally think of a house pet.

55. Perhaps noticing among the spectators a man known for loquacity in the assembly.

56. Garlands were worn not only by speakers in assembly but also at drinking-parties (symposia), neither of which citizen women could attend.

57. That is, Demeter and Kore, a woman's oath.

58. That is, in the audience. This Epigonos is unknown, although a man with this rare name is listed in a roughly contemporary inscription among the female members of a cult association.

59. The following speech, which imitates the conventions of public oratory (see Ober and Strauss 1990:264–65; Rothwell 1990:82–92), begins by making criticisms of the political status quo that are not essentially jocular and ends with the fantastic, but not illogical, proposition that women should take over the executive functions of men.

60. The criticisms Praxagora makes in this first part of her speech are virtually the same as had been made some fifteen years earlier in the parabasis of Aristophanes' *Frogs*.

61. The goddess of sexual enjoyment, a woman's oath.

62. The alliance of 395 between Athens and Thebes.

63. Because naval service was a source of income for the poor.

64. Hieronymus was a prominent general. In 392/1 Thrasyboulos had persuaded the assembly to reject a treaty with Sparta (proposed by Andokides in the extant speech, *On the Peace*) not (Praxagora alleges) for patriotic reasons but because it would have deprived him of the chance to hold a military command.

65. Praxagora emphasizes traditional women's activities, and the fact that men are envisioned as still being soldiers, because (as she will argue in detail later) the women are to take over only governance from the men, all other gender functions remaining as they were.

66. Where the Athenian Assembly was convened.

67. That is, those displaced in the last decade of the Peloponnesian War (413–404).

68. A distinguished orator who also owned a pottery business.

69. Punning on two senses of the verb *hypokrouein* "to attack" and to "assault sexually."

70. That is, when having sex.

71. Only the first 6000 assemblymen in attendance were paid.

72. Typical men's names.

73. "While the audience is laughing at Blepyros bereft of his garments, off-stage the men of Athens are being bereft of their powers in the Assembly. Aristophanes here uses visual means to convey a dramatic point symbolically," MacDowell 1995:311.

74. The name means, roughly, "pennypincher."

75. Ordinary Athenians would not typically own more than one cloak and one pair of boots.

76. Soft shoes that covered the ankles, worn by women (Stone 1981:227–29).

77. Kinesias was a contemporary dithyrambic poet whose music was so "airy" that comic poets imagined him as flying through the air like a bird.

78. The identity of these men is uncertain, but an ancient commentator says that Amynon was not a doctor but a "prostituted politician."

79. The goddess of childbirth.

80. A rope covered with vermilion and used to mark those late for assembly.

81. Shoemakers, being (like women) indoor workers, were stereotypically pale.

82. Parodying Achilleus' lament for Patroklos in Aischylos' play *Myrmidons*, with "those three obols" substituted for "the deceased."

83. See *Assemblywomen*, Introduction, n. 16.

84. Identity unknown, but evidently a poor man.

85. Using the hides as blankets.

86. In reality, the poor gathered at the bath-house not to bathe but to warm themselves by the furnace until they were thrown out by the bathkeeper.

87. A grain magnate who presumably gave out no baker's dozens.

88. That is, Praxagora in disguise.

89. Apparently an effeminate-looking young man.

90. For the secret rites of this festival honoring Demeter and Kore, which only women attended and for which they established their own "government," see *Women at the Thesmophoria*, Introduction 2.

91. Since neither a woman's oath nor her testimony was recognized as legally valid, witnesses would in any case be pointless.

92. That is, old men; fear of a reversal of men's conventional sexual dominance underlies the following jokes.

93. Athena, as protectress of Athens.

94. In which case the midwife would expect to get payment (or a gift) of more than three obols.

95. In introducing the debate Aristophanes elides the distinction between theater and assembly, a sign that he is addressing comic advice to the polis.

96. Blepyros' alignment of himself with the spectators ("for us") indicates that Praxagora, like hero(in)es in previous plays, is addressing her recommendations to all the men in Athens.

97. This is not to be a gender-reversal: the men are asked to do nothing on their part, for example, domestic chores.

98. That is, a prostitute; at Athens they were either slaves owned by a pimp, a brothel-keeper or some other kind of master, or they were resident aliens.

99. The terms of the following sexual regulations make it clear that Praxagora wants both the ugly and the lower classes of both sexes to get their rights.

100. Presumably a man who could be called ugly and/or lower class.

101. Essentially the same question that Glaukon asks Sokrates in Plato's proposal for community of children in *Republic* (461c).

102. This man was for some reason associated with dung-eating.

103. For weaving, the housewife's characteristic work, see *Lysistrata*, n. 122.

104. Aristophanes assumes, probably correctly, that most ordinary men would enthusiastically accept such a fantastic inversion of real-life experience.

105. The category "slave-girls" here excludes prostitutes, who have been discussed already.

106. Men found abundant pubic hair unappealing in a woman; see *Lysistrata*, nn. 45, 168.

107. Her plan accomplished, Praxagora has no further need to appear onstage, and we shall not see her again. But she is not forgotten, since we are periodically reminded that she is at work in the city center and that her plan is being triumphantly realized: see Introduction 3.

108. For an analysis of this scene, a representative debate between a cooperative, law-abiding citizen and a self-interested scoff-law, see Rothwell 1990:60–66.

109. See *Lysistrata*, n. 143. This parade of utensils—a new kind of "civic festival"—aptly symbolizes the new replacement of the polis by the household; recall the women's conversion (described in the previous scene) of the polis's governmental apparatus into dining-halls and kitchens.

110. Since the Greeks had no alarm clocks, the Neighbor is probably addressing his rooster!

111. Not the tragic poet, who had died some 15 years earlier, but the son of Adeimantos of Myrrhinous and protégé of the general Konon; after the failure of his tax plan, his name came to denote a score of forty in games of dice.

112. For analyses of this episode, which illustrates, like the Kinesias-Myrrhine scene in *Lysistrata*, the sexual consequences of the heroine's plot, see Said 1979, Henderson 1987:118–19, Rothwell 1990:66–72, MacDowell 1995:317–20.

113. A dildo: see *Lysistrata*, n. 48.

114. Classical Greeks associated fellatio (stereotypically a specialty of older prostitutes) with Lesbos, as some do today with France.

115. The reciprocal erotic passion between Epigenes and the girl is the first such "romantic" relationship portrayed in surviving Greek drama.

116. A musician and composer of erotic songs, Charixene (the name means "nice to strangers") had apparently attracted (or persisted in trying to attract) lovers after she had begun to grow old.

117. A legendary robber who fitted his victims to a bed by stretching those who were too short and trimming those who were too long; there is also a pun on the verb *prokrouein*, "to bang" (sexually).

118. According to Attic law, no woman could transact any business for more than the value of one *medimnos* of barley (the equivalent of an average family's weekly groceries) without the permission of her male head of household; for this and other financial regulations concerning women see Foxhall 1989.

119. The origin of this proverb, indicating ultimate compulsion, is unclear.

120. The following routine, in which Epigenes equates going to bed with the old woman with his own funeral, comically reverses the familiar poetic connection (for which see Barringer 1991) between a woman's marriage and her death.

121. Waxen garlands were used in funerals.

122. Not a very cogent argument: since Praxagora, unlike Plato (*Republic* 5), has not planned to separate mothers from their newborn children, mothers and children will still be able to identify one another. But the argument is persuasive enough to deter the First Old Woman.

123. A horrible bogey-woman.

124. This law ordered that those accused of injuring the Athenian people should be bound and face (not fuck!) the charge before the people.

125. The tipsy maid reminds us that in the new regime women have taken control of the household stores, including the wine: in *Women at the Thesmophoria* the women complain of male strictness about allowing access to the stores.

126. In the Greek this list of foods is combined into one huge word, the longest attested word in any Indo-European language.

## Appendix

1. Parodying the opening of Euripides' *Hekabe*. Thearion was a renowned contemporary baker.

2. Probably referring to Aiolosikon's daughters.

3. If this refers to women's diaphanous clothing, the singers may be a semichorus of men, but the cloak in question (exomis) is elsewhere worn by men.

4. Someone reports a dream-epiphany of Amphiaraos.

5. Feminine gender.

6. A place on the frontier of Attika where corpses were cast out.

7. Poor fare.

8. Tentatively reconstructing the corrupt citation.

9. Probably of a sexual posture.

10. Female birds of certain species were thought to be capable of impregnation by the wind, and eggs so produced would never hatch. "Wind-egg" was also used of parthenogenetic births.

11. Punning on kore (girl) and koris (bedbug).

12. Meaning unclear: perhaps a slang- or "brand"-name for a cosmetic or perfume.

13. Meaning unclear.

14. Masculine gender.

15. Plural.

16. Feminine gender.

17. For the tragic poet Agathon see the prologue of *Women at the Thesmophoria*.

18. Possibly "my wife."

19. Euripides' IT 30–33 had called him swift (the root meaning of his name).

20. With Bergk's emendation: "hearth" MSS.

21. Or possibly Dorilaos; punning in any case on *periallos*, loins.

22. Stephen of Byzantion 413.8: "Lemnos is named after the so-called Great Goddess they call Lemnos, to whom maidens are sacrificed;" see fr.386.

23. Personified as a female in the play.

24. Probably Poesy herself.

25. Apparently the play by Strattis named after the famous tragic actor.

26. Two women discuss dildoes.

27. Feminine plural gender.

28. Parodying Euripides, fr. 968 N., "you will be the bitch of light-bearing Hekate."

29. Perhaps metaphorically of deflowering a maiden.

30. Variant "you'll be beaten"; with either reading the victim is female.

31. For Ariphrades the cunnilinctor, who moved in sophistic circles and may have been a comic poet, see Ar. *Knights* 1280–89.

32. Usually explained as referring to the expensiveness, or the larcenousness, of the courtesans for whom Korinth was famous.

# Bibliography

## Abbreviations

| | |
|---|---|
| AJA | American Journal of Archaeology |
| AS | Ancient Society |
| BMCR | Bryn Mawr Classical Review |
| CA | Classical Antiquity |
| CGITA | Cahiers du groupe interdisciplinaire du théâtre antique |
| CP | Classical Philology |
| CQ | Classical Quarterly |
| EMC | Échos du monde classique/Classical Views |
| G&R | Greece and Rome |
| GRBS | Greek, Roman and Byzantine Studies |
| JHS | Journal of Hellenic Studies |
| JWCI | Journal of the Warburg and Courtauld Institutes |
| MC | Museum Criticum |
| PCPS | Proceedings of the Cambridge Philogical Society |
| QS | Quaderni di storia |
| TAPA | Transactions of the American Philological Association |
| ZPE | Zeitschrift für Papyrologie und Epigraphik |

Assaël, J. 1985. "Misogynie et féminisme chez Aristophane et chez Euripide," *Pallas* 32:91–103.

Austin, Colin and Olson, S. Douglas. 2004. *Aristophanes Thesmophoriazusae. Edited with Introduction and Commentary.* Oxford University Press: Oxford.

Barringer, J. M. 1991. "Europa and the Nereids: Wedding or Funeral?" *AJA* 95:657–67.

Blok, J. and Mason, P., eds. 1987. *Sexual Asymmetry: Studies in Ancient Society.* J. C. Gieben: Amsterdam.

Blundell, Sue. 1995. *Women in Ancient Greece.* Harvard University Press: Cambridge, MA.

Bobrick, E. 1997. "The Tyranny of Roles: Playacting and Privilege in Aristophanes' *Thesmophoriazusae*," in Dobrov 1997, 177–97.

Boedeker, Deborah and Raaflaub, Kurt, eds. 1998. *Democracy, Empire, and the Arts in Fifth-Century Athens*. Harvard University Press: Cambridge, MA.

Boegehold, A. and Scafuro, A., eds. 1994. *Athenian Identity and Civic Ideology*. Johns Hopkins University Press: Baltimore.

Bonnamour, J. and Delavault, H., eds. 1979. *Aristophane, les femmes et la cité*. E. N. S.: Fontenay-aux-Roses.

Bowie, Angus M. 1993. *Aristophanes. Myth, Ritual and Comedy*. Cambridge University Press: Cambridge.

Brumfield, A. C. 1981. *The Festivals of Demeter and Their Relation to the Agricultural Year*. Arno Press: New York.

Burkert, Walter. 1970. "Jason, Hypsipyle and New Fire at Lemnos," CQ 20:1–16.

——. 1983. *Homo Necans*, trans. P. Bing. University of California Press: Berkeley.

——. 1985. *Greek Religion*, trans. J. Raffan. Harvard University Press: Cambridge, MA.

Caldwell, R. 1989. *The Origin of the Gods. A Psychoanalytic Study of Greek Theogonic Myth*. Oxford University Press: Oxford.

Carlson, Susan and McGlew, James, eds. 2000. *Performing the Politics of European Drama*. University of Northern Iowa: Cedar Falls.

Cartledge, P. 1981a. "Spartan Wives: Liberation or Licence?" CQ 31:84–105.

——. 1981b. "The Politics of Spartan Pederasty," PCPS 27:17–36.

——. 1993. "The Silent Women of Thucydides: 2.45.2 Re-viewed," in Rosen-Farrell, 125–32.

Chaniotis, A. 2007. "Theatre Rituals," in Wilson 2007, 48–66.

Cohen, David. 1989. "Seclusion, Separation, and the Status of Women in Classical Athens," G&R 36:3–15.

——. 1991. *Law, Sexuality, and Society. The enforcement of morals in classical Athens*. Cambridge University Press: Cambridge.

Cole, S. 1984. "The Social Functions of Rituals of Maturation: The Koureion and the Arkteia," ZPE 55:233–44.

——. 1993. "Procession and Celebration at the Dionysia," in Scodel, 25–38.

Collard, Christopher et al., eds. 1995. *Euripides. Selected Fragmentary Plays I*. Aris and Phillips: Warminster.

Collard, Christopher and Cropp, Martin, eds. 2008–9. *Euripides VII and VIII: Fragments*. Loeb Classical Library/Harvard University Press: Cambridge, MA.

Connelly, Joan B. 2007. *Portrait of a Priestess: Women and Ritual in Ancient Greece*. Princeton University Press: Princeton.

Coulon, Victor. 1928. *Aristophane IV*. Budé: Paris.

Cowan, R. 2008. "Nothing to Do with Phaedra? Aristophanes, *Thesmophoriazusae* 497–501," CQ 58:315–20.

Csapo, Eric and Slater, William J. 1995. *The Context of Ancient Drama*. University of Michigan Press: Ann Arbor.

Davidson, James. 1999. *Courtesans and Fishcakes. The Consuming Passions of Classical Athens*. Harper-Collins: London and New York.

Detienne, M. 1989. "The Violence of Wellborn Ladies: Women in the Thesmophoria," in Detienne-Vernant, 129–47.

Detienne, Marcel and Vernant, Jean-Pierre. 1989. *The Cuisine of Sacrifice among the Greeks*, trans. P. Wissing. University of Chicago Press: Chicago.

Dillon, M. 1987. "The Lysistrata as a Post-Dekeleian Peace-Play," *TAPA* 117.97–104.

Dobrov, Gregory, ed. 1997. *The City as Comedy: Society and Representation in Athenian Drama*. University of North Carolina Press: Chapel Hill/London.

——. 2008. *A Companion to Greek Comedy*. Brill: Leiden.

Dover, Sir Kenneth. 1972. *Aristophanic Comedy*. University of California Press: Berkeley.

——. 1974. *Greek Popular Morality in the Time of Plato and Aristotle*. University of California Press: Berkeley.

——. 1978. *Greek Homosexuality*. Harvard University Press: Cambridge, MA.

DuBois, Page. 1982. *Centaurs and Amazons*. University of Michigan Press: Ann Arbor.

Edwards, A. 1991. "Aristophanes' Comic Poetics," *TAPA* 121:157–79.

——. 1993. "Historicizing the Popular Grotesque: Bakhtin's Rabelais and Attic Old Comedy," in Scodel, 89–117.

Faraone, C. A. 1997. "Salvation and Female Heroics in the Parodos of Aristophanes' Lysistrata," *JHS* 117:38–59.

——. 2006. "Priestess and Courtesan: The Ambivalence of Female Leadership in Aristophanes' Lysistrata," in Faraone and McClure, 207–23.

Faraone, Christopher A. and McClure, Laura K., eds. 2006. *Prostitutes and Courtesans in the Ancient World*. University of Wisconsin Press: Madison.

Fletcher, J. 1999. "Sacrificial Bodies and the Body of the Text in Aristophanes' Lysistrata," *Ramus* 28:108–25.

Foley, Helene, ed. 1981a. *Reflections of Women in Antiquity*. Gordon & Breach: New York.

——. 1981b. "The Conception of Women in Athenian Drama," in Foley, 127–68.

——. 1982. "The Female Intruder Reconsidered: Women in Aristophanes' Lysistrata and Ecclesiazusae," *CP* 77:1–21.

——. 1994. *The Homeric Hymn to Demeter: Translation, Commentary and Interpretive Essays*. Princeton University Press: Princeton.

Fowler, D. 1989. "How the Lysistrata Works," *EMC* 40:245–49.

Foxhall, L. 1989. "Household, Gender and Property in Classical Athens," *CQ* 39:22–44.

Gamel, M.-K. 2002. "From *Thesmophoriazousai* to the *The Julie Thesmo Show*: Adaption, Performance, Reception, *AJPh*," 123:465–99.

Gardner, J. 1989. "Aristophanes and Male Anxiety—The Defence of the Oikos," *G&R* 36:51–62.

Gilbert, J. 1995. "Review of Taafe," BMCR, 7 May.

Golden, M. 1988. "Male Chauvinists and Pigs," EMC 32:1–12.

Goldhill, S. 1990. "The Great Dionysia and Civic Ideology," in Winkler-Zeitlin, 97–129.

——. 1994. "Representing Democracy: Women at the Great Dionysia," in Osborne-Hornblower, 347–69.

Gould, J. P. 1980. "Law, Custom and Myth: Aspects of the Social Position of Women in Classical Athens," JHS 100:38–59.

Grant, M. and Kitzinger, R., eds. 1988. Civilization of the Ancient Mediterranean, 3 vols. Scribner's: New York.

Hall, E. M. 1989. "The Archer Scene in Aristophanes' Thesmophoriazusae," Philologus 133:38–54.

Halliwell, S. 1993. Plato: Republic 5. Aris and Phillips: Warminster.

——. 2002. "Aristophanic Sex: The Erotics of Shamelessness," in Nussbaum and Sihvola, 120–42.

——. 2008. Greek Laughter. A Study of Cultural Psychology from Homer to Early Christianity. Cambridge University Press: Cambridge.

Halperin, David M. 1990. One Hundred Years of Homosexuality. Routledge: New York.

Halperin, D. M., Winkler, J. J. and Zeitlin, F. I. 1990. Before Sexuality. The Construction of Erotic Experience in the Ancient World. Princeton University Press: Princeton.

Hansen, H. 1976. "Aristophanes' Thesmophoriazusae: Theme, Structure and Production," Philologus 120:165–85.

Harriott, R. M. 1985. "Lysistrata: Action and Theme," in Redmond, 11–22.

Harvey, David and Wilkins, John, eds. 2000. The Rivals of Aristophanes: Studies in Athenian Old Comedy. Duckworth: London.

Hawkins, T. 2001. "Seducing a Misanthrope: Timon the Philogynist in Aristophanes' Lysistrata," GRBS 42:143–62.

Henderson, Jeffrey. 1987a. Aristophanes' Lysistrata. Edited with Introduction and Commentary. Oxford University Press: Oxford.

——. 1987b. "Older Women in Attic Old Comedy," TAPA 117:105–29.

——. 1988. "Greek Attitudes Toward Sex," in Grant-Kitzinger, vol. 2:1249–63.

——. 1990. "The Demos and the Comic Competition," in Winkler-Zeitlin, 271–313.

——. 1991a. The Maculate Muse. Obscene Language in Attic Comedy. Oxford University Press: Oxford.

——. 1991b. "Women and the Athenian Dramatic Festivals," TAPA 121:133–47.

——. 1998. "Attic Old Comedy, Frank Speech, and Democracy," in Boedeker and Raaflaub, 255–73.

——. 1998–2007. Aristophanes. Edited and Translated (5 vols.). Loeb Classical Library: Cambridge MA.

——. 2000. "Pherekrates and the Women of Old Comedy," in Harvey and Wilkins, 135–50.

———. 2002. "Strumpets on Stage: The Early Comic Hetaera," *Dioniso* NS 1:78–87.

———. 2007. "Drama and Democracy," in Samons, 179–95.

Henry, Madeleine M. 1995. *Prisoner of History: Aspasia of Miletus and Her Biographical Tradition.* Oxford University Press: Oxford.

Hubbard, Thomas K. 1991. *The Mask of Comedy: Aristophanes and the Intertextual Parabasis.* Cornell University Press: Ithaca.

Just, Roger. 1989. *Women in Athenian Law and Society.* Routledge: London.

Kallet Marм, L. 1993. "Thucydides 2.45.2 and the Status of War Widows in Periklean Athens," in Rosen and Farrell, 133–43.

Keuls, Eva. 1985. *The Reign of the Phallus: Sexual Politics in Ancient Athens.* Harper & Row: New York.

Kilmer, Martin F. 1982. "Genital Phobia and Depilation," *JHS* 102:104–12.

———. 1993. *Greek Erotica.* Duckworth: London.

Konstan, D. 1993. "Aristophanes' *Lysistrata.* Women and the Body Politic," in Sommerstein et al., 431–44.

Lada-Richards, I. 1997/98. " 'Estrangement' or 'Reincarnation'? Performers and Performance on the Classical Athenian Stage," *Arion* 5:66–107.

Larson, Jennifer. 1995. *Greek Heroine Cults.* University of Wisconsin Press: Madison.

Lattimore, Richmond. 1942. *Themes in Greek and Latin Epitaphs.* Illinois Studies in Language and Literature 28.

Levine, D. 1987. "*Lysistrata* and *Bacchae*: Structure, Gender, and 'Women on Top'," *Helios* 14:29–38.

Longo, O. 1990. "The Theater of the Polis," in Winkler-Zeitlin, 12–19.

López Férez, J. A., ed. 1998. *La Comedia Griega y su Influencia en la Literatura Española.* Ediciones Clásicas Madrid: Madrid.

Loraux, Nicole. 1980/81. "L'acropole comique," *AS* 11/12:119–50.

———. 1993. *The Children of Athena.* Translated by C. Levine. Princeton University Press: Princeton.

MacDowell, Douglas M. 1995. *Aristophanes and Athens.* Oxford University Press: Oxford.

Maitland, J. and Buch, J. 1997. "Translating the Metaphor: Problems Solved and Circumvented in Staging Aristophanes' *Thesmophoriazusae*," in Zimmermann 1997, 153–69.

Martin, R. P. 1987. "Fire on the Mountain: *Lysistrata* and the Lemnian Women," *CA* 6:78–105.

Mastromarco, Giuseppe and Totaro, Piero, eds. 2006. *Commedie di Aristofane II.* UTET: Turin.

McClees, Helen. 1920. *A Study of Women in the Attic Inscriptions.* Columbia University Press: New York.

Minieri, L. 1982. "Vini usus feminis ignotus," *Labeo* 28:150–63.

Muecke, F. 1982. "A Portrait of the Artist as a Young Woman," *CQ* 32:41–55.

Nussbaum, Martha C. and Sihvola, Juha. eds. 2002. *The Sleep of Reason: Erotic Experience and Sexual Ethics in Ancient Greece and Rome.* University of Chicago Press: Chicago/London.

O'Higgins, Laurie. 2003. *Women and Humor in Classical Greece*. Cambridge University Press: Cambridge.

Ober, J. and Strauss, B. 1990. "Drama, Political Rhetoric, and the Discourse of Athenian Democracy," in Winkler and Zeitlin, 237–70.

Olson, S. Douglas. 1988. "The 'Love-Duet' in Aristophanes' *Ecclesiazusae*," CQ 38:328–30.

———. 2007. *Broken Laughter: Select Fragments of Greek Comedy*. Oxford University Press: Oxford.

Osborne, R. 1993. "Women and Sacrifice in Classical Greece," CQ 43:392–405.

Osborne, Robin and Hornblower, Simon, eds. 1994. *Ritual, Finance, Politics. Athenian Democratic Accounts Presented to David Lewis*. Oxford University Press: Oxford.

Ostwald, Martin. 1986. *From Popular Sovereignty to the Sovereignty of Law*. University of California Press: Berkeley.

Parke, Herbert W. 1977. *Festivals of the Athenians*. Cornell University Press: Ithaca.

Parker, Robert. 1983. *Miasma. Pollution and Purification in Early Greek Religion*. Oxford University Press: Oxford.

Parisinou, E. 2000. " 'Lighting' the World of Women: Lamps and Torches in the Hands of Women in the Late Archaic and Classical Periods," G&R 47:19–43.

Patterson, C. 1986. "Hai Attikai: The Other Athenians," *Helios* 13:49–67.

Pembroke, S. 1967. "The Ancient Idea of Matriarchy," *JWCI* 30:1–35.

Pickard-Cambridge, Sir Arthur. 1988. *The Dramatic Festivals of Athens*, 2nd ed., revised by J. Gould and D. M. Lewis. Oxford University Press: Oxford.

Platter, Charles. 2007. *Aristophanes and the Carnival of Genres*. The Johns Hopkins University Press: Baltimore.

Powell, A., ed. 1990. *Euripides, Women and Sexuality*. Routledge: London.

Reckford, Kenneth J. 1987. *Aristophanes' Old-and-New Comedy*. University of North Carolina Press: Chapel Hill.

Redmond, John, ed. 1985. *Themes in Drama VII: Drama, Sex and Politics*. Cambridge University Press: Cambridge.

Revermann, Martin. 2006. *Comic Business: Theatricality, Dramatic Technique, and Performance Contexts of Aristophanic Comedy*. Oxford University Press: Oxford.

Rhodes, P. J. 2003. "Nothing to Do with Democracy: Athenian Drama and the Polis," *JHS* 123:104–19.

Rosen, Ralph and Farrell, Joseph, eds. 1993. *Nomodeiktes. Greek Studies in Honor of Martin Ostwald*. University of Michigan Press: Ann Arbor.

Rothwell, Kenneth S., Jr. 1990. *Politics and Persuasion in Aristophanes' Ecclesiazusae*. Brill: Leiden.

Said, S. 1979. "L' *Assemblée des femmes: les femmes, l' économie et la politique*," in Bonnamour, J. and Delavault, H. eds. *Aristophane, les femmes et la cité*. E.N.S: Fontenay-aux-Roses, 33–69.

———. 1987. "Travestis et travestissements dans les comédies d' Aristophanes," *CGITA* 3:217–48.

Samons, Loren J. 2007. *The Cambridge Companion to the Age of Pericles*. Cambridge University Press: Cambridge.

Schaps, David. 1977. "The Woman Least Mentioned: Etiquette and Women's Names," CQ 27:323–30.

——. 1979. *The Economic Rights of Women in Ancient Greece.* Edinburgh University Press: Edinburgh.

——. 1982. "The Women of Greece in Wartime," CP 77:193–213.

Scodel, Ruth, ed. 1993. *Theater and Society in the Classical World.* University of Michigan Press: Ann Arbor.

Seidensticker, Bernd. 1982. *Palintonos Harmonia. Studien zu komischen Elementen in der griechischen Tragödie.* Vandenhoeck and Ruprecht: Göttingen.

Shaw, M. 1975. "The Female Intruder: Women in Fifth-Century Drama," CP 70:255–66.

Silk, Michael S. 2000. *Aristophanes and the Definition of Comedy.* Oxford University Press: Oxford.

Slater, Niall W. 2002. *Spectator Politics: Metatheatre and Performance in Aristophanes.* University of Pennsylvania Press: Philadelphia.

Simon, Erika. 1983. *The Festivals of Attica. An Archaeological Commentary.* University of Wisconsin Press: Madison.

Sommerstein, Alan H. 1980. "The Naming of Women in Greek and Roman Comedy," QS 11:393–418 reprinted in Sommerstein 2009a:43–69.

——. 1984. "Aristophanes and the Demon Poverty," CQ 34:314–33.

——. 1990. The Comedies of Aristophanes, vol. 7. *Lysistrata.* Aris and Phillips: Warminster.

——. 1994. The Comedies of Aristophanes, vol. 8. *Thesmophoriazusae.* Aris and Phillips: Warminster.

——. 1998a. The Comedies of Aristophanes, vol. 8. *Ecclesiazusae.* Aris and Phillips: Warminster.

——. 1998b. "The Theatre Audience and the Demos," in López Férez, 43–62.

——. 2000. "Nudity, Obscenity and Power: Modes of Female Assertiveness in Aristophanes," in Carlson and McGlew, 9–24 and (with addenda) Sommerstein 2009, 237–53.

——. 2009a. *Talking About Laughter and Other Studies in Greek Comedy.* Oxford University Press: Oxford.

——. 2009b. "The Language of Athenian Women," in Sommerstein 2009, 15–42.

——. 2009c. "Lysistrata the Warrior," in Sommerstein 2009, 223–36.

Sommerstein, Alan H. et al., eds. 1993. *Tragedy, Comedy and the Polis.* Levante Editori: Bari.

Sourvinou-Inwood, Christiane. 1988. *Studies in Girls' Transitions.* Kardamitsa: Athens.

Stone, Laura. 1981. *Costume in Aristophanic Comedy.* Ayer: New York.

Strauss, Barry S. 1986. *Athens after the Peloponnesian War.* Cornell University Press: Ithaca.

Stroup, S. C. 2004. "Designing Women: Aristophanes' *Lysistrata* and the 'Hetairization' of the Greek Wife," *Arethusa* 37:37–73.

Taafe, Lauren K. 1991. "The Illusion of Gender Disguise in Aristophanes' *Ecclesiazusae,*" *Helios* 18:91–112.

——. 1993. *Aristophanes and Women.* Routledge: London.

Taplin, O. 1986. "Fifth-Century Tragedy and Comedy: A Synkrisis," *JHS* 106:163–74.

——. 1993. *Comic Angels and Other Approaches to Greek Drama through Vase-Paintings*. Clarendon Press: Oxford.

Thür, G., ed. 1994. *Symposion 1993. Vorträge zur griechischen und hellenistischen Rechtsgeschichte*. Böhlau: Köln.

Turner, Judy. 1983. Hiereiai. *Acquisition of Feminine Priesthoods in Ancient Greece*. diss. Santa Barbara.

Tyrrell, William B. 1984. *Amazons: A Study in Athenian Mythmaking*. Johns Hopkins University Press: Baltimore.

Tzanetou, A. 2002. "Something to Do with Demeter: Ritual and Performance in Aristophanes' *Women at the Thesmophoria*," *AJP* 123:329–67.

Ussher, Robert G. 1973. *Aristophanes Ecclesiazusae*. Oxford University Press: Oxford.

Vaio, J. 1973. "The Manipulation of Theme and Action in Aristophanes' *Lysistrata*," *GRBS* 14:369–80.

Van Steen, Gonda. 2000. *Venom in Verse: Aristophanes in Modern Greece*. Princeton University Press: Princeton.

——. 2002. "Trying (on) Gender: Modern Greek Productions of Aristophanes' *Thesmophoriazousae*," *AJP* 123:407–27.

Versnel, H. S. 1987. "Wife and Helpmate: Women of Ancient Athens in Anthropological Perspective," in Blok and Mason, 59–86.

Wallace, R. W. 1994a. "Private Lives and Public Enemies: Freedom of Thought in Classical Athens," in Boegehold and Scafuro, 127–55.

——. 1994b. "The Athenian Laws Against Slander," in Thür, 109–24.

West, Martin L. 1992. *Ancient Greek Music*. Oxford University Press: Oxford.

Whitehead, David. 1986. *The Demes of Attica 508/7–ca. 250 B.C.* Princeton University Press: Princeton.

Willi, Andreas. 2003. *The Languages of Aristophanes. Aspects of Linguistic Variation in Classical Attic Greek*. Oxford Classical Monographs: Oxford.

Wilson, Nigel G. 2007. *Aristophanis Fabulae II*. Oxford University Press: Oxford.

Wilson, Peter J. 2000. *The Athenian Institution of the Khoregia: The Chorus, the City and the Stage*. Cambridge University Press: Cambridge.

Wilson, Peter J., ed. 2007. *The Greek Theatre and Festivals*. Oxford University Press: Oxford.

Winkler, J. J. and Zeitlin, F. I., eds. 1990. *Nothing to Do with Dionysos? The Social Meanings of Athenian Drama*. Princeton University Press: Princeton.

Winkler, John J. 1990. *The Constraints of Desire. The Anthropology of Sex and Gender in Ancient Greece*. Routledge: New York.

Zanetou, A. 2002. "Something to do with Demeter: Ritual and Performance in Aristophanes' *Women at the Thesmophoria*," *AJP* 123:329–67.

Zeitlin, F. I. 1981. "Travesties of Gender and Genre in Aristophanes' *Thesmophoriazusae*," in Foley 1981, 169–217.

———. 1982. "Cultic Models of the Female: Rites of Dionysus and Demeter," *Arethusa* 15:129–57.

———. 1985. "Playing the Other: Theater, Theatricality, and the Feminine in Greek Drama," *Representations* 11:63–94, reprinted in Winkler-Zeitlin 1990, 63–96.

Zimmermann, Bernhard, ed. 1997. *Griechisch-römische Komödie und Tragödie II = Drama 5*. M&P: Stuttgart.